Can my pony come too?

BALLYNASTRAGH BOOKS

Can my pony come too?

From an Idyllic Childhood Home in Tipperary
to a Challenging New Life in Australia

ROSEMARY ESMONDE PETERSWALD

Published by Ballynastragh Books
www.ballynastraghbooks.com.au
Email: peterswald@bigpond.com

ISBN: 978-0-9807807-4-1

Please refer to the National Library of Australia website for cataloguing in publication details.

Text and photographs copyright © 2016 Rosemary Esmonde Peterswald
This edition published in 2025.

Apart from any fair dealing for the purposes of private study, research, criticism or review, as permitted under the Copyright Act, no part may be reproduced by any process without written permission. Inquiries should be addressed to the publishers.

Cover and internal design by Luke Harris, Working Type Studio, Victoria, Australia
www.workingtype.com.au
Editor: Ormé Harris

Cover Photo: Sitting on Clown with Eugene, Dibs, Viv and Gill holding Porky at Reidsdale.

National Library of Australia Cataloguing-in-Publication entry:
Creator: Peterswald, Rosemary, author.
Title: Can my pony come too? : from an idyllic childhood home in
 Tipperary to a challenging new life in
 Australia / Rosemary Esmonde Peterswald.
ISBN: 9780980780741 (paperback)
Subjects: Peterswald, Rosemary.
 Peterswald, Rosemary--Family.
 Women--Australia--Biography.
 Irish--Australia--Biography.
 Immigrants--Australia--Biography.
Dewey Number: 920.720994

To my parents,
Owen and Antonia (Toni) Esmonde

When I think of these days I think also of other episodes and personalities. I think of Lieutenant-Commander Eugene Esmonde, VC, DSO...and other Irish heroes that I could easily recite, and then I must confess that bitterness by Britain against the Irish race dies in my heart.
　　—Winston Churchill...1945

Table of Contents

Chapter 1 Till We Meet Again 1

Chapter 2 County Wicklow 7

Chapter 3 An Irish Family 13

Chapter 4 Drominagh 24

Chapter 5 An Irish Hero 37

Chapter 6 On the Shores of the Shannon 50

Chapter 7 Across the Lake at Clonmoylan 55

Chapter 8 A Time of the Raj 65

Chapter 9 Leaving for Down Under 74

Chapter 10 On the High Seas 78

Chapter 11 Arriving to the Unexpected 85

Chapter 12 Irish Bush Family at Reidsdale 93

Chapter 13 Moving to the National Capital 111

Chapter 14 Ijong Street…Not Drominagh but Ours 132

Chapter 15 The Reluctant Student, Rose Bay 138

Chapter 16 A Fortunate Meeting 143

Chapter 17 Falling in Love 150

Chapter 18 Leaving the Nest for Papua New Guinea 159

Chapter 19 A Tropical Wedding 178

Chapter 20 Tapini…and Life as a PIR Officer's Wife 182

Chapter 21 A Settler's Wife…Lae 197

Chapter 22	Back Home and Off to War	204
Chapter 23	Waiting for the Returning Soldier	209
Chapter 24	Adjusting Again…Kapooka	219
Chapter 25	Wewak in the Sepik	227
Chapter 26	Home To Aus and a New Career	256
Chapter 27	Our Own Drominagh	265
Chapter 28	Ireland Revisited	274
Chapter 29	A New Life in Tassie	283
Chapter 30	*She'll be Apples* at Koonya	292
Chapter 31	Overcoming Adversity…Hobart	321
Chapter 32	Finding Our Feet and Sea Legs	327
Chapter 33	Heading North on *Reveille*	334
Chapter 34	From Humble Beginnings…Starting Peterswalds	338
Chapter 35	The Next Generation and *Oceania*	352
Chapter 36	A Setback with a Silver Lining	364
Chapter 37	*Sea Dreams* in the Med	369

Epilogue 376

And Then There Was … 383

Acknowledgements 403

References 404

About the Author 405

Chapter 1

Til we Meet Again

It was summertime in Ireland with every hedgerow seemingly in bloom. There were golden haystacks in emerald fields and a warm west wind blew pollen through the air.

'Not the sort of day for someone to die,' my mother told me sadly over the phone from Cloneen, the ancient bluestone cottage in County Wicklow, where she and my father had lived for the past twenty-three years in the small village of Glendalough.

Yet it was on this August morning in 1993, with birds singing and squirrels foraging in his beloved garden meandering down to the Glendasin River that my father left us. When my mother rang, I was in the midst of an arctic winter on the small island of Tasmania, with a roaring 40s' southerly gale battering our windowpanes and a log fire burning in the hearth.

My last precious weeks with him are etched clearly in my mind.

The Irish countryside was splashed with great dobs of yellow gorse and purple heather when I'd drive to Dublin from Cloneen to visit him in the stark hospital ward, where he lay in a bed of crisp white sheets staring vacantly at a desolate grey wall and a grim courtyard of weeds.

Each morning I would serve my mother breakfast in bed and then take off in my parents' tiny red Fiat through the village of Glendalough and past the thatched-roofed gift shop which they ran in the 70s and 80s. Leaving Laragh and Anamoe villages, I would scuttle over the Avonmore River's ancient bridge, passing the mansion of Daniel Day Lewis and a sprawling stone-walled estate belonging to the manager of U2, or so I'm told.

Ireland too is more interested in celebrities than in local identities. Mia Farrow lived close-by and was spotted in the antique shop. My father adored the elegant Dana Wynter, another local, who was still a great beauty into her sixties with her lustrous dark hair and unlined creamy skin. Even I would stop in my tracks as she floated by.

There was no hope for my father we were told. The inevitable would happen. I was here in Ireland to say goodbye. Sadness was my constant cohort, yet in some strange way, this short period was one of the most contented I've spent in my life. A time of reminiscing about my childhood, as I pushed on between ancient stone walls that meandered and climbed, twisting and turning below the shadowy outline of Sugarloaf Mountain, my father's favourite, towering halfway to the clouds.

One morning, with the sun breaking through a thick grey mist, I stopped to let an elderly farmer, Dermott, cross the road with his flock of sheep. He had known my parents for many years and was, according to my mother, *the salt of the earth* until the demon drink turned him into the devil himself. Trudging slowly to my car, he leaned a gnarled wooden walking stick against the door and lit a well-worn pipe, as his dog, Ellie, herded the grateful flock into the abundant field of grass and daffodils, through the narrow opening in a stone wall.

Dermott tilted his somewhat tattered tweed cap in my

direction. 'Top of the morning to you, Teeny,' he beamed, his wizened elfin face creasing into a thousand hard-earned wrinkles.

After my sister Deborah (Dibs) proclaimed that I was 'teeny weeny' when she first saw me, I have always been known as Teeny by my family. I was the fifth and last surviving child.

Dermott was keen to pass the time of day, as is typical of most Irishmen, particularly after a couple of pints. However, this morning he looked quite sober and he didn't appear to be suffering any ill effects from the night before either.

I told him I was on the way to my father in hospital.

'Will you be giving himself my best wishes?' he said with a genuine warmth to his thick brogue. 'And what would be the matter with Mr Esmonde that be keeping him in hospital for so long now?'

When I explained it was cancer that had now taken a hold, he cast his watery eyes to heaven.

'Ah! I thought as much. I'd not be wishing that on any person, let alone such a grand gentleman as he be. Would you be telling his good lady we all be thinking of her?' And then with a wave and a 'God be with you', he followed his dog through the hole in the wall.

I pressed on through Roundwood (supposedly the highest village in all of Ireland), lined with ivy-covered cottages and cosy pubs with bright Guinness signs, which seemed to beckon me.

Ignoring their eager bidding, I drove on through many more miles of stone walls, patchwork fields and thick hedgerows, until I was negotiating the busy N11 highway junction at the small village of Kilmacanoge. Passing the Avoca Handweavers Mill, I skirted the seaside town of Bray, scooting past the tinkers' ramshackle campsite on the verge of the road.

The tinkers, now known as travellers, would be huddled in a tight group around a makeshift fireplace. Runny-nosed children with raggedy trousers held up by pieces of string played happily in the mud and a few clapped-out cars were carelessly strewn against the hedgerow. A little further on a piebald horse and a grey donkey were tied to a fence, and a couple of scrawny dogs loitered nearby.

Even though it was not a salubrious hospital where my father was dying, it was friendly. The nurses were curious about Tasmania, and although during the month I was visiting my father, most of the patients in his ward died, they seemed a happy lot on the whole.

Seamus, an elderly retired publican believed he was being entertained by fairies in the garden. When we obviously couldn't see them, he suggested they had probably gone to Grafton Street to shop.

Maybe it was because of the medicine given to a dying man.

If so, I supposed there could be a worse fate in a long life as it drew to a close.

In any case my father and I assured him that he'd have a most enjoyable time in the evening when his friends returned. Now, seemingly satisfied, he smiled contentedly and nestled down for a sleep.

These times, as I sat by my father's bed, were when I assured him: 'Yes, you will be home soon and I'll be there waiting for you.'

But he didn't come home and I wasn't there waiting for him.

In Ireland they often don't believe in telling the dying they're dying. Not like in Australia where everyone must know exactly what's happening. I think I prefer the Irish way.

One morning I collected Father Doyle, the gregarious and elderly retired priest, who was a great friend of my parents.

Chapter 1   Til we Meet Again

As he drove with me he turned his jovial ruddy face beneath a healthy crop of snowy hair in my direction and pronounced: 'Well to be sure now, Rosemary, what's the point of telling the poor man he's dying? Has the good soul not got enough on his plate just now – to be worrying himself about that?'

After morning tea with my father, I'd return through the mountains to Glendalough to collect my mother so she too could visit him. Sometimes we stopped for tea and scones in the grounds of the Avoca Handweavers Mill, browsing through the shelves crammed with items for the tourists to buy.

This once grand old home is today a thriving restaurant and gift shop, set amidst newly mown lawns and tall fir trees, and reached by driving over a stone bridge spanning a running brook. My mother adores sitting with a light lunch and a glass of wine under one of the bright umbrellas in the tranquil grounds rolling down to the brook, or searching for presents to send home to the great-grandchildren in Australia. Or she might, as she did last time we were there, strike up a conversation with another old-timer from Dublin, pulling apart the Irish rugby team, discussing the good old times, the troubles in the north, or the general appalling nature and performance of Irish politicians. In particular she disliked Bertie Ahern, the gregarious Taoiseach (Prime Minister) who at the time was scandalously living with his mistress, but still attending family functions with his long-suffering wife as he'd devotedly promised his elderly mother that, as a good Catholic boy, he'd never get a divorce.

But my mother was only concerned about his questionable financial dealings and policies, not his morals.

The drugs they pumped into my father made him not himself at all. He too started to see fairies in the courtyard. My sister, Viv, who had come over from Wales where she lives, ranted and raved until the doctor, a morose elongated string of a man with a grey overworked complexion, changed the dosage and also gave him back his half Valium a day, which he'd taken for years; ever since he'd frightened us when he'd suffered a near fatal heart attack on discovering a flock of stray sheep devouring his much loved garden of colourful shrubs and flowers at Cloneen.

The dour doctor seemed doubtful, but probably fearful of Viv's fiery black eyes, and no doubt overcome with her great beauty, as most men are, changed the drugs anyway – ensuring that my father's quick mind came back from where it was hiding. However, it was devastating to see this once strong and agile man lying listlessly on a hospital bed, as he fought courageously, rallying somewhere between life and death.

One freezing day he slipped into unconsciousness. I organised for my mother to be picked up and informed all of the family. The resident priest arrived to give the last rites. When my mother arrived, my father had regained consciousness, in fact was quite chirpy, giving her a beaming smile, thus proving me a liar.

CHAPTER 2

County Wicklow

Glendalough, as the name denotes, is the 'Glen of the two lakes'.

It nestles in a valley surrounded by Derrybawn, Lugcluff, and Camaderry Mountains in a scene of serene beauty. From Dublin one enters the village from the east, passing the shoulder of the legendary Trooperstown Mountain before meandering through the small village of Laragh and then onto Glendalough itself. Glendalough today is a great tourist Mecca, particularly in the summer months when tourists make the streets almost impassable.

It was to Glendalough that the entrepreneurial St Kevin came as a young hermit in the 5th century, establishing himself in a cave on a cliff overlooking the upper and larger of the two lakes. After a while, he gathered quite a following, so it wasn't long before a monastic settlement was established, eventually developing into a university instructing up to 3000 students from all over Europe, contributing to Ireland's reputation as 'The Land of Saints and Scholars'. Only the ruins of the stone buildings and of course St Kevin's Tower itself, built as a *lookout* post and a refuge from marauding Danes, remains today, for sadly troops of spoilsport Englishmen did their utmost to destroy it all in 1398. There is also the cemetery where I've spent hours wandering amongst the graves. The crumbling remains of St Saviour's Abbey, St Kevin's Kitchen, a small cathedral, Our Lady's church, and an arched gatehouse are still evident.

The year before he died my father took great delight in showing me through the fancy new Glendalough Visitor Centre, which sits under a tall arbour of oaks and horse chestnuts in a verdant field, in springtime a vivid canvas of wildflowers, tulips, and daffodils, before the small wooden bridge to the Bottom Lake. There is also the Upper Lake, reached by driving on past St Kevin's Tower to the picnic grounds surrounding this vast stretch of water, the colours of which vary enormously from a sparkling blue on a warm summer's day to an unwelcoming grey in the winter months. For hours we'd amble in the late twilight, along the shores of the Bottom Lake, as my father regaled me with stories of times gone by, for history was his forté.

When his legs began to let him down, I should have realised that his cancer had taken a firm hold.

Cloneen, over three hundred years old, was originally a forge for the mines, then a labourers' cottage. Sitting snugly in the shadow of Camaderry Mountain, separating the two valleys at the very spot where they merge into one, a few hundred yards from the village of Glendalough, it had been the home of my parents since 1969 when they returned to Ireland from Australia. It nestles into the crook of a small stone-walled lane and perches on the side of the Glendasin River. In my parents' day a green door opened to a stone-flagged entrance hall leading to the cosy sitting room, with a picture window overlooking the garden rambling down to the river. A small desk in the sitting room was where my father, who was well into his eighties at the time, wrote his memoir, *The Way Things Happened* in a dozen exercise books, which I brought home to Australia. My sister, Gill, typed them up and my brother, Eugene, had them published for the family.

We all cried as we read them, only realising his great talent after he had died.

At the rear, through the dining room, was the sunny kitchen with a fuel stove and a much later addition of an electric oven. When lying in the old claw bath, with its antiquated hot water system gurgling happily in the corner, the window thrown open to the sound of the Glendasin River crashing over the moss-covered rocks below, I used to breathe in the crisp cool country air and feel utterly contented.

My father built a grotto on the Glendasin River at Cloneen for the battered statue of The Blessed Virgin Mary at whose faded and chipped feet we had recited the Rosary over many years, wherever we lived – especially in outback Australia. There had been no shrine for her before; not even at Drominagh, my father's family home, a great Victorian mansion on the shores of Lough Derg in County Tipperary, my birthplace.

In Cloneen's front garden, my father had turned a barren field into an oasis of wildflowers, begonias, fuscias, petunias and roses, amidst hedges of purple lavender and rosemary. A stone bird bath rested next to a slab table with a couple of tattered wicker chairs where my parents took their tea most summer days.

For centuries folk have walked what we all call the 'river walk'. Without doubt one of the loveliest walks of the world, it meanders up the eastern side of the Glendasin River where rabbits scuttle, hedgehogs ferret and wild deer graze in the thick woods. On the western side is the Wicklow Gap Road where a cluster of whitewashed cottages nestle into the hillside with thick smoke billowing from tall chimneys. Whenever

I looked across at those chimneys, I just knew that a warm loaf of Irish Soda bread was about to be taken off the huge stone hearth in the kitchen down below and slathered in thick butter and jam.

Autumn twilights, now indelibly etched in my mind, are when I enjoyed the river walk most, with the amber trees seeming to bounce back as if reflected and the leaves chasing each other along the gravel path.

There's even a sandy beach where the local children come and swim in the summer, lazing in the fleeting rays of sunshine. Outcrops of speckled rocks jut high into the air, as if meticulously carved by a gifted hand centuries ago. One of these, St Kevin's Rock, is supposed to heal all illnesses when you sit upon its surface.

A local fellow, Sean McGuire, with a twinkle in his eye, arrived on my parents' doorstep one evening as we sat around the dining room table, to tell us with great glee: 'Come lay down your knives and forks. Bring your drinks I've found the rock'.

I wondered if I brought my father home from the hospital in Dublin and sat him on that rock if his cancer would go away; however, the doctor looking after him didn't appear to be the type of man to be taken in by such fanciful ideas.

At Cloneen, we would be informed that meals were ready by the battered brass gong which had once summoned my father and the workers from the fields of Drominagh. On formal occasions, the richly polished cedar dining room table would be laid with the remaining cherished china (which had survived after our arduous Australian trip forty years before), our Waterford crystal glassware and the family silver.

Father Doyle was not your typical priest. One day, when I was visiting Cloneen, we invited him for dinner. Around the table sat my parents, Pat and Una from *The Cottage* over the field (in reality The Mansion), the wonderful Imelda, who looked after my parents for many years, and Imelda's husband, Kevin. We had a grand night; much was imbibed by all, except my father, who stuck to his enforced no-drinking pledge, having partaken of one tipple too many in his younger days. There was much merriment and, on leaving, Father Doyle said cheerily: 'Well now…will you be my guests at the Presbytery one night next week? I'll be ringing to let you know what night that might be.'

As he'd partaken of the odd drop of whisky and his memory was not the greatest at the best of times, we felt it was highly unlikely he would remember this kind invitation.

We thought no more about it until we were at the end of a fine meal at the kitchen table at Cloneen on Tuesday of the following week when the phone rang and Father Doyle's housekeeper, Eileen, inquired politely of my father as to where we might be?

When he informed her that we were sitting around the dinner table, she promptly replied: 'Well now, the good Father is doing the very same thing – waiting for you to join him.'

As my mother and I'd consumed a glass of her favourite cream sherry at the cocktail hour and a glass of good riesling with our meal we were feeling rather merry, not to mention adequately fed.

'Don't be so silly, Owen. There's no way we can go,' my mother exclaimed, seeing the determined look on my father's face – a look that told us in no uncertain terms we should immediately up stakes and hastily drive to the presbytery. 'How could we possibly eat another thing?' she bemoaned.

'We must,' my father stated firmly. 'It was obviously a misunderstanding. Father Doyle is expecting us.'

A Catholic priest in Ireland, unless he's blotted his copybook like many around the world have, is even today treated with the greatest of respect, particularly by the elderly. And so it was that my mother and I packed up the table, hurriedly dabbed on some lipstick, grabbed our handbags and overcoats from the stone vestibule by the front door and piled into the small Fiat where my father was anxiously waiting. Ten minutes later we joined Father Doyle at the presbytery. Needless to say he was delighted to see us, with not a mention as to why we were late. Shortly we were sat down to not one, but five beautifully prepared courses, cooked, and served by Eileen.

Gazing around between courses, I noticed the dining room was furnished to the hilt with Father Doyle's family heirlooms; the table was also brimming with polished silver and fine china. It seemed to me at the time, that this home of the parish priest was somewhat grander than one would have imagined. Yet, in true tradition, it was as cold as ice. For, although it was in the middle of a freezing Irish winter, it would not seem to be in good form for the priest to be enjoying *too* many comforts of this world. Maybe he didn't notice the cold. Or perhaps the whisky kept him warm.

CHAPTER 3

An Irish Family

Even though my father, Owen James Esmonde, born May 15, 1905, left school at fourteen, he was a self-taught, well-read learned man.

Three months after I deserted him there in Ireland to return to Tasmania he sadly did pass away. Fortunately, Viv had organised for him to leave the institution-like hospital in Dublin to be admitted to Clonmanan, a stately Georgian mansion recently turned into a nursing home in County Wicklow, and set in acres of picturesque gardens, dotted with tall fir trees, a favourite of his since his days in Drominagh.

'Yet,' my mother lamented, 'he always sat with his back to the fir trees. For ages I couldn't work out why – until I realised they reminded him too much of Drominagh.'

I faxed him every day from Tasmania and sent him a Koala bear for his bedside. It had a Vegemite jumper and he loved it.

It was August 23rd when he left us – the day after my brother, Eugene's birthday.

My mother, now alone, had carried out his wishes, burying him in Terryglass by the River Shannon in County Tipperary near Drominagh. They had returned to Ireland from Australia in 1969 to run the gift shop managed for many years by my father's recently deceased brother, Jimmy. This was fortunate (if not for poor Uncle Jimmy) as my father believed that to attain Heaven he needed to die in the Land of Saints and Scholars, in sight of his 'Lordly Shannon'. He was grateful for the opportunities Australia had given his family; however, Ireland was his home.

My grandfather, Dr John Esmonde, a flamboyant well-known Irish doctor (a Licentiate of the Royal College of Surgeons and of the Apothecaries Hall) and Nationalist Parliamentary Member for North Tipperary, died suddenly in 1915 when my father was just nine years old; the cause of his death appearing to be controversial at the time.

In all the cuttings I have in my possession, and there are hundreds from both Irish and English newspapers proclaiming his sad demise, they all said he died of pneumonia.

Not so, my father's half-brother wrote furiously to the Editor, in answer to the newspaper reports: *He died of a heart attack brought on by the hard work he had to carry out as the Royal Army Medical Corps Officer in Tipperary and its surrounds during the Great War. He was overworked so much that this caused his heart attack and subsequent death.*

I gather they were understaffed in the RAMC at this time and a great deal of Tipperary's medical needs fell to my grandfather, with little help.

One of the cuttings at the time of his death describe him: *After the outbreak of the great European war, Dr Esmonde took a leading part in urging that Nationalist Ireland should do her share in curbing the ambition and frustrating the designs of Prussian militarism, and he gave practical proof of the faith that was in him by joining the Royal Army Medical Corps. He was gazetted a Captain and was stationed with the Irish Brigade in County Tipperary, where Lt. William Redmond, MP, son of the Irish leader was also in training. The deceased gentleman was of a kindly and amiable disposition, he was a staunch friend and in social life was a delightful acquaintance.'

It goes on to say: *He was an earnest Home Ruler and a loyal and popular member of the Irish Party and did yeoman service for the Nationalist cause, particularly in England where he was in frequent request as a speaker held to urge Ireland's claim to National Self Government.'*

How I wish I had met him.

I remember my father drawing heavily on his pipe and telling me that our family had its recorded origins in the 9th Century in one Eric Osmond, a page to Duke William 1 of Normandy. This connection with the rulers of Normandy continued with the marriage of a later member of the family to Isabella, daughter of Duke Robert, father of William the Conqueror in 1016. Over time the family acquired the surname de Estmonde and later de Esmonde through journeys to the Middle East in the early crusades for the recovery of the Holy places. From the crusades sprang the family crest, Malo, Mori Quam Foedare, meaning 'Had rather die than be dishonoured'.

Sir Geoffrey de Estmonte, knight, was one of a party of 30 Norman knights who came to Ireland. They and their followers were less than happy with their expectations of the successors to William the Conqueror and hence took up the challenge to come to the aid of Dermot McMurrogh (King of Leinster) in his fight against the Ard Ri (High King of Ireland), Rory O'Connor. Unbeknown to Dermott and Henry 11 of England, these trusty and gallant Norman knights felt that they could found an independent Norman Kingdom of Ireland.

This plot was abruptly put to an end when the Earl of Pembroke (Strongbow), dispatched his army, asserting Henry's overlordship. Sir Geoffrey, however, settled at Lymbrick in Co Wexford, where Sir James de Estmonte, Knight, built a Norman Keep on the site of the Moat and Bailey in 1235.

Henry Esmonde (present form of our name) was Seneschal of Wexford 1249-1270. He died without having any children and the castle, Lymbrick, fell into disuse and later ruins.

The Esmondes also built castles at Johnstown, County Wexford, Huntington, Co Carlow and Ballynastragh, Co Wexford. However, Ballynastragh, sitting on a plot of land granted to the family in the eleventh century, is sadly the only original property still remaining in the Esmonde family. And, needless to say, the money and other grandeurs have long since dissipated, so that sadly by the time we left for Australia in 1954, for our branch of the family anyway, there was little to show for what my forebears had gallantly fought for and gained through grants for services rendered.

In 1625, Lawrence, Lord Esmonde, built Huntington Castle on lands granted in the reign of Charles 1, lands that were in dispute between the local O'Kavanagh and O'Neill clans. Over the centuries the original tower house has been added to. But the most amazing addition is relatively recent. A fully fledged Egyptian temple in what would have been the dungeon.

Huntington Castle was supposedly the first private building in the twenty-six counties of Ireland to be wired for electricity. It has a history, as my Aer Lingus, *Cara* magazine, told me on my last visit to my mother at Cloneen, 'to which the word chequered barely does justice'. This was enough for me to pick up the phone and make an appointment with the Durdin-Robertson family, descendants of Lord Esmonde, like myself, who now reside there. Today parts of the castle are open to the public. It is also the foundation centre of an international pagan movement with almost 24,000 members.

Was it not enough that 'Bad Lord Esmonde', as he was known, denounced the Catholic faith in order to be made a

Lord? Now paganism! What next! I was beyond curiosity as to what I would find.

As I drove one sunny August morning through the emerald countryside into the picturesque town of Clonegal and over the River Slaney, the river of healing, I turned left into the magnificent avenue of yews. When I caught a glimpse of Huntington Castle through the sun-streaked leaves on the giant trees, I could see that it is one of the finest examples of Jacobean architecture remaining in Ireland today. As I moved slowly down the avenue, I thought that the old saying that the Anglo-Irish Ascendancy was known as the *Raj in the Rain* became almost a lie, as the warm rays of sunshine shone on this ancient bastion standing sentinel in the midst of manicured lawns surrounded by 180 acres of the richest land in Ireland.

David, the present owner and my distant cousin by marriage, met me in the walled garden to the rear of the castle where chickens foraged beneath heavily laden fruit trees and a few pieces of rickety farm machinery were pushed against the drystone walls. He ushered me inside to the sunny kitchen with the delicious aroma of baking coming from the fuel stove in the corner. Soon I was sitting around the scrubbed pine table in the centre of the room sipping from a steaming cup of tea, nibbling a piece of thick soda bread slathered in butter and homemade jam. It was then that his aunt, the wonderful and exotic Olivia, flounced into the room.

Eighty-six-year-old Olivia Robertson, the matriarch of Huntington at that time, is one of the few people in the world to have been on speaking terms with WB Yeats and Mick Jagger – both visitors to Huntington Castle over the years. She reminded me of Gypsy Rose…long flowing hair draping over upright shoulders as if it was a netted black mantilla, flouncing dress, dark flashing eyes and expressive hands.

'You're an Esmonde,' she said with aplomb, in her fine upper-crust accent.

'Yes. I am. From Australia…Tasmania actually…'

A robin redbreast landed stealthily on the stone windowsill, pecked at the shining glass, and stared hopefully inside.

'Oh! I've read about Tasmania – such a fascinating island,' Olivia said, looking me up and down as if I was a horse she was about to add to her stables. 'I've always loved the Esmonde women. So much more interesting than the men.'

Somewhat taken aback, I thought of all the Esmonde men who had died in the wars; the doctors come politicians, like my grandfather; those who were hanged on O'Connell's Bridge for their faith; those who had won Victoria Crosses fighting for Britain; my great uncle who'd travelled the world writing his hunting memoirs; those who were missionaries in Africa, including one who'd bravely given up the priesthood to marry a dark foreigner (causing such a furore that one would have assumed he'd murdered the Pope or at the very least an archbishop); my father; my brother.

Had she not met them? Not heard of them? Somehow I couldn't help feeling slightly chuffed.

'Not that I don't find some men enthralling,' she chuckled, moving to the stove to fiddle with the copper kettle. 'Now Stanley, what a divine man he was.'

It took me a moment to realise she was referring to Stanley Kubrick, the director of the movie, 'Barry Lyndon', partly filmed at Huntington Castle. A contradictory vision of dapperly clad gentlemen, ornately dressed ladies, shining black horses and grand rooms, together with the dreadful soul-destroying poverty of those less fortunate, flitted through my mind as I recalled the film I'd watched over and over again. And as she sat down, both Olivia and I agreed that a young

Ryan O'Neill, who played the film's hero, was at that time one of the sexiest stars of the big screen.

'David, you must show Rosemary the hole in the wall where her ancestor was shot. And don't forget to tell her about the ghosts,' Olivia gushed, pushing her chair back from the ancient table and scraping the heavy wooden legs on the stone floor.

'Ghosts?' I queried.

'Oh yes! Bishop Leslie, Bishop of Limerick who was here in the 18th Century still comes to visit. And of course, Ailish O'Flaherty, the first wife of Lord Esmonde and granddaughter of Grace O'Malley, visits often, wailing and combing her long hair. She usually comes at night with a white cat.'

'Oh!'

I looked at the sprightly Olivia and wondered if in a hundred years' time there may not be another Esmonde being entertained in this very same kitchen and being told: 'Ah! Yes! Ghosts. Olivia, now she calls in frequently. Long dark hair, darting eyes. She lived here in the twenty and twenty-first centuries. Ran the Temple of Isis.'

I took another sip of tea and placed my cup back on the saucer.

'How did the Fellowship of Isis start?' I asked Olivia.

'My brother, Derry, Baron Strathloch, an Anglican clergyman,' she pronounced with fervour, 'was on a train journey to Bolton when he was suddenly hit with a message: God was a woman!'

'Wow?' I exclaimed.

Having been brought up to believe God was definitely a man, yet having read the novel, the *Da Vinci Code*, assuring me Mary Magdalene had married Jesus and produced a son, I decided anything could be possible.

'Yes,' Olivia went on, with the assured knowledge her brother was definitely right. 'That's when he came back to Ireland and set up a shrine to Isis.'

'May I have a look?' I asked tentatively.

'Not today,' she said, shaking her head with vigour. 'It's all closed up. Perhaps sometime in the future.'

I didn't like to take it any further. As it was, I was grateful enough that I was here. Perhaps I'd get a peep at the shrine another day. With that, Olivia tossed her mane over her shoulder and flouncing out of the room she left David to show me around the castle and grounds.

The doors were studded; hand-carved-ceilinged rooms contained leather-bound books, paintings, Victorian memorabilia, family silver and furniture. Sure enough, a hole in the wall in the front room caused by a Muscat ball verified the felling of an Esmonde several centuries earlier.

In the dining room, a huge stained-glass window depicted the family tree. I photographed it twice, wondering as I did what my ancestors would have thought of modern day technology! It was beyond wonder.

In the next room buffalo heads and tiger skins hung from the stone walls. On from that was a magnificent conservatory with succulent green grapes, almost ripe for the picking, hanging low over deep wickerwork chairs with plush feathered cushions. The bedrooms we wandered through had some of the grandest four-poster beds I'd ever seen.

Leaving the splendid rooms of the castle behind, we strolled out to the gardens where legend has it that the Tuatha de Danann, the original tribe of Ireland, had made it one of their hallowed sites. After stopping for David to take a photo of me in front of the castle, and I of him, we meandered across the lawns to the Yew Walk, canopied with ancient yew trees planted by the Esmondes in the early 17th century. From there we went to the Lime Tree walk overlooking the Esmonde fishing ponds. In the distance was the wonderful river Derry, the dividing line between counties Carlow and Wexford. Huntington Castle and its grounds are actually situated on what is called the Crow's Foot, the coming together of the splendid Rivers Slaney and Derry. Looking back to the fortress, I could see the traditional trees of Ireland: alders, birches, and hawthorns casting refined shadows over the formal newly mowed lawns, while to the front of the castle hardy young workmen mixed cement to fix the centuries-old steps leading up to the entrance.

Back in the house I met David's charming auburn-haired wife, Moira, Scottish, like my mother, yet born and brought up in Italy, and his pretty daughter, Sarah, home from England for a study break. After signing the *special* visitors' book, one that had to be fetched from the private rooms above, we wandered outside and stood on the porch. For some time we gazed over the gardens and across to the gently sloping fields where my ancestors would have ridden their battle-weary horses weighed down with heavy armour.

Shortly, I bade David, Moira, and the wonderful Olivia farewell and got in my car. With a final wave I drove down the long avenue, turning right into Clonegal where I stopped at the post office to buy a couple of hand-painted postcards of Huntington Castle to send back to Australia. By the river's edge I sat on a wooden bench and watched a family of ducks playing within the tall reeds, whilst all around me was the song of birds and the gentle tune of water lapping across the stones.

After writing on the postcards, I dropped them into the green box by the post office before venturing home along the road winding through the thick hedgerows and fields to my mother waiting in the garden at Cloneen. She was to have come with me, but age and tired legs let her down. Besides, years before she'd taken this very same trip with my daughter, Charlotte, and my father. She assures me that David's mother, dressed to the nines, was wheeled out on a rickety wooden trolley to meet them. Having had a stroke sometime before, this was her only mode of transport. Unable to move a limb, she chatted away happily, although Charlotte, only fairly young at the time, was somewhat alarmed at the proceedings.

A few days after my visit to the castle, my mother felt up to a drive. After lunch at the picturesque gardens and restaurant at Rathwood near Tallow, a favourite haunt of both of ours, we wound our way through the narrow lanes back to Huntington. As my mother was unable to get out of the car, David came and talked to her through the window and pointed out the original Irish flag flying from the turrets of the castle.

A flag with an Irish harp in the centre. A flag long in retirement in modern day Ireland, but a flag my mother remembered well. A flag that made that long trip to Australia with us all those years ago, and back again to Ireland.

Ballynastragh Castle, the Esmondes' family's home in County Wexford, was tragically burned down in the Irish Civil War in 1922. With the burning of this magnificent turreted castle many treasures accumulated over the centuries were sadly lost. A new house was built on the site and the children of my father's half-brother, Sir Anthony, the 16th Baronet, and his wife, his cousin, Ethne Moira Grattan, a descendant of the Rt Hon. Oliver Henry Grattan, the great Irish orator, still live there today.

On my last visit to Ballynastragh, my cousin Alice brought out a tender roast, or joint as it is still called in Ireland, and carved it into huge portions, serving it up with piping hot potatoes and greens, as we chatted around the very same table Oliver Cromwell had sat at centuries ago. His initials and those of his soldiers carved into the ancient wood are still highly visible.

Sir Thomas Gratten Esmonde wrote a wonderful book, *Gentleman the Queen*, a supposedly fictional account of the Esmondes at Ballynastragh (in a fantasy style) describing the tragic burning of the old house in the Civil War. I'm lucky enough to have a rare copy in my possession. It is a remarkable account, if not slightly controversial in today's times.

Thankfully Ballynastragh was rebuilt, the smaller house far less imposing than the original castle. As only my cousin, Barty, not farm hands and labourers, keeps the magnificent grounds and picturesque lake in order, there is some overgrowth and a sunken wooden rowboat at the partly submerged jetty. Luckily, a number of family portraits stored elsewhere at the time of the fire, gaze down haughtily from lofty walls. A large portrait of Queen Christina of Sweden, the inspiration for Sir Thomas Gratten Esmonde's novel, hangs regally besides the French windows. Bird life nests in the ancient trees next to Barty's busy farm machinery business.

Chapter 4

Drominagh

Drominagh, a three-storey early Georgian house where my father spent much of his youth and where I was born, is in a wonderful piece of Ireland nestled into the shores of Lough Derg and reached by a tree-lined avenue with timber fences encasing over a hundred acres of richly fertile fields. It was built in 1721 and was called Castle Biggs until my great-grandfather bought it in 1866. Finding this a 'dreadful name' he renamed it Drominagh, which means a place where ivy grows and which was the original name of the area.

At its most impressive when the ivy-clad walls are in leaf, this grandly proportioned residence is now richly panelled inside with antique English timbers. (My parents had preferred lighter pastel painted interior walls in their day.) It boasts fireplaces in all of the rooms and a central regal staircase. Upstairs are the bedrooms and sitting rooms and on the ground level are the reception and dining rooms and an immense stone-flagged kitchen. The scullery and gun room open to the cobble-stoned courtyard with the stables and work rooms adjoining.

My father's family were lucky to be raised in this paradise brimming with bird and animal life and to be taught by the steward and his son *Old Danny* and *Young Danny* how to ride and shoot with the best of them. By the shore of the glorious

Lough Derg, were the ruins of the old O'Kennedy's Castle, where my father and his siblings played imaginative games about past marauders crossing the lake from the distant purple Tipperary Mountains.

My father told us that his earliest memories of Drominagh were of a large and somewhat disorderly family returning to live there after his father moved from London when he was four years old. On one occasion, when they were entertaining their English neighbour, Lady Austin, at high tea conversation was interrupted by a procession of a drake and six ducks arriving unheralded, quacking loudly, touring the room and eventually retiring, satisfied that everything was in order and that formal greetings had been bestowed on the honoured guests. My father was sure Lady Austin would have 'dined out' on this story for some time, reporting to her friends back in England that the peculiar standards attributed to Irish country gentry, were in fact, as painted.

I understand now how my father would have died a broken man if he had not been given that opportunity to realise his dreams and see Drominagh by Lough Derg again, despite being happy 'in exile' in Australia.

My grandfather, Dr John Esmonde, sired two broods, one in the late eighteen-hundreds to Rose McGuiness, and a second in the early nineteen-hundreds to Eily O'Sullivan, of whom my father was the eldest.

There were also three daughters by my grandfather's first marriage. Rose died at the turn of the twentieth century and a few years later my grandfather married my grandmother, Eily, (whom we called Gargy), who bore him a girl and six boys of which my father was the oldest. My grandmother was a descendant of O'Sullivan Prince of Bere and Bantry, famous in Irish history for his leadership of the arduous 'long march'. Photographs from earlier days show her as a beautiful woman, slim with lustrous dark hair and deeply set Irish eyes, which many of her children inherited, as did some of her grandchildren.

On her husband's death, my grandmother, Eily, was forced to buy Drominagh from her step children, due to a provision put in my great-grandmother's will that Drominagh and its lands should go to the first half of the family. Fortunately for all, Eily had a small income from a family trust fund, enabling her to hold on to Drominagh. Even so, things were more than tight for a widow with seven small offspring to raise and educate. She was also providing a home to most of the first family as well. My father Owen, was not yet ten, his brother Donal, eight, Witham, seven, and the twins, Eugene and Jimmy, just five years old. The only girl, Carmel, and the youngest, Paddy, were barely walking.

My father went to school at Downside Abbey run by the Dominican Order, just twelve miles south of Bath in England where he and his brothers enjoyed a life with pets. One such animal was a mischievous cygnet my father and his brothers had reared at Drominagh and took back to Downside, not an easy feat considering the trip took a couple of days with a crossing of the Irish Sea. It was housed in a large box and fed and watered regularly and arrived at Downside in fine fettle, whereupon the understanding headmaster built him a concrete tank with a wooden ramp and there it remained, apart from sojourns on the lawns, eventually becoming the school mascot, surviving for many years after my father and his brothers had left.

Initially, my father undertook this arduous trip to Downside on his own. In later years his brothers joined him in the pony and trap from Drominagh to the railway station at Cloughjordon ten miles away, then by train to Dublin. Thereafter it was across the sea by steamer and another long train trip to Downside. It was a daunting trip for a seasoned traveller in the middle of the Great War, let alone a small boy on his own, and later accompanying his smaller brothers.

One cold winter's evening, with smoke spiralling from his pipe as we sat by Cloneen's small drawing-room fire my father said, sighing, 'It would have been far more appropriate if I'd been sent to an Irish school, followed by agricultural college in Ireland, which of course would have made me better equipped for the running of Drominagh later on.'

His education did not equip him for the land, yet he gained a great love of history, geography and literature, which became his lifetime pursuits and pleasures.

Most of this travelling to and from Downside was carried out during the turbulent years of the 1st World War. The old city of Dublin Steam Packet Company's vessels, *Munster and Leinster*, made these crossings from what was then Kingstown (and is now known as Dun Laoghaire) to Holyhead.

As Ireland was also in the throes of the War of Independence, these ships were used by the British government as troop transporters, carrying whatever passengers could fit in.

'Schoolboys were given priority as they could be squeezed in almost anywhere,' my father said. 'One long night I stood terrified on the after deck, clinging on for dear life in a howling storm, with monstrous freezing waves crashing all around me. Under no circumstances was I allowed downstairs.'

The Leinster was later sunk by the Germans, just ten miles from Dun Laoghaire, with great loss of life, including a cousin of my father's, Thomas Esmonde. At this time there were about 20 Irish boys at Downside, travelling back and forth across the waters between Ireland and England.

The Esmonde brothers spent their years at Downside learning (although they did not excel in this, particularly Latin), and playing rugby and cricket (which my father didn't excel at either).

'However,' he told me, chuckling, 'I once caught a ball in my cupped hands when sleeping in the outer field and woke up suddenly to thunderous applause. But this was against Lord Dunalley's eleven at Nenagh in Tipperary, not at Downside.'

Their travelling companions comprised, amongst others, Dermot, the son of the unforgettable poet, novelist, playwright, great wit, and world-renowned drinker, Oliver St John Gogarty. Many an hour was spent having breakfast at the Gogartys' huge house in Dublin, filling in time before the train left for Tipperary. This is when my father's sister, Carmel first met Dermot, whom she later married. The wedding, a grand affair, was held in a marquee set up in the manicured lawns of Drominagh.

'The only hitch,' my mother told me with a laugh, 'being that the Bishop refused to allow another Dermot, Dermot Magillicuddy, son of the lovable and titled 'The Magillicuddy of the Reeks' to be best man as he was not a Catholic. At the last minute, Carmel's brother Paddy was roped in and Donal officiated.'

Oliver St John Gogarty described the wedding in one of his poems he wrote about my Uncle Eugene VC, DSO.

Of all the feasts that are jovial
A wedding feast is the best of all.
And now I am fondly recalling one
When your only sister married my son.

Chapter 4   Drominagh

And the tents were set and the tables spread
On lawns with branches overhead
And the bright air lingered, with music plied
On fields by the Shannon's broad-margined side

The wide still river too smooth for foam
As wide as the meadows around your home
The lake-like river that shone full brimmed
And half the day with its shining rimmed
To lend some rays of immortal mirth
To your ancient home on the dreaming earth.

Oliver St John Gogarty.

Back in his schooldays my father's mother had acquired a Model T Ford; however, this was taken over by the Republican forces for use in the guerrilla war being fought against the British occupation forces. She was pleased when it was returned in good order – with a brand new engine!

In their later school years, my grandmother bought a modest villa in Wimbledon Park, London, where the younger children were enrolled at Wimbledon College as day boarders. My father and the elder boys visited for long weekends and holidays.

'Drominagh was left in the very capable hands of Old Danny,' my father told us, 'with my mother in remote control in London until she returned to Drominagh in 1923. This is when she requested I return with her to run the farming lands, a request I could not refuse.'

During this period in London, my father and his brothers spent time with their school friend, Cyril McCormack, son of the famous Irish Tenor, Count John McCormack. My father said he was one of the few people, apart from the famous tenor's family, who could claim to have had the honour of hearing John McCormack sing to guests after tea in his own house.

At that time in history, ninety years ago, not one of the Irish gentry was supposed to speak with an Irish brogue. Hence all these elaborate schooling arrangements ensured that the brothers spoke with the most educated of English accents. Even now, I'm often asked why I don't speak with a brogue and I have to go into long explanations as to my parents' education. An Irish brogue is one of the loveliest in the world. Fortunately it is much encouraged nowadays and is a joy to listen to, both in speech and song.

Back then England was again at peace regarding the Great War, yet she was still at war with Ireland. Hence travel was often liable to be disrupted at any time by military operations. This of course was the bitter, tragic and bloody Civil War, which shook Ireland in 1922 and 1923 until the forces of the new Free State gained the upper hand and were able to establish law and order once again throughout the land. The bitterness of this Civil War, setting brother against brother, (and when Ballynastragh Castle was burned down), continued to bedevil Irish politics for generations. It has not subsided, even to this very day.

After spending some time working in the National Bank at the London Grosvenor Branch, and living in Wimbledon, where he commuted to work on a very smart BSA motor cycle with side car, my father managed to get a transfer to the Bank at Nenagh in Tipperary when his mother returned to Drominagh from her extended stay in London in 1923. With my father running the farming side of Drominagh, as well as working in the bank, and with the help of *Young Danny*, many of the younger Esmondes, including the half-brothers and -sisters, happily gathered here for part of the summer where long twilights were spent sitting languidly under one of the fir or lime trees, gazing out to the shimmering lake.

My father fell in love with my mother, Eira Margaret Antonia Mackenzie (Toni) in the summer of 1936 when she came to stay with her Aunt Winnie, at her stately home, Clonmoylan, on the other side of Lough Derg from Drominagh.

Alec Hingston, an old friend of the family, (the one I sent to collect my mother when I thought my father was about to depart this world), says of my mother as he knew her in 1936, 'Toni was a rare beauty. We were all a little in love with her, yet it was your father who won her heart.'

He told me this after he picked me up at Dublin Airport that May, when my father was dying and I'd flown in from Tasmania. Alec, too, knew the magic of Drominagh, having spent many of his school holidays as part of the Esmonde clan – for at the time his parents were living abroad in Kenya, not regarded as a healthy environment for a young boy. Hence he was dispatched to his grandparents back home in Ireland, who farmed the poor boy out to various friends and relations around England and Ireland (a normal occurrence at the time for many children, including my mother, whose parents were living in India during her school days). He, unlike all the Esmonde boys, who were educated in England, attended Blackrock College in Dublin where my brother Eugene went for a time before we moved to Australia. Alec's other grandmother was the noted writer, Katherine Tynan, whose daughter, Pamela Hinkson, wrote one of her many books while living at Drominagh.

'She stayed with us for quite a few months in 1939,' my mother told me, 'during which time she co-wrote, *Seventy*

Years Young, Memories of Elizabeth, Countess of Fingal, (Daisy), a fascinating liberated woman who married the 11th Earl of Fingal in 1883 when she was just seventeen. I remember Pamela was rather demanding, but as she was a PG (Paying Guest), and we needed the money desperately, we could do little but put up with her demands. And in fact a lot of the time she was great fun and very interesting.'

Recently my eldest daughter, Charlotte, picked up a new edition of this book and gave it to my mother, not knowing the connection. Needless to say my mother has hardly put it down since, as it's at least seventy years since she last read it and it's the most marvellous record of the times and people of that intriguing era.

Pamela also wrote a wonderful book called *Irish Gold*, which was actually set at Drominagh and is still available through online bookshops selling rare books.

My father described meeting my mother: 'In July, the 'Red Boat' arrived from Clonmoylan. It included a very beautiful young lady and her fiancé. She was Eira Margaret Antonia Mackenzie, niece of Winnie's, and as far as I was concerned the fiancé was rather superfluous, as I was extremely taken straight away. In fact before the summer was out I was very much in love and more than sad that she was out of reach.'

Fortunately the Red Boat arrived again in the August of the following year. This time the fiancé had been left behind and my mother was free. As my father states: 'This was very satisfactory from my point of view.' With the excuse of returning a lost earring, he traversed the lake in his small sailing boat from the Tipperary side to where Clonmoylan, a two-storey gabled house stood graciously on the Galway shores opposite, adjoined by a walled garden with wisteria and geraniums tumbling happily into beds of roses and vegetables.

An apple orchard and a myriad of stone fruit trees dotted the gently sloping lawns which ran into the fields rolling down to the lake.

In this splendid setting, my mother's enchanting Aunt Winnie, with her long thick flaxen hair often tied up in a neat bun, was now looking after numerous nieces and nephews, who'd returned from abroad, together with her own brood of four. Often she would throw magnificent weekend house parties, with the guests partaking in sailing competitions, boisterous games of tennis, or duck shooting. Sometimes the guests arrived on horseback, by boat across the lake, or by pony and trap.

It was during this time that my father eventually won my mother's heart. However, it took a couple of visits across the Irish Sea to London before matters were finalised and he arrived home to Drominagh to announce to his mother, Eily, that he and Toni, the daughter of George Henry Louis Mackenzie of Coul, Inverness, Scotland, were now an engaged couple. Not a notion that thrilled my grandmother in the least, having been used to having her eldest son to herself, not to mention at her every beck and call.

My mother was not just a rare beauty; more importantly as far as the Esmonde clan was concerned, she was also a skilled tennis player – a great asset to the competitive brothers, and in particular as a doubles partner to her new husband. My father, as always being humble at such times, said he was a fairly indifferent player himself and gives all the credit for their successes in the many competitions around Tipperary and Galway to my mother. As she only just missed out on playing at Wimbledon, a great feat for a woman at the time, perhaps his humility was well placed.

The marriage took place on the 19th February, 1938, at

the Garrison Church, Farnborough in England – from the house of my mother's cousins, General Sir Brian and Lady Taylor. My mother's uncle, Father Hugh Pope, was to have conducted the service. As he suddenly became ill at the last minute they were lucky to have my father's brother, Donal, as a guest. Fortunately for all, Donal had not long been ordained a Catholic priest, hence was able to step into the breach, performing his duty with great aplomb, with my mother's young nieces, Deirdre and Phillida, as bridesmaids.

They look a handsome couple standing on an Indian rug in the lush garden at Farnborough this misty February morning. My mother's wedding dress is not unlike many of the fashions of these modern times, my father resplendent in his morning suit.

Spending their honeymoon on the Tyrol near Innsbruck at Ehrwald in Austria, they took a chairlift up the Zugspitz on the border of Austria and Germany.

'We were amongst the last people to walk the tunnel into Germany shortly before it closed during the war,' my mother told me as we looked at an old snap of them skiing on the alps.

Back at Drominagh after the honeymoon, my father endeavoured to make a living, but it was not always easy as the economy in Ireland was in dire straits, with the Great Depression casting a gloomy shadow over the entire land. Needless to say it was also somewhat difficult for the new bride, as Eily still saw herself as lady of the house.

It was only when we were leaving for Australia many years later that she called my mother aside, explaining her unreasonable attitude: 'I just imagined when you married Owen you'd become another member of the family. Like one of my children,' she told my mother apologetically, with compassion in her thickly lashed troubled eyes. 'Looking back,

I should have realised you'd want to have a say in how the household was run.'

My grandmother wrote a novel at this time, called *Inistaig*, about a couple living in a large mansion in Tipperary with the husband's mother. It described an idyllic household in perfect harmony.

'Not quite the truth,' my mother told me recently with a smile. 'Yet its royalties brought in much needed funds when it was serialised in the American *Notre Dame* magazine, so it was a blessing in a way…giving us some sort of security for a while.'

I've hunted everywhere for a copy. So far I've been unsuccessful.

Any spare time from running Drominagh's estate back then was spent hunting or dapping on the lake and fishing when the trout were biting, playing tennis or sailing with the brothers and Carmel when they returned from England and other parts of the world. For a time, before the war, it was a wonderful carefree existence, apart from financial woes.

Dapping on Lough Derg was one of my father's greatest loves. It is almost a religion in Ireland, particularly on Lough Derg, one of the few limestone lakes that breed the mayfly in the months of May and early June.

Sir Thomas Gratton Esmonde wrote in his book *Hunting Memories* in the 1920s: 'May Fly rising; come at once.'

> This telegram on my London breakfast table puts thought of all else out of my head: *The irresistible call of the wild is in my ears and nothing else matters. But of all the dapping districts, I prefer Lough Derg, and I know of no place where this fishing is to be carried on amid more romantic surroundings or lovelier scenery. And nowhere are there better fish, heavier or stronger fighters than in the great lake to whose shores I have brought my readers.*

I last read from this book of my uncle's when I was having a couple of weeks in Paris, one of my favourite cities. Once more I rummaged amongst the shelves of old books and magazines in the quaint and renowned Shakespeare's Book Shop, a special haunt of mine, and found a rare copy hidden behind other dust-covered books on the top floor. I took the somewhat battered copy and sat at the tiny window shrouded in the splendid purple early spring flowers of a Virginia creeper and read for over an hour. I almost felt as though I was there at Drominagh too, with my uncle, my father and his siblings as they donned their long waders and hauled the wooden row boat through the rushes for a day's fishing on the lake. I also looked at Shakespeare's for copies of the *Notre Dame* magazine with my grandmother's articles. Alas, none were to be found.

My mother assures me that even my father would admit he wasn't the best of farmers, with most of his orders being shouted out of the bathroom window on the second floor of Drominagh (when he was having a shave) to the workmen in the cobbled courtyard down below. Only recently I stood at that very same window and imagined him doing just that. Not quite the normal way farms are managed. Yet, what is normal, particularly in Ireland – and particularly in the Esmonde family? After all, this was a family who'd lost John Esmonde in 1798 to a political hanging by the British on O'Connell's Bridge in Dublin. His son was on his way to tell his father he'd been given a reprieve. Tragically, when he got there his father was dangling from the hangman's noose. Undaunted by this atrocious act by the British, the son went on to serve in the British Navy, captaining the notorious frigate, *Lion,* into battle.

CHAPTER 5

An Irish Hero

The Second World War changed many things at Drominagh, as each of the brothers decided to cross the channel and join the British forces in their fight against Germany and its allies, leaving Eily and my mother to run the estate. Eugene, VC, DSO, my father's younger brother and Jimmy's twin was the tragic star, yet the others deserved immense praise too.

Eugene died aged just thirty-two while serving in the British Fleet Air Arm in 1942, leading a flight of Swordfish in the Channel Dash chase of the *Prince Eugen, Gneisenau* and *Scharnhorst* and was awarded the Victoria Cross posthumously.

Codenamed Fuller, the surface and aerial British planners' view was that the German ships would pass the straits of Dover in darkness and could therefore be attacked safely by the vintage Swordfish in the protective cloak of night and without the need for fighter escort.

How wrong that was.

On Wednesday 11th February, Eugene left Manston, where he was stationed with his 825 squadron and travelled to London to receive his newly awarded Distinguished Service Order (DSO) (for his effort in sinking the great German battleship, *The Bismarck in* May 1941) from the King. Unbeknown to him, whilst he was happily celebrating his award back at Manston, the German Admiral Ciliax issued orders for *The Scharnhorst*, followed by *Gneisenau, Prinz Eugen* and accompanying surface escorts to slip out of Brest at 9.15pm undetected. After a series of mishaps and errors by the RAF and RN, they sailed on for another thirteen hours before they were spotted. All hell let loose. On the 12th February Eugene was faced with the unthinkable – a daytime attack. The odds against the Swordfish were high, but Eugene had no intention of sending his Squadron out on a suicide mission. Yet that is what it virtually ended up being.

'Forget all you've learned of a night time attack,' he told his Squadron. 'We'll attack in sub-flights in line astern at a height of 50 feet. We'll have plenty of fighter cover so you won't have to worry too much about enemy aircraft.'

Wing Commander John Gleave, the RAF Station Commander at Manston, met Eugene as he walked to his aircraft and wished him good luck.

Gleave said, 'The look on his face shook me. It was the face of a man already dead. It shocked me as nothing had before, nor has done since.'

Apart from Eugene's Victoria Cross, eighteen men of 825 Squadron were all decorated, thirteen of them posthumously. Eugene's body was washed up on the banks of the Thames Estuary many weeks later. He was identified by a small gold ring on his left little finger bearing the word Jerusalem, part of the Esmonde family's coat of arms. A few days later he was given a Royal military funeral at Gillingham cemetery with all the trimmings befitting a hero.

On the 3rd March, 1942, my grandmother received the following letter:

I am commanded by My Lords, Commissioners of the Admiralty, to inform you that the King has been graciously pleased to award the Victoria Cross to your son, Lieutenant-Commander Eugene Esmonde, DSO, Royal Navy for valour, in the action in which he lost his life.

On the morning of Thursday, the 12th of February, 1942, Lieutenant-Commander Esmonde, in command of a Squadron of the Fleet Air Arm, was told that the German Battle Cruisers Scharnhorst and Gneisenau and the Cruiser Prince Eugen, strongly escorted by some thirty surface craft, were entering the Straits of Dover, and that his Squadron must attack before they reached the sandbanks North East of Calais.

Lieutenant-Commander Esmonde knew well that his enterprise was desperate. Soon after noon, he and his Squadron of six Swordfish set course for the enemy, and after ten minutes' flight were attacked by a strong force of fighters. Touch was lost with his fighter escort and in the action which followed, all his aircraft were damaged. He flew on, cool and resolute, serenely challenging hopeless odds, to encounter the deadly fire of the Battle Cruisers and their Escort, which shattered the port wing of his aircraft. Undismayed, he led his Squadron on, straight into this inferno of fire. Almost at once he was shot down; but his Squadron launched a determined attack, in which at least one torpedo is believed to have struck the German Battle Cruisers, and from which not one of the six aircraft returned.

His high courage and splendid resolution will live in the traditions of the Royal Navy, and remain for many a generation a fine and stirring memory.

I am to express Their Lordships' pleasure at this, the

highest mark of His Majesty's appreciation and their deep regret that your son did not live to receive it.
I am, Madam,
Your obedient Servant.
HR Markham.

As I mentioned, the day before his tragic death, Eugene received the DSO for his action in launching a torpedo at *The Bismarck*, which hit the ship and slowed it down before the British navy finally finished it off. In foul weather, and against strong head winds, on the 24th May, 1941, he led a strike of nine Swordfish armed with torpedoes from the aircraft carrier *Victorious*. Sighting the Bismarck some eight miles ahead, he led the Squadron into attack. Flying though intense anti-aircraft fire and sustaining some damage, the Squadron pressed home the attack, claiming a torpedo hit on the starboard side of *The Bismarck*, which finally sank on the 27th May.

Eugene was not the only Esmonde involved with the fate of *The Bismarck*. The next day, the Admiral of the Fleet took his destroyers in to attack the wounded battleship. Second in this line was the impudent little ship *Zulu*, her engineer officer being Eugene's debonair older brother, Lieutenant-Commander Witham Esmonde. Witham said that to try and get the engines to put out more speed, everyone on board had to grab tables, chairs and anything else they could lay their hands on, and hurl them into the boilers.

And in a convoy fewer than 20 miles from the Swordfish action, Eugene's twin brother, Jimmy, was sailing home from his job in the mines of the Gold Coast in Africa when their boat was torpedoed. Fortunately he survived.

Oliver St John Gogarty (the father of Eugene's sister

Carmel's husband, Dermot) wrote a poem in Eugene's honour... the first verse being:

> *Eugene well got!!! Well born, I mean.*
> *Of Norman knights on the Irish scene,*
> *Who threw in their lot with the Irish lot*
> *And with them for liberty turned and fought.*
> *If I were told of the Clan Esmonde,*
> *The best would be known of Ireland.*

My father proudly received the Victoria Cross for his brother from King George V1, (of *The King's Speech*) together with his mother, Eily, in her wheel chair, having been partially crippled in an accident where she hit her head on the door frame of a chicken shed at Drominagh some years before.

Eily's youngest son, Paddy, stood proudly on the other side of her wheel chair as the King presented the Cross.

King George had kindly arranged for a special plane to fly from England to collect Eily, Carmel, and Paddy from Sydenham, Belfast. The plane came from Lee On Solent, Eugene's station, and was flown by a fellow Lieutenant Commander and a great friend of his. Arriving in dreadful weather the tiny plane ferried the contingent across the Irish Sea to Sealands, Chester; then to London where they landed at Hendon and met up with my father. The 5th Sea Lord had sent his own personal Bentley. By six o'clock they were in London drinking tea at the popular Welbeck Hotel.

When asked if she was tired, after the long, arduous journey from deep in the countryside of neutral Ireland to war-torn London, my grandmother seemed surprised. 'No. Of course not,' she stated airily. 'Why should I be?'

At ten o'clock the following morning, 17th March, St

Patrick's Day, a day befitting such an occasion and with shamrocks pinned to their lapels, the party drove to Buckingham Palace where a wicker bath chair awaited my grandmother. A few minutes later my father and Paddy carried her inside to the front row. Shortly, King George arrived and when the time came to hand over the award he leaned down, telling my grandmother how he had met Eugene not long before – when he had proudly pinned on his DSO.

Paddy tells us that the King's manner to his mother was lovely. He says: 'The beauty of those few minutes was indescribable and I remember feeling as I stood there and watched in a daze of admiration that Eugene was not far away. The King shook my mother by the hand and smiled and he looked at Owen and me and shook our hands.'

A few days later my grandmother returned to Drominagh, where my mother and my two elder sisters, Deborah, aged four, and Gill, two, waited. The noble grey walls of Drominagh once more received a symbol of an Esmonde who had done his duty in the service of England.

The *Tattler* and *Bystander* reported in bold print, along with a large photograph of my grandmother, my father, and Uncle Paddy:

> *Wearing the shamrock of St Patrick, Mrs Esmonde was accompanied by her sons, Pilot Officer Owen Esmonde and Captain Patrick Esmonde when she went to Buckingham Palace to receive the VC.*

The article went on to say: *The King asked Mrs Esmonde: 'How many sons do you have fighting in the services at present, Mrs Esmonde?'*

She answered bravely: 'Only four now, Your Majesty.'

My father became a reluctant media star, as his photo, together with his mother's and Paddy's, blazed out from nearly every newspaper in England and Ireland at the time. Needless to say, being rather shy, this caused him some consternation, but as he was so enormously proud of his younger brother, and mourned his loss dreadfully, he was happy to do all he could to honour him and commemorate his memory, as well as be a staunch support for his mother and the rest of the family.

The first Esmonde Victoria Cross was won by Captain Thomas Esmonde, my great uncle, in the Crimea…*for repeatedly rescuing wounded under fire of shell and grape shot, and particularly for extinguishing a fireball before it could betray the position of his men.*

After my grandmother died, my father was the custodian of Eugene's Victoria Cross until his own death. For many years, along with the family silver, it spent time in the vaults of the Bank of Ireland at Rathdrum. Now its home is with the Imperial War Museum in England, having been loaned to them by my brother, Eugene, Uncle Eugene's namesake, born soon after his untimely death, whose care it was entrusted to after my father's death.

In the week before the Queen's Diamond Jubilee, I was lucky enough to go to the museum with my daughter, Charlotte, to view the display, together with the display for Thomas Esmonde. We also went to a commemorative lunch for Victoria Cross and George Cross holders at the Union Jack Club and a service at St Martin-in-the-Field where Prince Charles and his wife, Camilla, were the honoured guests. I was also fortunate to meet two of our Australian Victoria Cross holders, Keith Payne, who was awarded his cross for a heroic act in the Vietnam War and Ben Roberts-Smith who was a hero in the war in Afghanistan. It was a memorable day and both Charlotte and I were extremely proud to be representing my uncle.

Eugene Esmonde, VC, DSO, was also one of the first pilots to fly with Imperial Airways, later Qantas, on the Australian route.

Some years before he joined the RAF, thinking he had a vocation to be a Catholic Priest, Eugene spent a few years studying to be a Mill Hill Father at St Peter's College, Freshfield, so that he could become a missionary. It wasn't long before he discovered this was not for him. About the only point of agreement between him and the good Fathers was on his unsuitability for missionary work. It was an odd choice of career from the beginning.

Small and wiry (he was only five feet six) with a round face and mischievous deeply set Irish eyes, he was a strange mixture of fun, intellectualism, sober mindedness, and native shrewdness.

He parted with the Fathers on excellent terms, promptly deciding on a more civilised and thoroughly dangerous occupation – the air. In 1928 he joined the Royal Air Force with a short service commission, at once volunteering to take part in bomber operations over the sea, a decidedly risky affair not many of those early pioneers cared to chance. There was no Fleet Air Arm in those days, and although the Navy operated several aircraft carriers, the first biplane bombers attached to them were manned by the RAF.

From the RAF he joined Imperial Airways and, for the next five years from age twenty-three, he played a major and active role in the emergence of the world's initial commercial flights. Amongst other feats he flew Catalina Flying Boats across the world to Darwin for Imperial Airways, where he delivered the first surcharged airmail to Australia and the first internal airmails in India to the Viceroy and his wife, Lord and Lady Linlithgow. By 1936 he ranked high on the list of experienced long haul pilots, then almost all employed by Imperial Airways. His co-pilots referred to him as the 'smallest meteor alive'. He was never conscious of his lack of inches, his vital personality making it almost unnoticeable to others. If a friend made jocular reference to it he would laugh: 'Yes, but if the engines pack up you lot need a parachute. All I need is a pocket-handkerchief.'

But where was that pocket-handkerchief when he needed it most?

Hitler's ranting reached a crescendo at the Nuremburg Rally in 1938 and the Esmondes' paradox came out in Eugene. While he was Irish to his bootstraps, he realised Britain was the only defence against a fascist Germany threatening the liberty of the whole world. He, like a lot of Irishmen, was prepared to fight and if necessary give his life for freedom. Yet in January 1939 he was faced with a dilemma. Could he afford to give up a good salary from Imperial Airways in return for a dubious future in one of His Majesty's armed forces?

The solution to his troubles came from the Admiralty. The Navy had formed the Fleet Air Arm some years earlier, but lacked trained pilots to give it backbone. Eugene was well known for his expertise on the flight deck of carriers and his name was recalled with admiration by those responsible for this young branch of the Navy. He was asked to join – with the rank of Lieutenant Commander with a guarantee of service for at least fifteen years, which was important to him, as he wanted to help his mother and my father with the running costs of Drominagh.

With his usual humour he sent a letter to the Admiralty asking: *Does the guarantee of fifteen years' service at least, prevent me from becoming an Admiral?*

The Secretary to the Board of Admiralty replied in similar vein: *Not at all. If you elect to remain in the Service you might well become an Admiral, if that is really what you want.*

Unfortunately his wish, whimsical as it may have been, was not to be granted, yet for the number of years he was with the Fleet Air Arm he sent money home to help with the upkeep of Drominagh – where years before he'd landed a Gypsy Moth in the 22-acre field at the back of the house, much to the delight of the rest of the family. However, he baulked at Paddy's request to pass his share of Drominagh over to his mother and my father who'd kept it going for so long, while the others all pursued their own careers. Eugene felt his career in the Services would probably be short lived. So he wanted to have Drominagh to come home to without feeling he was just a guest. This, in hindsight, I can quite understand; however, my mother told me: 'At the time it caused quite a bit of angst.'

Ironically, on his death, his share went to his mother anyway, as the sole beneficiary of his will.

Supposedly, he was a great party man and like most Irishmen enjoyed the odd tipple. The telling of his escapades grew better with each drink.

I asked my mother if he was good looking. 'Lord no,' she laughed. 'When I first saw him walking across the lawns at Drominagh I thought he was the new gardener. Even then I thought he was a very unimposing gardener. But he had great charm.'

Similar to most heroes he had a certain recklessness to him. My mother also told me that on his last trip back to Drominagh before he was killed, he relished the peace and quiet of the familiar surroundings away from the traumas of war.

'It's something I'll always take with me,' he told her. 'And keep close to my heart.'

When she asked him if he was ever afraid of flying on operations, he replied: 'I'm always afraid of being afraid, Toni.'

I have in my possession Winston Churchill's victory speech titled: 'Forward Till the Whole Task Is Done,' where he mentions amongst other matters:

> *When I think of these days I think also of other episodes and personalities. I think of Lieutenant-Commander Eugene Esmonde, VC, DSO, of Lance Corporal Kenneally, VC, and Captain Fegen, VC, and other Irish heroes that I could easily recite, and then I must confess that bitterness by Britain against the Irish race dies in my heart. I can only pray that in years, which I shall not see, the shame will be forgotten and the glories will endure, and that the peoples of the British Isles as of the British Commonwealth of Nations will walk together in mutual comprehension and forgiveness...*
> —*Winston Churchill. May 13th 1945.*

My mother told me that this speech infuriated the Esmonde family enormously, for they felt Churchill had been fairly unprofessional in his approach to the organisation of the Channel Dash and its aftermath. Unfortunately for all, Churchill was also wrong in his prediction that the conflict in Ireland would pass, particularly in the counties of the north.

Eugene's many letters from abroad to his mother at home in Drominagh describe in great detail his passion for flying and the adventures of which he partook. He had a wonderful relationship with his mother, and not being married, he told her of his exploits, feelings and hopes for the future as if she were his companion. There was one where he tells how he had to dramatically crash land in the desert after engine trouble. He and his passengers, whom he'd picked up in Karachi, survived for several days with little water and provisions before a rescue party thankfully arrived. Much longer and they'd all have perished in the intense heat.

The first letter I have of his is written on Imperial Airways letterhead on the 17th of December 1934 when he was flying to Australia. After crossing over to Paris he travelled by train to Brindisi in Italy, where he took command of his flight – and where Rob and I anchored on our yacht, *Sea Dreams*, seventy-five years later. The last letter is written shortly before his death.

All Esmonde brothers served in the English forces during the war, apart from Donal, who became a Mill Hill Missionary priest in Kenya. My father, after a short course at Uxbridge, was posted to Sheffield Balloon Barrage as a Pilot Officer in the RAF Volunteer Reserve. Being thirty-seven at the time he was mainly restricted to Administration, which frustrated him enormously.

Witham, in the Royal Navy, was awarded the Distinguished Service Cross (DSC) for his service on HMS *Mowri*.

Paddy, a doctor in the Royal Medical Corps, was awarded the Military Cross, finishing his career as a medical officer at Sandhurst Military College.

Much to my joy, the Irish Government has now decided to honour its Irish heroes who fought for Britain during the wars. Previously there was a definite feeling that they should not be acclaimed, due to Ireland's neutrality, but most of all her animosity towards Britain. In fact Thomas Esmonde, VC, and Eugene Esmonde, VC, DSO, were hardly acknowledged at all in their own country, a tragedy I found difficult to believe. For surely, by fighting for freedom, the enemy of Britain and her allies, Ireland, as her near neighbour, had more to gain than most.

'This lack of recognition was a great sorrow to your grandmother,' my mother told me. 'When you think how her five sons readily joined up and one lost his life you can imagine how she felt.'

I might point out here that it's almost unheard of to find a family with two Victoria Crosses, let alone an Irish family fighting for England when Ireland was neutral, and with some controversy as to where her allegiance lay.

CHAPTER 6

On the Shores of the Shannon

I began my life at Drominagh as a ten-day-old baby in 1946. I howled my way into this world at the busy Rotunda hospital in the heart of Dublin on the 4th September. My godfather was the renowned Rickard Deasy, squire of the beautiful estate, Gurtray, not far from Drominagh and who was famous in Ireland as head of the Irish Farmers Association and leader of the notorious Irish Farmers March in 1967. My godmother was Rosemary Esmonde, my father's spinster half-sister, with whom I kept in touch until her death many years after we arrived in Australia. She was, in fact, a great favourite of mine, not least because of her long flowing hair that fell to her knees like a spindly spider's web, but also because every birthday I'd receive a cheque for the amount of years I was turning. This finally petered out when I became twenty-one.

I don't remember Drominagh from that stage as I was only eighteen months when I left; however, I do remember it from the many visits I've had there since. One particular trip I recall was in 1979 when I took my two daughters, Charlotte and Georgina, aged eleven and seven, to visit the land of my birth, the first time I'd returned there since leaving in 1954.

After a week or so at Cloneen in Glendalough we drove down with my parents to Tipperary to stay in a traditional Irish cottage at Puckaun on Lough Derg. With great glee my father showed us his beloved Drominagh and O'Kennedy's castle where he and his siblings had played amongst the ruins as children. We scrambled to the top and admired the expansive view of the Shannon River where the thick callows crawled with waterfowl, golden plovers, ducks and a myriad of other bird life. It was a cold day, the lake was big and an icy wind blew across from the Tipperary Mountains shrouded in thick clouds. Shortly after our ascent of the castle it sadly collapsed in a heap of rubble. The present owners had removed the ivy, which my father assured me had been holding it together for centuries. Being one of the oldest castles in Ireland its sad demise made the front page of the *Irish Times*.

The stables brought back memories of my parents' horses, Dalmi and Jane, waiting excitedly for the hunt. No matter what the weather conditions, my father loved these events until the time he was severely injured with a split kidney and had to fight for his own life. Both of my parents were competent hunters. Summers were wonderful times of swimming, lazing and hunting.

On Dublin trips my parents stayed at a private hotel and frequented clubs in the evenings, including the United Arts Club, which my mother described as a most convivial and inspirational venue, with artists and poets including Jack B Yeates, brother of WB Yeates, and Oliver St John Gogarty, gracing its grand rooms. She said, 'It was a wonderful time of fun and gaiety.'

My mother adored the lavish Hunt Balls and the August Dublin Horse Show with the associated grand ball in the evening at which my father wore his 'hunting pink' and the ladies, silks and taffetas. They sometimes attended the rowdy dances at the leading Dublin hotels, including the famous Gresham and the Shelbourne.

'Although it was great fun,' my mother added with a laugh, in case I thought they were totally frivolous, 'it wasn't all parties. There was a lot of scrimping and saving…and hard work too.'

One of my parents' ventures at Drominagh was to run charters up and down the Shannon River on *The Wayfarer*; a wonderful old wooden houseboat, which my father turned into 'a smart white cruiser with green topsides'. They found *The Wayfarer* in June, 1938, where she was moored in the docks at Portumna on Lough Derg. She was originally brought from Gloucester on the Avon by Sir Robert Woods, a renowned Dublin surgeon, and was towed from there to Kingstown in April 1917. After a few more owners she came into the grateful hands of my parents.

Privacy for the young couple at Drominagh was difficult to attain with my grandmother in residence, so *The Wayfarer* provided a needy haven. Recently, I discovered my father's log books from that time. There seemed to be a lot of time spent 'recovering with a strong whisky down below'. Not dissimilar to what we've done over the years after a stormy ride on our own yachts, although now, as we sail the Mediterranean on *Sea Dreams* it's an icy cool *vino* that we relish at the end of a long hot day.

Not all the charters on *The Wayfarer* were incident free. One late summer's afternoon my father was happily chugging along with a half a dozen passengers when he noticed that the deck chair and the elderly lady who'd been on it, dozing off her lunch and wine, were missing! An hysterical scream alarmed him and he swivelled around to see the deck chair bobbing along and a cream calico tent-like apparition flailing its tentacles in terror in the air, screaming raucously, 'Help! Help!' Fully dressed, my father leaped into the water and with a life raft, rescued her, but lost the deck chair. Fifty years later, my father chuckled with mirth when telling us this tale as we sat on Rob's and my yacht, *The Charlotte Rose*, fishing in Tasmanian waters. 'She was extremely forgiving and appeared at cocktail hour in fine form,' he said as he hauled in a flathead, one of twenty we'd caught that day.

Our log books on all of the yachts we've owned sound remarkably similar to my father's. Most times the weather is better 'elsewhere', yet the satisfaction of dropping anchor in a new and undiscovered destination is second to none.

During the war years, shopping was done by bicycle to Terryglass some 10 miles away or by sailboat across the lake to Portumna. This was the time of petrol rations. Even *The Wayfarer* could only be used sparingly. My mother tells of many times coming home from Terryglass with her bicycle laden down with Christmas presents for the children waiting anxiously for Santa Claus. Needless to say, Santa was not overly generous during the war years and an orange was a great surprise.

Drominagh is a lucky house. When the Esmondes sold it in 1947 it went to a wonderful family who still have it today. They're extremely generous to the Esmondes and each year Viv and her family come over from Wales, spending two weeks there (joined occasionally by those of us who happen to be in Ireland), and pretend that it is 'like the old times'. But my mother refuses to stay in Drominagh, saying it would bring back too many memories. However, she'll come with one of us to visit for a few hours from time to time. One year she stayed with Rob and me in the glorious Gertalougha Private Hotel next door, which is once again a private home, now belonging to the Getty family. From there we walked through the woods to Drominagh to have afternoon tea with the delightful caretaker, Helen, who welcomed us all with open arms.

We often dream of buying Drominagh back, but even if the owners wanted to sell, it remains a dream. Besides, who would look after her – with four of us in Australia and Viv in Wales?

CHAPTER 7

Across the Lake at Clonmoylan

Clonmoylan on the other side of Lough Derg and in County Galway, where we moved to in 1947 when I was eighteen months old, looks much the same today as when I lived there as a child, apart from a central heating system throughout and a new sunroom added to the front overlooking the lake. Only last month I visited for old times' sake and was kindly ushered into the kitchen at the back where, just like at Drominagh, the original Aga takes centre stage.

The only difference when driving up the long wooded avenue is that the apple orchard has long gone.

In 1947 many of our goods and chattels were ferried in a small rowing boat across the lake from Drominagh with my father at the helm. The rest he carted by tractor towing a trailer.

When we drove for the last time down the long avenue from Drominagh, we passed the stone gatehouse, where the faithful Boyle family, who'd served the Esmondes for so many years, were standing with tears in their eyes.

It was then that Gill was heard to lament in her usual compassionate way. 'This old house is going to be very lonely without us.'

No doubt it was – not just for us but for all the Esmondes who'd enjoyed her serenity, happiness and sadness for so many decades before. But it was no longer possible for us to continue life at Drominagh. Finances were stretched to the limit, overdrafts were not viable and prospects of matters improving were grim indeed. Sadly there was no alternative other than to sell up and buy something smaller. Fortunately that something smaller happened to be Clonmoylan across the lake where my father had first met my mother at her Aunt Winnie's. My father felt that the harvest from Clonmoylan's apple orchard, together with poultry farming, would provide him with enough income to see us through.

My parents felt the move more than we did. I can only imagine my father's feelings in leaving his wonderful childhood home – a home that had given so much, but taken as well. Eily must have felt this too. Little did we realise that we had taken the first step towards our new life in Australia.

Unlike my siblings, I didn't have a nanny, but often ate with Mary, the young maid and Brownie, my father's worker on the farm and in the orchard, in the kitchen. I am still nostalgic for the heady aroma of baking, the warmth of the Aga with clothes drying above it on cold mornings, wet gumboots by the grate and Mary's sweet smell of soap and onions.

A large cobblestone dairy off the kitchen, where pails of fresh milk were laden with thick cream on top and the old wooden churner that we used to help Mary make butter with stood in the corner, led to the stable yards and workshops. Here we would annoy the ever-patient Brownie until he came and did whatever task we could beg him to do, whether it be to help catch the horses or mend whatever we'd broken before our parents could see.

My father turned a small first floor room into a tiny chapel where he housed our statue of the Blessed Virgin. Likewise, a dining room eventually became a bed sitter for Eily when visiting from Dublin.

On the shores of the lake my father built a jetty, much like the one he'd built in Drominagh years ago. I used to catch my legs between the wooden slats and I remember I had to wear a rubber swimming cap, which pulled my hair dreadfully. I also wore a red woollen swimming suit, which was immensely itchy and I seemed to spend most of my time in gumboots handed down from my older siblings. Even on Eugene's First Communion day, as a photo of the day shows, I'm dressed in my Sunday best, with my gumboots on. Although, when I brought this up with my mother recently she assured me I did *not* go to the communion service in gumboots. Obviously they'd been prised off my feet before then.

The jetty where we tied the row boats up became the centre of activities for us children as we played and swam amidst the rushes – with the older ones mucking around in the small row boat. I swam in the shallows inside a huge rubber tyre or was pushed around in a contraption my father made – called the 'bog cart', which consisted of a wooden platform on two drums, and created waves for the others to dive under, giving me the greatest excitement.

Oh the simple joys of youth!

Deborah (Dibs) and Gill were the 'big ones'; Viv and I 'the little ones'. Poor Eugene was stuck in the middle. Dibs and Eugene look very alike – their huge blue-grey eyes ringed by eyelashes as thick and long as hollyhocks (from my father's side) – with the rest of us having the brown eyes of my mother's side.

When it wasn't raining, our adored small brown mare, Peggy, took us in the trap to Sunday mass, with my father holding the reins and my mother beside him clasping her tweed hat in one hand, and her other arm wrapped around me. The rest of the family perched in the back. We were devastated to find Peggy dead in the fields from old age. She was tolerant of most games but hated double decking as Viv and I discovered one freezing morning when she dumped us unceremoniously on the ground, scaring my father, who came running to check for signs of life. 'Fortunately,' he said, 'there was plenty of it and rather noisy it was too.'

We also worshipped, but were somewhat wary of Merrylegs, a cunning and devilish grey Connemara pony, whose greatest trick was to fly under the nearest fence with whoever was on board. Years later I acquired another Merrylegs in our Australian Drominagh. She did exactly the same thing. Merrylegs at Clonmoylan could only be coaxed to move forward if Gill or Eugene banged on two cake tins with sticks, whereupon she would take off like a rocket, with whoever was on board hanging on for dear life.

Powers Cross, two miles away, was our closest village, 'village' really being too grand a word for the one shop housing the post office. Viv, only five at the time, rode her small bike there regularly to do the messages, stopping off for a bite to eat at one of the farms on the way – a different and safer world then.

When we were passing a donkey and a foal in a field on the road to Portumna, my small voice was heard from the back of the van: 'Slow 'em down, Dad...want to see baby donkey.'

My father, being a soft touch as far as I was concerned, was eventually persuaded to allow Early Mist to become part of our family. Related to a mule, he was stubborn, but I loved him dearly, often bringing him up to the kitchen door to be fed scraps by the ever-patient Mary, once even bringing him inside by the Aga when it was very cold. He bluntly refused to do what I wanted. However, with his huge floppy ears, mournful eyes, and furry coat he had me wrapped around his hoof, so to speak.

Viv was allowed to ride a somewhat easier addition to the family, Billy Boy, a chestnut Galloway but to my annoyance I was only allowed to ride him if being led. Viv was not allowed to jump him but did so frequently, swearing Brownie and me to secrecy.

Dibs and Gill, being a bit older, rode for miles to join the local hunt and would often arrive home, soaked to the skin well after dark. Gill in fact got so lost after one hunt meet that she had to take shelter with a local farmer, where eventually my worried parents found her sitting by the huge peat fire drinking hot chocolate. No matter how cold the weather was we were always outside, even if there was three feet of snow covering the ground – when Brownie would attach Peggy to the snow cart and continue to do his chores with all of us helping.

Viv was the adventurer of the family, always in one escapade after the other, usually with me, just 18 months younger, as her accomplice. She had the beauty of a princess with her dark curls, peaches and cream complexion and luminous brown eyes flashing brightly like polished chestnuts. Needless to say she could wrap anyone around her finger, particularly Brownie who called her 'the worst girl in central Europe!' Why central Europe we could never work out.

Brownie went on in later life to win the largest lottery in Ireland. Yet, until the day he died, he still lived in the same cottage he'd built when we left him to come to Australia.

'What would I be wanting to move for?' he said, raising his hat and scratching his mop of thick grey hair when I last visited him. 'Haven't I got all I want here?'

Inside his white-washed cottage I sat with him by the fire,

sipping steaming cups of tea listening to him talk longingly of his days at Clonmoylan.

'Sure, there's never been another family like you lot,' he said with a chuckle. 'We were all devastated when you left for Australia. But look at you now. Who would have thought young Teeny would have turned into such a fine lass. And Viv... well,' he laughed out loud. 'Never in a month of Sundays would I have thought that one would have survived to be a teenager, let alone the grand lady she is now.'

Although we children were finding Clonmoylan paradise, it was not quite the same for my parents. Once again they were finding it hard to make a living in these difficult times in Ireland, especially with five young children to educate. Being in an isolated part of East Galway, boarding schools were the only option – costing an arm and a leg.

Somehow they scrounged the money to send Dibs and Gill to board with the Sacré Coeur nuns at Mount Anville at Dundrum in Dublin; Eugene to Killashee and then Blackrock College, while Viv and I managed to continue the Esmonde tradition of going through an amazing number of governesses at home in Clonmoylan.

We were not the easiest of children to teach; many poor governesses came and left in a very short space of time. We spent hours thinking up scams to scare them off. On more than one occasion we were successful, much to the horror of my parents who'd spent many a day enticing these kind young women to up stakes from Dublin and come and work in the wilds of outback Galway in the first place.

In the early days at Clonmoylan, on the occasions when we didn't have a governess, the older ones would ride their bikes to the one-teacher school at Shragh some five miles away. Or if it was in the trap with Merrylegs, they'd set off with

Merrryleg's lunch in a chaff bag. She would then spend the day with neighbours next door to the school until they were ready for the return trip. A couple of times I was allowed to travel with them and sit in to see what real school was like. I didn't go to a proper school until I was eight and in Australia.

The local undertaker had a horse-drawn hearse, known as the Coff, often seen standing outside a Corpse House, where a recently deceased would be laid out for respects to be duly paid. We soon worked out that this was a great place for children to acquire sweets and other delicious treats, so a few times we'd drop in after school to pay our respects, hovering around until finally someone offered us something from the table. I remember thinking that the Coff horses were a bizarre combination, with not much thought going into matching them in size, colour or status. Sometimes a tiny pony was harnessed with a huge 17-hand workhorse, making for a comical sight, let alone a rather bumpy ride for the corpse in the coffin.

Electricity came to Clonmoylan early in the 1950s, causing great excitement. Before that we had kerosene lamps to read by and only the wood-fired Aga to cook on. When going to bed in the long dark winter evenings, we'd ascend the three flights of stairs carrying our small painted china lanterns firmly in our hands, carefully placing them on the table beside our bed where they'd remain until my mother or father came to say goodnight, safely blowing them out.

In front of Clonmoylan was Friar's Island to which we'd row over in the small wooden boat to explore with great delight. Alive with wild goats and feral cats it boasted a rat-infested ruin. The herd of goats started when Mrs Conary, our ironing lady, who lived at Powers Cross, would bring Eugene a kid goat as a present now and then, much to my father's horror, who banished them to the island. Needless to say, before too long they were breeding in healthy numbers.

My remembrances are of Irish summers of long golden twilights, picnics under the beech tree on the lawn, adults in deck chairs with children on thick blankets spread at their feet, the smell of newly cut hay and lavender, and the sight of mayflies and midgets jumping on the lake.

I also remember wintertime at Clonmoylan fondly, the freezing cold, sometimes snow, when we loved to roast marshmallows and horse chestnuts in one of the huge roaring peat fires. Christmas was particularly magical when my father handed out presents from the huge tree which we'd cut down from the woods, standing next to the drawing room fire. A large traditional Christmas lunch followed where Brownie and Mary sat down with the family, with my grandmother, when she was in residence, presiding over all. Afterwards we'd rug up and go for a long walk, often in the snow, then come back inside to a delicious tea of scones and sandwiches (which my parents always had at about five, followed by supper at eight or nine) play cards, charades, or dress-ups. Later we'd fall into bed – exhausted, but happy children

Tinkers were also a real fear for us children. They'd arrive up the driveway at Clonmoylan quite unexpectedly. Although we were sure they were coming to 'get us', they were in fact just selling their wares. The tinkers or gypsies of those days were an accepted part of Irish folklore; managing to survive by sharpening utensils, selling colourful rugs or doing odd jobs. Irish tinkers are mostly descendants of those who'd been forced to take to the roads during the great famines of the 19th Century, never resettling anywhere and often travelling in brightly covered horse-drawn caravans, much the same as tourists hire today to see the countryside.

Chapter 7 Across the Lake at Clonmoylan

It was my great joy to help my father do the chores around the farm and in particular feed the chickens. I didn't get my name 'Teeny' for nothing, fitting easily into a bucket, which he'd hang on the fence whilst he did his jobs.

One morning when I was slightly older I ran ahead to open the chicken gate and called back in great excitement, 'Daddy, Daddy…come quickly and look. The chickens are all asleep.'

Needless to say, my father was not as thrilled as I was about this exciting find of mine for the dozens of chickens were more than asleep. A fox had killed the lot, and having had his fill, left the rest massacred on the ground. As this was one of our ventures paying well at the Galway markets, my father stood there devastated.

'I think that nearly finished him. Me too,' my mother told me, raising her eyes to heaven, 'as sadly the apple crop had failed that year as well.'

Maybe these setbacks contributed to why our life at Clonmoylan was about to come to a close. That year at the Dublin Horse Show my father was offered a job in Australia to manage a large coastal sheep property in New South Wales. For some time my parents had been considering migrating to another country. This job offer is what clinched it.

Little did my father know what lay in store for him.

The economy of Ireland at this period, and in particular on the land, was still not good. Educating five children at boarding school seemed insurmountable on the amount of money Clonmoylan was bringing in, even before the chicken and orchard failure. There were numerous enticing advertising promotions for Australia, South Africa and Canada in the Irish papers, encouraging the movement of many a family from their home country to a new and challenging life in a far-off land.

We were about to take up this challenge.

I think it was also a case 'that the grass is greener on the other side of the fence'. In this case the other side of the world. Other forces were at work too. My grandmother was still living with us and I think my parents felt it was time to do something on their own. Gargy was a great influence on us all, in particular, her eldest son. It was no easier for my mother at Clonmoylan, than it had been back in the early days at Drominagh.

During this time at Clonmoylan my grandmother was becoming more and more demanding, which undoubtedly put a great strain on my parents' marriage.

As I write this story, however, I've great respect for the arduous job she had in bringing up her seven children on her own at Drominagh. And how she achieved a certain amount of fame with her writings; the talent she portrayed in her paintings; the many languages she taught herself; the strength she showed with the early death of her husband and then the tragic loss of her adored son, Eugene.

It was a pity that I was just seven years old when I last saw her. If I'd been older, would I have appreciated her more? I surely think so. I look at the relationship I have with my five grandchildren today, and wish I could have had the same enjoyment with her. I'm glad, that like her, I have my story telling, and that she can play a part in it.

However, I have no doubt in my mind that she played a part in my parents' decision to move to Australia.

CHAPTER 8

A Time of the Raj

Before we left for Australia, Lillian Mackenzie, my maternal grandmother, known as Granny Mac, also came to stay at Clonmoylan. At my tender age she appeared to be a softer lady than my father's mother. Yet she was just as tough in many respects as Eily, but with a happier and more jovial nature. Even then she had beautiful dark hair, a peaches and cream complexion and the most amazing twinkling eyes.

Granny Mac died many years after we came to Australia; but not before my mother had returned to Ireland to settle her into a private hotel in the seaside suburb of Greystanes where she could still enjoy a glass of sherry and a game of Bridge.

'Even in her eighties,' my mother told me, 'she loved male company, refusing point blank to stay any place where she could not enjoy their presence. Every day, without fail, she strolled from the hotel down the road to the Copper Kettle, a small tea-shop, where she had a pot of tea and an iced cake with a few gentlemen who joined her at her table.'

Sadly, I never met her husband, George Henry Louis Mackenzie, my grandfather. Only recently I unearthed a photo of him in his Scottish kilt and beret, eye monocle to his left eye. He looks more than impressive in an eccentric sort of way.

At four years old my mother was sent to board at the Sacré

Coeur Convent at Tunbridge Wells in England where she remained until her mother returned two years later from India for a two-year stay. When her mother went back to India my mother returned to Tunbridge Wells.

'I never had a Christmas with my father, who was trying to make his fortune in jute broking in India until I was seventeen, although my mother came home nearly every two years until I was older. Then I went for four years without seeing them at all,' she told me.

Many of her school holidays were spent with aunts and uncles in Ireland or remaining at Tunbridge Wells with the 'good nuns' or visiting school friends. She assured me that children of the time were quite often treated like her. With no planes, the only mode of transport was boats and the trip from India to England would have taken six weeks or so.

Most of my mother's parents' generation living abroad had been brought up to believe that children must be sent home to good and very expensive private schools in the UK. Hence so many children, like my mother, rarely knew the security of a settled and permanent home.

'It was the way things were,' she said matter of factly. 'For it was assumed that if children were not educated back in England, their accents and characters would be ruined by the Indian influences. An agonising experience for both children and parents. In a way I was lucky for I'd never known the warmth, colour and exotic aromas of India, and I loved my time at Tunbridge Wells. For some poor children the sudden immersion in the cold, grey corridors of England's button-up society was sheer misery after the freedom of their adopted land.'

She told me that most of her parents' lives were lived either 'well off or totally broke'. Jute broking was erratic – due mainly to the gambling on the Gunny market (raw jute). The British in India at the time were status-conscious and snobbish. The Indian civil service administrators were known as the 'Heaven-born' and then there were the armed services, followed by the businessmen or merchant class known as the *box-wallahs*, a class to which my grandfather belonged. Although trade was the reason why the British were in India in the first place, the *box-wallah* caste was the least prestigious.

'However, being a gentleman of some standing from the British Isles my father was accepted more than others,' my mother told me.

Zita, my mother's eldest sister, who my mother told me was a true beauty with straight auburn hair and luminous dark brown eyes, was born in Alipore, a very 'up-social' suburb of Calcutta. This was before my grandparents moved to Ballygunge and then Barrackpore, where they had a spacious bungalow with a luxuriant tropical garden rambling down to the River Hooghly (made famous by Rumer Godden's book, *The River*, and the subsequent film). In 1930, Zita became engaged to Phillip Burch, a dashing officer with the Duke of Cornwall's light infantry whom she'd met when he was recuperating with a broken ankle and staying with her parents. On a visit back to England before her wedding, Zita duly organised for my mother to sail to India to join their parents. So at just seventeen in July, 1930 my mother set forth on the six-week voyage in the charge of the captain.

'There was a canvas swimming pool on board the ship,' she told me. 'We used to play deck quoits and in the evening we changed for dinner. Most of the women had dozens of evening dresses. I had just two, both fairly plain. After dinner, there was dancing. I loved it all.' She gave a small smile. 'Straight out of boarding school, I was somewhat naive and innocent;

however, the doctor and purser took me under their wing. For it was a well-known fact that the chief officer had an eye for the women, particularly young ones.' She laughed. 'If I was unlucky enough to be holed up in a cupboard with him, whilst playing the popular game *Sardines*, the purser would be close at hand. He even took me ashore when he went to do the ship's banking at the ports we passed through, making sure the chief officer could not harass me in his absence.' She stopped talking for a moment and I could see a twinkle in her beautiful hazel eyes. 'He did a good job, for I landed in India as innocent and uninstructed in the ways of the world as I was when I walked out the doors of Tunbridge Wells for the last time.'

Some months later the purser and doctor arrived at Barrackpore and took her to a memorable dinner at the famous restaurant, Firpos in Chowingree, where the popular Angelo Firpo, renowned for his scrumptious dishes, reigned supreme over this popular establishment situated next door to the Oberoi Grand Hotel. When not eating at Firpos, the genteel were often found at Pelitis, owned by the celebrated, Frederico Pelitis (who'd tutored Angelo Firpo in the fine art of cooking), where a quick lunch cost one pound and fifty pence. In Firpos the average bill was about two pound fifty. Both sound horrendously expensive for the day; however, my mother assures me Firpos was worth every penny. Sadly it closed down in the 1960s, so I'm unlikely to ever put it to the test.

When the boat from England arrived at Calcutta my mother's parents met her at the docks. Having not seen her for four years they found it difficult to recognise their daughter. She had now grown into a tall and beautiful young woman.

'It was like strangers meeting for the first time and that gap was never really closed,' she told me sadly, holding a photograph of her debonair father in her hands.

Later, after a fine welcoming lunch in town, their driver drove the family home to Barrackpore, sixteen miles from Calcutta.

'I remember being so taken with it all, the women in bright saris, the heady aromas, the rickshaws everywhere, and cows sitting in the middle of the roads. Even the poor beggars had a certain charm. It was total chaos. But I just adored it.

'My parents' bungalow was amidst a magical garden of tropical flowers and native bushes bursting with vibrant colours,' my mother reminisced. 'There were violets, hopheads, balerias, frangipani, jasmine vines, orchids, clematis, and the wonderful purple and pink pride of India trees. I immediately fell in love with India and its people (the natives not the Brits), from the moment I was there.'

My mother related many tales about her social life in India, visiting clubs, especially the Saturday Club (the Slap) for tennis, horse riding, swimming, badminton and bridge, high teas and grand balls. It was the heady days of the Raj. My vivacious grandmother would have been a source of delight to the young officers from the barracks (although my mother was sometimes embarrassed by her extraversion) as she entertained them on piano with hits of the day.

My mother adored her friend, Indira, the Maharani of Cooch Behar, a glamorous and wealthy widow, who was refused entry to the Saturday Club but would hold lavish parties of her own for which she was famous.

Tragically, after my mother had a memorable holiday on a houseboat in Shrinigar with Zita and Phillip, things changed for the worse.

'In 1932 my father lost all his money and my parents and I returned to England, leaving Zita and Phillip in Meerut,' she told me. 'When we arrived at Dover after the long six-week voyage, we were met with the devastating news of Phillip's sudden death from rabies as a result of a bite from his beloved dog.'

It was a tragic loss of a fine man, whom my mother always mourned. She told me, my Rob, as a young army officer, always reminded her of Phillip.

My mother stayed in England during this period, where she kept the *wolf from the door* by setting her hand to all sorts of jobs. She, like many of her convent-educated contemporaries, was untrained for any position of great help in a time like this, although she'd passed her Matric with flying colours. She was supposedly destined for a 'good marriage' in India, until things fell apart. The *fishing fleet*, as it was described, was when young women came to India to visit their relations and hopefully find a dashing *beau* at the same time.

Undaunted, my mother first found a job working in the ski resort of Arosa in the district of Plessur belonging to the canton of Graubunden in Switzerland, looking after a young girl called Maria, where she stayed for six months, often competing in snow races, both on skis and on horses. When back in England, she found employment as a telephonist, (a great help later in our initial time in Australia). She also secured work in the Strand Palace Hotel and the Savoy, more on her wits than any training. She had no shorthand and typing, which of course was what was required in those days. Her charm and good looks got her by and even the Aga Khan was rather taken by her and her Irish friend, Moira, taking them out on the town on more than one occasion when he stayed at the Savoy.

'He was a very charming man,' she told me, but took it no further than that, despite my probing. 'And I enjoyed my time at the Savoy, even though I only earned thirty shillings a week, fifteen of which went on board. Moira was great fun and we often went out dancing. I remember walking back to the Savoy the week before Christmas and seeing Wallis Simpson driving by. Standing on the side of the road, we joined a group who started singing and shouting out: *Hark the Herald Angels sing, Wallis Simpson stole our King.* She really was very unpopular.'

This is also the period when my mother became engaged to Tony Marks, whose family ran a country hotel in Farnborough, Hampshire. This as we know didn't work out, to the great satisfaction of my father.

'Sadly,' she said, 'Tony was killed in an air raid in London during the Second World War.' She paused and took a sip from her sherry glass. 'After some time back in Ireland, when things weren't going quite as they should have been within the marriage, both financially and otherwise, my mother returned to India to take up a position as housekeeper with the Nizam of Hyderabad. She'd rather courageously answered an advertisement the Nizam's household had placed in a London newspaper. She stayed in this position for two years sending money home to my father each month. He was now also living in Clonmoylan, helping Aunt Winnie with the farm.' She smiled. 'It appeared to be a platonic relationship. Eventually my father went to Scotland and managed the estates of a Mrs Robertson, a mysterious lady, who later became his companion. I received a letter from my father just before we left for Australia in 1954,' she continued, 'wishing me good luck. As travelling between Ireland and Great Britain was prohibited during the war and finances were so bad after the war it was many years since I'd seen him. And of course once we left for Australia I was sadly never to see him again.'

Granny Mac eventually left India and returned to Ireland to live on her own, whilst my grandfather remained with

Mrs Robertson until his death in 1960 at age eighty-eight. On her death, a number of years later, when we were trying hard to make ends meet in Australia, Mrs Robertson kindly bequeathed my mother some much-needed money (twelve thousand pounds). It was quite unexpected, as my mother was not sure that Mrs Robertson even knew where we were all living at the time. It was money we could well do with; hence we were all eternally grateful to the generous, if mysterious, Aisla Robertson.

My mother assures me she has no idea where she spent the years from when she was two until four and started at Tunbridge Wells.

When there, my mother sat with the nuns in their pews and chewed on their rosary beads.

'It was a lovely country setting,' she told me, 'with beautiful gardens, a stone fountain, which I fell into at aged four, and acres of rolling fields and woods.'

In later years, after the First World War, which saw them take shelter from Zeppelin raids down in the cellar, she spent one lot of school holidays with Brigid O'Malley and her father, who had been presumed killed in action during the War, only to arrive back to tragically find his wife was married to another. A situation no doubt repeated across the country time and time again. Heartbroken, he took his daughter and my mother to Parknasilla, a magnificent hotel on the Ring of Kerry in Ireland for a few weeks' holiday, where seventy-five years later she asked me to take her again. Although unable to walk the glorious grounds rolling down to Kenmare Bay, she sat by the window in the drawing room where we partook of high tea. Later we dressed for cocktails before being escorted to our places in the plush dining room overlooking the grounds, which rolled down to the bay where she'd sat all those years before.

Over the years, Parknasilla has been a retreat for many well-known identities from around the world, including the past Taoiseach, Berty Ahern, who holidays there each summer.

In 1954, as my parents tossed the big move to Australia around, it was not just my father's mother we would be leaving behind. It was also Granny Mac. So all in all it was a huge decision to up stakes and leave.

'I suppose as I'd spent so much of my life without my parents that I didn't think it odd at the time,' my mother told me, when I asked if she and my father hadn't felt guilty about leaving both of my grandmothers behind in Ireland. 'Besides, I thought it wouldn't be long before we could come back to visit.' She smiled wryly. 'Mind you, it was a lot longer than I thought.'

Chapter 9

Leaving for Down Under

I remember my father announcing to us one evening, as we gathered around the roaring fire in the drawing room of Clonmoylan, that he had successfully negotiated with the gentleman from the Dublin Horse Show. He now had a Manager's job waiting for him in New South Wales on the gentleman's large coastal sheep property. He was to sail out first on the P & O cruise liner, the *Orcades*. My mother and the rest of us would follow a couple of months later on the *Oronsay*. This would give my father a chance to settle into his new job and find us a house to live in, as accommodation in Australia at the time was as scarce as hens' teeth.

It didn't quite work out like this. To a seven year old our proposed move to the other end of the world was a great adventure. I wasn't too worried about the details. We'd seen some enticing brochures of various countries. Australia looked by far the most colourful and exciting – with its endless white sandy beaches, jumping kangaroos, cute koala bears, scraggly gumtrees and wonderful cornflower blue skies. What's more, the boat trip sounded out of this world. Much to my delight, I noticed that the *Oronsay* even had a swimming pool.

'It's always hot in Australia. And you can ride your horses to school and tie them up under a gumtree,' my mother told us with a knowing smile, as we stared at her in awe.

Chapter 9   Leaving for Down Under

Looking out of the window, at the rain pelting down, and with Early Mist, Billy Boy and Merrylegs sheltering under a sodden tree, this move was starting to sound like heaven on a stick.

'Yet,' my mother told me, 'I noticed the older ones, Dibs and Gill particularly, although excited, were worried. No doubt they were concerned about what they'd be leaving behind in Ireland to start a new life in a strange country, for they both had made good friends at Mount Anville and the thought of starting all over again in a new school, let alone a new country, was daunting.'

Even Eugene was now settled into Blackrock College with a tight group of friends. However, all I could think about was how I would be able to ride my own horse to school in the bright Australian sunlight and swim in the warm surf.

'I know I was naïve,' my mother said, 'yet somehow I felt the move would solve our financial problems. For there was no way we could continue to send Dibs, Gill and Eugene to boarding school. And then of course there was you and Viv to think of later. Even keeping the food on your plates was becoming harder and harder as our debts grew each month! We could possibly have sold Clonmoylan and moved somewhere else, but Ireland was in such a depression that Australia looked like a very attractive cloud with a wonderful silver lining.'

My father left for Australia on 17th February, 1954. With mixed feelings, we saw him off at the North Wall in Dublin for his crossing to Liverpool. From there he was to continue by train to London, where he would board the P&O liner, the *Orcades*. We were to follow in six weeks. I can hardly imagine how my mother felt at this stage, seeing her husband off to an unknown land on the other side of the world, leaving us all behind; while ahead for her was the daunting prospect of a long boat trip with five children ranging in age from seven to fifteen.

My father had to tie up the fraying ends of the existence we were about to discard before he left for Australia. In practical terms, this meant auctioning most of the furniture, much of it antiques, and other less select pieces, which had made the trip from Drominagh across the lake to Clonmoylan those years before. Most of our silver and crockery my father packed himself in large packing cases for the long journey to Australia. Some of the valuable Worcester china didn't make it unscathed. Much was in pieces when it arrived, putting extra strain on my parents when it was unpacked later in Canberra. I think my mother finally forgave my father just before he died for this sloppy packing.

Clonmoylan was put on the market with a real estate agent in Limerick. Shortly a retired colonial doctor made us an offer, which my parents accepted. It was a sad decision, but having made it there was no looking back or time for regrets. My mother's great saying was: 'Having made your bed you must lie in it.'

This was certainly the case here.

Leaving Clonmoylan behind, we moved to a small brick bungalow in Putland Avenue, Bray, south of Dublin, to await our departure for Australia.

My donkey, Early Mist, was given a new home with a family in the village and I cried myself dry against his soft furry neck as I said goodbye. The dogs, Eugene's Timmy, Gill's Shadow and Viv's cat, Bunty, went to friends. Merrylegs and Billy Boy were found homes and were sadly loaded up in horse floats and taken away, our pleas that we be allowed to take them having been callously dismissed by our parents.

My father said of the time we left Clonmoylan: 'We said farewell to Clonmoylan, which had been our home for seven years; seven years of country life beside our beloved Shannon.

Years which, although not entirely carefree for Toni and me, had been wonderfully so for the children during their early years.'

The seaside town of Bray, where we spent the few months waiting to leave for Australia, holds fond memories for me. I remember the long walks by the sea, the air ringing with the caw of seagulls and the fun of having other children close by. We'd never had neighbours as such, so the novelty of having playmates to horse around with, play hop-scotch or build sandcastles on the beach, never wore off. I loved the pounding waves on the shore and the tangy smell of seaweed.

One rainy morning, minus my two front teeth, I stood in the church wearing a brand new white embroidered dress and veil made by my mother, with all the family (apart from my father) looking on proudly at my First Communion. I placed the small piece of shamrock I was given carefully in my First Holy Communion book, treasuring it for many years. It may not have been the first piece of shamrock to make the long trip to Australia, but it was one of the most beloved.

CHAPTER 10

On the High Seas

After arriving in Sydney my father was picked up by family friends, the Frosts, who'd migrated to Australia not long before. After a few weeks at their house in Morriset on Lake Macquarie, north of Newcastle in New South Wales, he set off on a mammoth 440-mile drive that would take him through dry dusty roads to Bobingah, near the small towns of Nimmitabel and Bombala at an altitude of 1070m on the high Monaro plains not far from the Victorian border and the Snowy Mountains.

He had met his new employer, Jim Baker, a stocky bloke, well turned out in moleskins and a large felt hat, at the Australia Hotel in the heart of Sydney as arranged. Together, they drove out of the hustle and bustle of Sydney and onto the gravelled two-lane Hume Highway between Sydney and Canberra.

'Getting stuck behind a huge heavy transport with no way of passing made for a slow trip,' he said.

The countryside appeared deserted – for most of the potholed road ran through sprawling sheep stations with the homesteads out of sight behind the barren hills. They drove through the country towns of Campden, Mittagong, Moss Vale, Goulburn and on through Canberra before continuing south to the town of Cooma, the headquarters of the Snowy Mountains Hydro Electric Authority. At the time the largest engineering hydro scheme in the world was being built here, employing many new migrants from Europe. Taking twenty-five years to complete, it brought enormous benefit to all of Eastern Australia. Many a new migrant found the harsh conditions and hard slogging work unbearable. Tragically, an enormous number of lives were lost, quite often young and virile men, full of the hopes and dreams of a new life in a far better country than the one they'd left behind, struggling to cope with the aftermath of war. Sadly, what they found in their new land was sometimes harder to hack than what they'd fled from.

My father said of the drive at the time: 'It all seemed very desolate and strange after the emerald grasslands and trees of Ireland.'

During the long drive down from Sydney, Jim dropped a bombshell. My father was not to be the manager of Jim's new farm on the coast after all. He was merely to be a 'station hand' at Jim's 10,000-acre sheep station, Bobingah at Nimmitabel.

This didn't sound promising, but my father decided to hold his peace and see what awaited him.

Unfortunately what he found on arrival to this remote outpost was far from good.

He was shown his quarters, consisting of a falling down corrugated hut in the yard of the homestead, dunny outside – with the promise they'd inspect the new home tomorrow. Only now, after driving through that very same country, can I imagine my father's desolation at seeing these high-altitude drought-stricken, rolling khaki uplands with tusks of desiccated grass, dying gumtrees and endless rocky outcrops. The day I was there recently following his tracks, it was so hot and parched that the skeleton-like sheep looked close to death, the horses were dreadfully distressed and even the flies seemed to lack any will to live at all as they desperately clung to my soaked skin. And the ice-cream I'd bought melted before I'd a chance to get out of the shop, let alone back in the car.

Yet my father was there in April with the sub-zero winter about to set in, an even more daunting proposition. The promised new house he was shown comprised a corrugated iron shack in the middle of nowhere. Not a tree in sight. Cold as the Arctic. Wind howling. Snow to follow. No water or electricity. Not even a generator. The great job offered at the Dublin horse show turned out to be as the general dogsbody: chopper of wood, make a new garden out of an eighth of an acre of empty tins (which he did); milk one ferocious jersey cow to feed the cats (for some reason the family didn't drink fresh milk, only powdered) and any other job that no-one else felt like doing. To add insult to injury, his meagre dinner was left out for him on a fence post, where if he wasn't quick enough the rats got to it before he did.

Managerial skills were not a necessity. Survival skills certainly were.

No schools were nearby. He was told this wasn't necessary, for we'd become domestic servants in the homestead as we grew up. This proved to be the straw that broke the camel's – or in this case – proud Irishman's back.

He lay awake all of one night agonising as to what to do. Finally, after a month of slogging it out, he realised he'd been 'had'.

'Get out whilst you can,' he told himself, and this is what he did.

Meaning we had nowhere to go to when we were due to arrive on the *Oronsay* in a few weeks' time.

It certainly wasn't that my father was afraid of hard work. For despite hollering his instructions from the bathroom window at Drominagh, he'd then go down and join the workmen for a hard day's slog, and at Clonmoylan, he worked darn hard trying to make it work.

It was just that as he said: 'There were no prospects at all at this place – for any of you.'

He'd wanted a new life for us. This wasn't it. How he must have felt? Not knowing a soul, miles from anywhere? An Irishman, touching fifty, in a strange land with his large family arriving shortly? He had no possibility of stopping us – for the *Oronsay* was already on the high seas. It was certainly proving to be an adventure for him. Not one he'd imagined. In hindsight, an adventure he possibly should have foreseen.

Fortunately he'd bought himself an old Holden ute. 'The only cars for the Australian country,' he was told.

So after somehow extracting himself from this barren outpost and his new employers, back he drove in the Holden, up through the centre of New South Wales to his Irish friends, the Frosts at Morriset, where he made preparations for our arrival. Both families had been friends for years and the Frosts had spent many a summer at Drominagh and Clonmoylan. In fact it was because of the Frosts that we'd thought of Australia in the first place.

We, of course, knew nothing of our father's plight, as we enjoyed a month of the greatest excitement on the *Oronsay*. I learned how to swim in the ship's pool, which emptied from one side to the other depending on the lie of the ship, making it a bit of a challenge. We played quoits, table tennis, and shuttlecock. Somehow my mother managed to make us all elaborate costumes for a fancy dress party on deck to celebrate crossing the equator. Generally we made a nuisance of ourselves with the cabin crew, who allowed us into the kitchens and played chasey with us up and down the hallways.

On arriving in Sydney they seemed quite heartbroken when we disembarked. Needless to say we were all immensely sad saying goodbye to our new friends.

We'd followed much the same route as my father, stopping at Naples where Gill told me recently: 'I remember getting off the boat for the day and walking across a huge cobbled square. Then we went up some stairs to a cathedral to pray. I remember it as if it was yesterday.'

When Rob and I were staying on the island of Procida in the Bay of Naples, on *Sea Dreams*, I boarded a ferry across to Naples to search for distant memories. I jumped on a bus, which took me into the hills where I roamed amongst sun-splashed daffodil yellow and strawberry pink villas covered in purple and magenta bougainvillea, and with endless vistas out to the bay. Later I traipsed the winding chaotic streets in the centre of the city where washing was strewn across balconies; there was the piquant aroma of spices and olive oil permeating through shuttered windows; myriads of hassling hawkers and street vendors selling piping hot pizzas; a group of elderly men sitting on a wooden bench gossiping; dogs lolling in the shade, cats preening. Sadly, there were few memories from my distant past, apart from the stench of garbage that still litters the harbour, roads, and gutters. Anchored on *Sea Dreams* in the bay a few days earlier, piles of rubbish had floated by our stern, including condoms, tin cans and even a child's plastic chair and rubber car tyres.

When on the Oransay in Port Said in 1954, small rickety traders' boats came alongside selling leather camels of every imaginable size, jewellery, lengths of cloth and a wealth of other souvenirs, and clothing. A rope would be thrown up, which a passenger would tie to the railing and then purchases and money would be exchanged. I remember lying on the beach in the scorching sun in Ceylon, while my mother bartered with more local traders for tapestry bags, colourful beads, and leather pouffes (foot rests).

'We went with a group and had lunch at the magnificent Galle Face Hotel, the oldest hotel east of the Suez,' my mother told me nostalgically. 'It was listed as one of the 1,000 places to see before you die,' she laughed, 'so I thought we had to see it. It's in a magnificent setting facing the Indian Ocean. Louis Mountbatten used to holiday there.'

In the frantic squalor of India, although my mother was glad to be back in the country she loved so much, she was beside herself with worry.

'You hadn't been vaccinated for small pox, as you were sick with an ear infection when the rest of the family were vaccinated. Instead,' she said with a chuckle, 'I covered you in holy water and hoped for the best.'

Back on board the *Oronsay*, Viv and I were almost excommunicated. In those days it was supposedly a mortal sin for a Catholic to go into a non-Catholic service. Diligently, we sat through a great deal of the service before we realised something was amiss. With that, Viv grabbed my hand and we scurried out and hid behind a door in shame. Once again I was sworn to secrecy, Viv assuring me, hands waving in a flurry, dark eyes flashing: 'There's nothing for us now, Teeny. We'll definitely go to Hell.'

For weeks I believed her, until I finally worked up the courage to tell my mother what had happened and she reassured me the Good Lord would probably give us another chance.

Dibs fell out of her top bunk and broke her nose. She also fell madly in love with a fellow passenger, an Indian, who made a great fuss of the beautiful teenager as many did with Gill, who was now rapidly turning into a swan.

My mother told me recently: 'Despite having all of you in tow, I enjoyed ship life enormously. In a way it reminded me of that long journey I undertook to visit my parents in India so many years before. And everyone was very kind and helpful. Although,' she went on to say, 'the thought of the unknown (little did she realise how bad that would be, not having heard from my father as to his fate) and the homesickness for the life I'd left behind did get me down from time to time. But I was determined to make the best of it. After all,' she said with a deep sigh, when I asked her once again why it was (with my father touching fifty) they'd suddenly upped stakes and taken us across the world like that, 'it was originally my idea. I never thought for a moment your father would want to do such a thing. As it turned out, he was far more enthusiastic about it in the end than I was. By that stage I was wracked with second thoughts. However, he would have none of it. It became a sort of challenge.'

Chapter 11

Arriving to the Unexpected

We arrived in Australia on the 6th May, 1954, to the Fremantle Docks in Western Australia, where we were met by Jack Taylor, a rugged, jovial young man, the son of an Irish cattle dealer my parents had known back in Ireland, who gently took us under his wing and showed us around.

Even if our accents sometimes portrayed us as being well off, unfortunately this was not the case. What money we received from the sale of Clonmoylan, about four thousand pounds, was soon eaten up with farming debts, travelling and removal costs. A small amount was put aside for our beginnings in Australia.

'About one thousand pounds is all we arrived with,' my mother told me. 'Not a lot to get started in a new life. Maybe in hindsight we had stars in our eyes.'

The port at Fremantle bustled with activity. I loved the narrow winding streets, colourful fishermen's cottages, and sandstone buildings surrounding the port. But it was the butterfly blue water and the clear blue skies I loved the most. Hardly a cloud was to be seen. And even in May a stifling hot wind blew through the open windows of the car, ruffling our hair and filling our lungs. I couldn't believe we were actually here in Australia. That it wasn't just postcards and brochures we were looking at. During the long passage across the world, I was sometimes so homesick for Clonmoylan, our animals and Brownie and Mary, I cried often into my pillow. Now, fickle as I was, those thoughts were quickly hurled aside. Instead I was like a glass of fizzy lemonade bubbling over the top with excitement at the prospect of what our new life would be like.

A number of days later, after arriving through the heads into Sydney Harbour, my mother's exhilaration at seeing my father waiting for us to disembark at the docks was soon dissipated. Needless to say, she was less than impressed to find there was no job, no house and no prospect of either.

'It wasn't a promising start to our new life,' she told me with a wry grin.

She rallied around slightly, as we all jumped into the Holden ute – with our luggage following in a taxi. My father drove steadily in the busy peak hour traffic across Sydney Harbour Bridge, his familiar tweed hat perched high on his sunburnt head, his pipe firmly clasped between his teeth. Crowded in the back tray of the ute, we chatted ten to the dozen.

Unfortunately my mother's mood deteriorated again on being shown the dour and meagre rooms my father had organised for us in a run-down self-catering hostel in Neutral Bay, requiring the guests to have their own pots and pans, crockery and cutlery. We had none.

'A slight oversight on your father's behalf when he made the booking,' my mother told me. 'The humiliation of having to beg and scrounge is still engraved in my mind fifty years later.'

I was so overcome with the excitement of exploring the pokey hallways, fire escapes, and dark alleys that I didn't notice the lacking of the finer things at the time. Yet my first glimpse of Sydney Harbour is still etched in my mind. The Harbour Bridge appeared not nearly high enough for our monstrous liner to pass underneath. A number of years ago

Chapter 11 Arriving to the Unexpected

I sailed under the bridge on our yacht *Oceania* and sat on the deck looking up at the huge expanse of steel, remembering all those years ago doing just the same thing.

To a seven year old, who, up until then, had only had a few trips to Dublin, Sydney Harbour was awe inspiring. I remember the tall city buildings, the passenger ferries jostling for berths at Circular Quay, the brightly coloured sailing boats tacking to give way to the *Oronsay*, the wooded islands dotted amidst the expanse of blue water. There were sandy beaches and rambling houses and verdant gardens rolling down to the water's edge. So many of the suburban bungalows seemed to have red tiled roofs and, like Perth, the sky was the bluest blue. Perched on the eastern side of the harbour was an enormous sandstone Gothic building, Rose Bay Convent, later to become my boarding school.

Not far from the hostel we found a small café where we were enthralled with two new experiences: milk shakes in aluminium containers and fish and chips wrapped in newspaper. It was perfect autumn weather. About 70 degrees Fahrenheit. We relished the warmth after the cold Irish winter in the small bungalow in Bray.

Fortunately only a short time was spent in the inglorious hostel at Neutral Bay, before we children piled into the back tray of the Holden onto the Pacific highway to our new life in Australia. No thought of seatbelts here as we crouched around our luggage, waving excitedly to passing cars and truck drivers who tailed us. As soon as we left the suburbs and headed over the Hawkesbury River, we looked everywhere for a kangaroo or wallaby. Alas, none were to be seen. Compared to Ireland the countryside was open and barren. Flocks of dust-spattered sheep lolled under stands of gumtrees and huge dams were filled with muddy sludge. There was the golden glow of yellow wattle and a lot of the ground was covered in a mauve carpet that I later learned was the dreaded weed, Patterson's Curse. The houses, too, were different; often weatherboard with verandahs to the front and back to provide shade from the hot Australian sun. And beside each house there was a galvanised water tank and lots of ramshackle outhouse buildings. Further on, we drove amidst groves of orange and lemon trees and every now and then we went through a small dusty town with a rambling pub on each corner with dogs lying on the deep verandahs waiting for their masters to come outside. At one dilapidated pub there was even a horse tied to the railings, which threw us into great excitement. Along the curbs were dusty cars and fading billboards advertising beer, ice creams, Pepsi, Coca Cola, fish and chip cafés and milk bars. Each town seemed to have a couple of churches and what looked like schoolyards close by. Most of all I remember the smell. Of eucalypt, dust and sheep. And then there were the flies attacking us in swarms, getting up our noses and in our eyes.

'You swallowed one,' my mother told me. 'You nearly choked, until Gill knocked frantically on the cabin window and your father pulled over to the verge of the road and produced an old army issue water bottle he'd bought at a disposal store and you washed the fly down with tepid water.'

Fortunately the Frosts in Morriset had found us a place of sorts to live in, close to Lake Macquarie, and not far from their home in the grounds of the Morriset Mental Hospital, where Dr Frost was the resident physician. However, our new home was more like a garden shed, sitting amongst a stand of raggedy gumtrees on a dusty block set back from the potholed dirt road.

'It looked as if it was built out of matchsticks,' my mother laughed recently as we recalled that day we arrived. 'It didn't seem much bigger than a caravan.'

Attached to one side of the house was a rusty water tank. A small lean-to porch stuck out from the other side. Built on stumps, with tin caps to stop the ants and termites destroying the wood, it had glass paned windows tacked on as if they'd been put in as an afterthought and the corrugated iron roof was rusting, with the chimney falling apart. There was a small hutchie in the backyard, which we soon discovered was the lavatory or 'the dunny' as it was called in Australia. A word my parents never liked us to use…even if 'lavatory' seemed far too grand a word for such a building.

'I don't know what I thought,' my mother told me. 'I think I was in too much of a state of shock to think anything at all. It certainly wasn't what I had envisaged. But at least it was a roof over our heads.' She smiled. 'Somehow I imagined an Australian homestead with verandahs on all sides and horses tied up to the railing for you all to ride to school on. This was no way it. Certainly not what the brochures had portrayed.'

Inside, the house had a linoleum floor, faded and lifting. A green laminex table, a few chairs with ripped seats, and four steel beds were the odd bits of furniture my father had managed to scrounge. In one corner was a kitchen of sorts with an open shelf underneath the sink displaying a few battered pots and pans and odd bits of cutlery and crockery stacked away neatly.

'As it only had one room we put a blanket up to divide an area off for your father and me. You children slept on the verandah,' my mother said.

Sometimes Dibs and Gill went to the Frosts, and Eugene stayed with the St John of God Brothers at the school they ran for disadvantaged boys, nearby. The cheery brothers in their flowing habits were our saviours, along with the Frosts. Brother Celsius was our favourite; however, they were all kind, and some of them were even Irish, allaying our homesickness for a time.

I was dreadfully melancholy once the excitement wore off. Time and time again I dreamed I was back in Ireland sitting on the Aga early in the morning, chatting away to Mary, with the aroma of crispy bacon and a new loaf of Irish soda bread straight from the oven, or going to Powers Cross village with Peggy pulling the trap. I missed Brownie dreadfully and the flies in Australia were worse than the midges in Ireland had ever been. I cried at night and my mother comforted me, but I'm sure her homesickness was much deeper than mine, which tended to disappear when the first glimpse of morning light beamed through my window.

Most evenings we went to the brothers for a barbeque, something we hadn't experienced before. Afterwards we would attend Benediction. If we were lucky a film would follow. For years, until Brother Celsius died, our family kept in touch with the brothers, a couple of them coming to visit us. Eugene even went back there for school holidays once, glad to see a few of the boys he'd befriended.

My father busied himself whilst he searched for a job and a house for us all to live in together. He chopped wood for the fires, boiled water in the boiler for our baths, and tidied up the yard and surrounds. Through it all my parents remained optimistic when we were around; though every now and then I could sense the desolation in them both.

Ireland doesn't have snakes. Morriset certainly did. It's a well-known fact that St Patrick put his crook into the ground in Ireland, with it coming out in New Zealand. Hence the myth goes – he eradicated snakes in these two fortunate countries.

Australia was not to be so lucky.

Chapter 11 Arriving to the Unexpected

I never put my foot outside the bed without first checking to make sure there were no snakes underneath. I slept with the pillow over my head in case they joined me there. It was a long way from Drominagh and Clonmoylan in more ways than one.

Yet, for us children, the advantages of living in Australia were becoming more and more apparent. Even at this time of year the sun was hot and we could run around with little on. When we visited the Frost family we picnicked in their rambling garden and swam in the lake where we'd jump off a huge rubber tyre hanging from a weeping willow, in the process getting dreadfully sunburnt, long before sunscreen was the norm.

'If I hadn't had Knobs and Doreen,' my mother told me, 'I don't think I would have survived.'

The milkman picked us up each morning in his battered white truck to take us to the one-teacher primary school, with a Seventh Day Adventist teacher at Bonells Bay. Dibs, at fifteen, was the oldest in the school and of course she and Gill should have been in high school, but there wasn't one. As it was, we all shared the one bright and sunny classroom, sitting at penknife-engraved wooden lift-top desks. On the few days I attended I found this a good arrangement, for I could see the rest of the family at a glance, which curtailed my homesickness for my parents.

Like my mother, one of my greatest disappointments was that there didn't appear to be many horses tied up to the railings in the schoolyard. In fact there were none and my mother glossed over this promise she'd airily made to us back in Ireland.

'Perhaps it was an old brochure I was looking at,' she said. 'For I certainly saw horses tied up outside a school.'

Was Australia that desperate for migrants that the brochures had to lie? I wondered.

'When the Frosts travelled down to Sydney for a day or so, which they did from time to time,' she told me recently, 'we were able to stay in their house. Needless to say I thought this was bliss, as I could have a bath and the lavatory was inside.'

Living here at Bonells Bay was all very well. But my father had no job – and no prospect of one. Eugene couldn't spend the rest of his life living with the disadvantaged boys at St John of God, much as he seemed to be enjoying it, nor could we all live in this tiny house forever, with Dibs and Gill continuing their education in a one-teacher primary school. Feelers were put out to the Catholic Church throughout Australia. One day, after many decades of the rosary and novenas had been said by all the family to help with our search, a job was finally found. A house too. Not in Bonells Bay. But in the small community of Reidsdale many miles away to the south.

We were all sad to leave the Frosts, our new school friends, and the St John of God brothers; but at that stage we had no option.

CHAPTER 12

Irish Bush Family at Reidsdale

Reidsdale, a few miles south of the country town of Braidwood, was a tiny farming community at the head of the Araluen Valley on the Southern Tablelands of New South Wales. The Kennedys, an elderly couple who ran the post office, were retiring to Sydney and someone was needed urgently to replace them. We were the answer. The idea was that my mother would run the post office and telephone exchange and my father would work for Marcus Lyons who owned the surrounding land.

My father, mother, Viv and I arrived first in the Holden ute loaded up to the hilt. We looked not unlike the tinkers we'd left behind in Ireland, despite my mother's delicate pink floral dress and my father's dapper hat. Dibs, Gill and Eugene were to follow later with the Frosts.

'When your father thought we were all to live at Nimmitabel he'd scrounged a few pieces of furniture. This was ceremoniously brought out of storage and installed in our new house,' my mother told me one day at Cloneen, as we looked over some old photos.

Reidsdale's close-knit community of dairy farmers ran a co-operative cheese factory. It was rich country with the people nearly all of Irish descent. Such names as Maher, Hickey, Lyons and Thompson were the norm – in fact, the place was known as 'Irish Corner'. But even they found this family of Irish migrants somewhat of a novelty.

Despite our situation, appearances needed to be kept up. So with much care on Sunday morning we all dressed in our very best to attend Mass at the small chapel on the hill – my father in a dark suit; Viv and I in our new smocked floral pink dresses, which my mother had whipped up on a second-hand sewing machine she'd found in Morisset; Dibs and Gill in crisp white shirts and full skirts; Eugene with tie and long socks; my mother in a smart tweed suit and a green wide-brimmed woollen hat with a gold donkey brooch on the side. I thought how elegant and beautiful she looked against the farmer's wives, if not slightly out of place. The other families were friendly, doing their best to make us feel welcome, gently badgered into this from the pulpit by the local curate, Monsignor McKenna, a formidable Australian of Irish descent with a soft spot for the only Irish migrant family he'd encountered while serving in his expansive parish. With a great flourish of his ornate robes, he welcomed us into their midst, begging the locals to be kind to us, as we were so far away from home.

'This enthusiastic enveloping into the fold embarrassed your father and me no end,' my mother said.

Father O'Brien, a jovial young priest with a thatch of carrot hair, a gentle brogue, and who hailed from Tullamore in the heart of Ireland, was Monsignor McKenna's offsider, coming to Reidsdale every two weeks to conduct mass. His main claim to fame was that he once had played hurly for Ireland and was still a great sportsman. Over those early years in Australia he became almost part of our family. I suspect he was as homesick for his homeland as we were. And, despite being a priest, was somewhat charmed by the beautiful Dibs, as most men were.

I went to visit him not long ago in a retirement home in

Narooma on the New South Wales South Coast. He was just as jovial as I recalled. Over a cup of tea we reminisced about old times. I'd not seen him for forty-five years. Sadly, not long after my visit, he died when on a trip home to Ireland to catch up with his family. I think he must have realised his time was near, for shortly before my visit he'd posted Dibs a photograph taken at the Irish Embassy in the 1950s of himself and Dibs (looking divine in a navy blue dress with white flowers embroidered on the collar) talking to an elderly lady smoking a cigarette and wearing a white beret. I feel he'd cherished it all his life and wanted Dibs to have it.

Mass at Reidsdale was a social occasion with at least a good half hour put aside afterwards for gossip, tea, and home-cooked scones and cakes. Up near the church was the tennis court – an overgrown paddock with a high fence, a few scraggly white lines and a net of sorts in the middle. From memory even Father O'Brien used to join in when we played with tattered wooden racquets. He also played hurly with us, bestowing us each with a new stick he'd lovingly carved out of pieces of wood he'd scavenged in the countryside.

The Reidsdale Post Office, sited on a narrow dusty gravel road, was not a luxurious structure by any means. A steel gate led up a long potholed lane between paddocks sporting clumps of thistles and long wispy tusks of grass where sheep and cattle grazed. At the bottom of one paddock was a creek overhung with weeping willows, while right in the centre of the front paddock a lone apple tree stood.

'On the way to the school bus, we'd pick an apple off the tree for our lunchbox,' Dibs assures me.

As my father said at the time, '"House" was too grand a name to put on our new home.' The ceilings were rusted iron covered in spider webs, with tree branches protruding through the open crevices; the floors were unpainted wood with a few bits of torn lino here and there. None of the windows closed properly, only half the doors were in place and the plaster, stained brown with rain water, was peeling off the walls in most of the rooms. Perched on a raised hill to the rear of the building was an outside dunny. Apart from the terror of a red back spider biting my behind, it was a frightening walk to relieve oneself in the middle of the night. What's more, with the coldest winter the district was experiencing in years, most of the ground was covered in a deep white frost, so it was an excruciating chilly and slippery hike up there as well. We'd never in our wildest dreams imagined Australia being as cold as this; however, it wasn't long before we realised that our new country was a land of harsh extremes.

The only bath we had was a large tin tub we filled with water from the boiler, taking it in turns to wash ourselves by the fire inside. This was much easier when my father and Eugene were away, as modesty prevailed when they were in residence.

My father ingeniously set up a laundry tub outside under a gumtree, placing a couple of pipes into the ground to take the water, together with the dregs from the kitchen sink, some yards down the hill. Most of us shared the same bedroom and all the rooms opened onto each other and then onto the verandah – a style more suited to the tropics, not to the intense cold of our first Australian winter.

'Viv,' my mother told me, 'for some reason slept on a wire mattress on top of a disused bath tub to the side of the fire in the sitting room.'

Eugene slept on the verandah with his dog, Padraig, known as Porky, a brown Scottie mix, whom Viv had found in our first week in Australia at Morisset. In all the years he was with us he never let anyone, apart from the family, pat him. Possibly realising he and Eugene were two males up against four bossy sisters he appointed himself Eugene's guardian and protected him with his life. Later in Canberra, if Eugene was having a bath in the one and only bathroom, he'd sit on his pyjamas outside the door and growl at any of us who went past; and if we should have the audacity to knock on the door and tell his master to hurry up we were almost eaten alive.

The bats at Reidsdale were scary to say the least, sweeping down from the rafters like fighter jets about to drop a lethal bomb. Once again I slept with my head under the pillow, not just hiding from snakes this time. There were also many nights when it was hard to sleep for the sound of rats chewing on the woodwork.

'Do you remember the possum,' my mother asked me recently, 'a ferocious-looking beast clinging to the top of the bedroom door with a small baby in its pouch? There was no moving it no matter how hard we tried. We couldn't shut the door and had to go to bed with it there. Every time we went near the door it hissed and hit out with its claws. Your father and Eugene were away, so it lived in the house like this for days, until finally, thank God, it took off.'

To begin with we all went to St Bede's Good Samaritan Convent in Braidwood, catching the school bus about a mile away over the river, past the Lyons' stately farmhouse and up a steep hill. We mostly walked to the bus stop where we met up with a group of the local children. I hate to admit it, but we used to sit nails in the middle of the road, getting hugely excited when the bus driver, Mr Thompson, an elderly man of eternal patience, found he had a flat tyre a few miles further on, whereupon we'd all sit smugly watching him valiantly change the tyre with the help of one of the older boys.

Other times the bus would just break down on its own accord and it wasn't unusual for us to arrive at school close to lunchtime. The floor of the bus was riddled with holes, a bit like sitting on a cheese grater with the gravel road whizzing past underneath. I would curl my legs up under me as I was terrified a snake would wriggle up a hole when we stopped.

I was miserable at the convent, as apart from anything else the nuns seemed to have an avid aversion to Viv and me. We were forever being berated for our supposed misbehaviour; or being hit with a strap around our legs, or with a feather duster hard across the knuckles. Why we were not accepted was difficult to understand. Perhaps it was our accents (if we'd had broad Irish accents it might have been better), or perhaps they were not used to having new students at their school, let alone so many all at once. Or was it that the priests had made too much fuss of us? My mother suspected this was the case. Most of the pupils came from families who'd lived in the area all their lives. Suddenly this number of 'foreign' new students with all the attention being showered on them by the priests was more than the poor nuns could cope with.

Recently Viv told me: 'The nuns were always telling me I was dense.' This was anything but the truth; however, like me, Viv had never really been to a proper school before, apart from Bonells Bay, and the odd day at Shragh, and she was probably lacking in certain skills.

'You stupid girls,' Gill remembers them berating us. 'I thought coming from the land of Saints and Scholars you'd know more than this.'

Recently Eugene told me they were kinder to him. He vividly remembers Sister Margaret Mary, a rough and ready stocky young nun trying valiantly to teach him and the other boys how to play rugby, tucking up her habit and showing them how to form a ruck. Gill also remembers her on the sidelines of the netball games against the public school, jumping up and down in excitement and bellowing at the top of her voice: 'Bash 'em girls. Bash 'em.'

Dear Gill laughed as she remembered this. 'I thought she'd have a heart attack, but she was very good-natured and she did love Eugene. I think you and Viv were unlucky with the nuns you had, particularly Viv, who had a really vindictive one.'

The school was housed in a stark brick building next to the church and facing onto a bitumen square. The classrooms were like an iceberg and I constantly had chilblains. Many a day I played truant, with my parents' blessing. If this was what school was all about, I certainly didn't want to be part of it.

In later life I found some very kind nuns, but the Good Samaritan nun I had at Braidwood was not kind as I remember her. Maybe it was not her fault. Perhaps she was just part of a system that condoned such treatment. Spare the rod and spoil the child.

Between the nuns and the conditions in our meagre home we all suffered from dreadful homesickness, particularly my mother alone all day in the post office, except when the local people came into collect their mail.

'When you went to school and I was on my own, I often sat down and cried,' she told me as we sipped a glass of wine by the warm fire in the living room overlooking the garden at Cloneen. 'I think it was definitely worse for Dibs, Gill and Eugene than it was for you and Viv. They'd left school friends behind and were probably more aware of our situation.' She furrowed her brow and gave a sad smile. 'My heart went out to them. I remember Gill saying, when everyone was feeling particularly down in the dumps, "What can't be cured must be endured." She has always been the practical one. But I remember often thinking, what on earth have we done?'

My mother wasn't a whinger by any means, however, strongly setting her mind to making the best of things and running the post office efficiently.

The actual post office consisted of a small room attached to the side of the house. Here she sat in front of one of those party-line switchboards wearing headphones and plugging in different colour cords to connect the calls. She also had to be there for the local people to collect their mail.

'I remember that switchboard so well,' I said to her. 'You were more or less tied to it all day, weren't you?' Then I laughed. 'I remember Viv and I listening in to a few of the customers' conversations, much to your horror.'

She smiled. 'Yes, you two were devils. But you're right about me being tied to the switchboard. No call could be put through unless I was there to connect it. I had to be nearby for hours on end until closing it down at night, unless your father or one of the older ones could be coerced into giving me a break.'

For a moment we sat in silence reminiscing, with just the tick tock of the clock on the mantelpiece and Tassie, the canary I'd given her as a companion after my father died, chirping happily on the windowsill.

'John O'Brien's *Around the Boree Log*, particularly *The Little Irish Mother*, was my constant companion as I tried to learn about the Australian bush,' she told me.

Even today that slim volume sits by her bedside in Ireland, reminding her of a time when she was in her early forties with five children under sixteen and with no obvious prospects for a future in a new and strange land.

'I love reading it even now,' she said, picking the battered book up and opening the pages. 'It takes me back in time. A time I thought I'd like to forget. But a time I'm grateful to now look back on.' She laughed. 'We were mad, weren't we? But we survived. And look at you all now.'

Recalling that time, I'm filled with the greatest admiration for the way she coped. For this life in Reidsdale was an enormous contrast to the life she'd recently known back in Ireland – a life of maids, governesses and gardeners. Although she hadn't seen her father in years, at least her mother, sister and aunts were reasonably close by in Ireland. Here in Australia she had no-one, apart from the Frosts and us.

My mother was not sure in later years why they had made the move to Australia but believed they had done the right thing as we had received a good education to equip us for our adult lives. Her only regret was that we all, except Viv, lived so far from Ireland, her home in her twilight years.

When my father first died there were thoughts my mother would come back to Australia to live. But at that stage she was well in her eighties and getting residency would have been impossible. Viv had wanted her to go to Wales too. But in the end she decided to stay in Ireland where we all visit when we can. Much of the burden of making sure she's okay falls on Viv, who makes the trip across from Wales at least five or six times a year, however in recent times I too have been going over two or three times a year.

My father never seemed to let things in Reidsdale get him down, which it surely must have. I can imagine the adventure of the *big move* was now wearing thin and there was left only the dread and fear of being able to provide for us all – so far away from his family and friends.

I remember we prayed a lot. Maybe this helped.

Every night, after we finished the washing up in the rickety sink with a wooden washboard on the side, we knelt on the bare boards in the main room with a log fire roaring in the huge fireplace. Here we leaned against the tattered lounge chairs, reciting the five decades of the rosary with many trimmings on the end. The more depressed my parents got, the longer the trimmings became and the more our knees hurt as we eyed each other through our half-opened fingers with rosary beads entwined.

Without fail we always finished our prayers with the same anguished plea: 'St Patrick protect us from snakes and take care of us.'

There was of course no television and we only had a small radio. Praying, talking, playing games and reading were our entertainment once it got dark and we came inside. Being the middle of winter, the hours indoors were long indeed, but the burning gum logs kept us warm until we retired to our freezing-cold bedrooms and snuggled under the eiderdowns to hide from the jet planes lurking in the rafters.

My father carried out his duties for Marcus Lyons, building many miles of fences, digging hundreds of post holes by hand and clearing the land of thistles. He dug ditch after ditch and spent hours straightening wire with his bare hands. He never complained, working harder than he'd ever done before and harder than any man half his fifty years.

It was at this stage that it was decided, seeing as I was learning little and came home from school most days in tears, that St Bede's and I were not suited to each other, so I was taken out of the *good nuns'* hands and deposited at the Lyons' place across the road where Mrs Lyons did her best to tutor me, together with her youngest child, Laurie, also deigned to be better suited to the home classroom amongst the paddocks. Fortunately classes were for only part of the day. The rest of the time I spent with my mother at the post office or with my father toiling and chatting away companionably. With him I learned more than I could possibly have in any history class.

Stopping work now and then to fill his pipe from his leather pouch, he'd lift his hat from his rapidly balding head to wipe his furrowed brow and look out over the endless paddocks. He always seemed to have that worried look, though in later years he told me: 'My time in the paddocks at Reidsdale was actually very enjoyable as I surveyed the countryside from beside my post holes. If I'd not had the worry of your education I'd have really quite liked to stay there. Tried to make a living from the land.'

As it was, he'd pat me on the head and say how glad he was to have my company for a few hours. Then he'd continue to dig, with me prattling away by his side. My mother would often have made us sandwiches and a thermos of tea, which I'd cart up the hill and later we'd sit on a log under a gumtree devouring it. Quite often I had my grey pony, Timmy, lent to me by the Lyons, tied up to the log as well.

Was I spoiled, whilst the others slogged it out at St Bede's? Looking back I think so.

It wasn't long before we children began to love our new life at Reidsdale. As the weather got warmer we swam in the creek at the bottom of the front paddock and built a swing out of a piece of wood and a long rope, which we'd jump off. For hours we'd sit with a piece of meat hanging off a string to catch yabbies. On the side of the creek we'd light a fire and cook them, pulling off their tails. Using a dry twig we'd pull out the delicious meat and dip it in melted butter.

One day we got covered in leeches and my mother, who'd never seen a leech before – let alone a snake – rushed inside to call the local doctor.

'You must come at once,' she shrieked down the phone. 'My

children seem to have dozens of little snakes attached to their skins, biting and sucking blood.'

After being reassured by the doctor that we were not going to die and they were in fact only leeches, she managed to extradite them from our squirming bodies by burning a match to the end of each nasty wriggler. A long and laborious job, not to mention painful.

On many occasions we mustered sheep for the next-door neighbour, Peter Bopping who was Mrs Lyons' brother. He was a weather-beaten fellow who usually had a *roll your own* hanging from his sunburnt lips and wore a battered bushman's hat, with corks dangling from the rim. In his hand he carried a shabby leather whip, which he constantly flicked at the sheep. For hours he patiently taught us how to crack it and took us mustering.

I rode my beloved Timmy. Viv and Eugene shared Clown, a Piebald gelding of some fifteen hands. Dibs and Gill managed to borrow horses from Peter and the Lyons. We spent hours sitting around a campfire with Peter, who held us in awe with his tall yarns. He was only in his thirties at the time, but like most Australian bushman his deeply tanned and corrugated face made him appear older. Living on his every word, we eagerly learned more about life in the Australian bush than we could have from any camping book. He made us the best mugs of *billy tea*, as we perched around the burning coals at the end of a long day's mustering. We brought our own tin mugs and would wait excitedly for Peter to fill them up and throw us a piece of damper he'd cooked in his camp oven on the burning logs. We learned how to shear and crutch a sheep and some damn good Aussie slang words, which were to be of advantage to us all later on.

Only recently Eugene told me how Peter had taken him into the pub in Braidwood for a soft drink whilst Peter had a well-earned cold beer. The day before, Eugene, driving Peter's old ute, had run over his prize blue heeler when they were out mustering. Fortunately he didn't kill the dog and after a quick trip to the vet it was sitting in the back of Peter's truck, terrorising the locals outside the pub, where Peter was trying to cheer Eugene up.

'At least you didn't kill the bastard,' he said cheerfully, belying the fact the dog was a favourite he'd had for years. Unlike most working sheepdogs, which are relegated to a cold kennel outside, it slept on the bed beside him on the verandah. Needless to say Peter would have been devastated if Eugene had killed the poor mutt.

Eugene remembers a rather dapper fellow, dressed in a tweed sports coat, checked shirt and moleskins, coming over to introduce himself, having heard Peter was the man he needed to organise the shearing of his sheep on the property he'd newly acquired on the banks of the Shoalhaven River.

He removed a fancy Meerschaum pipe from his neatly moustached mouth and held out a hand. 'James Campbell-Brown,' he said in a highly polished Scots College accent. 'I believe you're name's Bopping and you're the good chap I need to shear my sheep.'

There was a moment's silence whilst Peter looked him up and down. Then he put his beer on the table and removed a soggy roll your own from between his smoke-stained teeth.

'G'day, Mr Brown,' he said, beckoning to an empty chair at the table next door. 'Pull up a chair.'

The man puffed out his chest. 'The name's Campbell-Brown, actually.'

A beat of silence. 'Not a problem, mate,' Peter said, eyeing him through dust-spattered lashes. 'In that case reckon you better be pulling up two chairs, eh.'

There were a number of sayings in Australia at the time, which we were unfamiliar with.

My mother got caught out dreadfully when asked to 'take a plate' to a function in a neighbour's house. Imagining the poor lady was short of crockery she took an empty china plate, much to the amusement of the other wives. Needless to say my mother was mortified.

She also got a fright when confronted with a 'g'day love,' by a down and out stranger at her door. Looking flustered and red in the face he told her he needed help as the 'bloody bomb' had blown up down the road.

Imagining the IRA or some such Australian radical group were terrorising the neighbourhood, my mother went into a bit of spin, until he explained that he needed some water to fill his car radiator up with.

The next day he turned up to say thank you. I feel he may have been rather smitten with the new postmistress. After a while my mother offered him a cup of tea, thinking he must be lonely. He declined, but asked if she had 'a cold tinnie' in the fridge. When she worked out he wasn't after a tin of baked beans or such he was somewhat put out to find she only had a bottle of sherry in the cupboard, which he declined.

Another time, a neighbour asked my mother if she could mind her children for a few hours, saying before she left: 'I hope they won't get in the road.'

'No, of course they won't,' my mother assured her, sounding a bit put out. 'I never let my children play down on the road. They may get hit by a car.'

The neighbour looked somewhat perplexed, until they came to an understanding that the children would not be allowed to get in my mother's way.

But the saying that really got her was when she was sitting

next to a local farmer at the Lyons' house. Suddenly he jumped up and said. 'Hold on a sec, dear, I'm just off to see a man about a dog. You wait here and I'll top up your drink when I come back.'

As it was about ten o'clock at night she wondered where the man with the dog was and why her companion had suddenly needed to go and see him. Seeing my mother on her own, my father came over and sat down beside her. He asked where the farmer had gone.

'To see a man about a dog.'

My father looked around. 'At this hour.'

'Evidently.'

When the farmer returned my mother asked him how he had got on. How was the dog?

He gave her an odd sort of look and then burst out laughing. 'It's a saying we have in Australia when we need to go and relieve ourselves.'

'I'd never heard such an expression before,' my mother told me with a laugh. 'A very odd one indeed.'

We met Steve Forsant, a jovial, bearded gentleman, who owned a horse-drawn brightly coloured wagon. We met him on one of our trips down the Araluen Valley, a beautiful green basin with the sweet aroma of orange and lemon trees filling the air. On the way we stopped on an outcrop of rocks, looking down onto the extensive dale.

My father later said: 'My memory of this place is the complete silence. In the middle of a hot Australian day, all life seemed to sleep and not even a bird chirped. It was a silence of tangible quality.'

We were having an outing in the Holden. Steve, a barrel of a man (a nun later told my mother he looked the image of St Joseph), was running tearooms overlooking the valley. Being thirsty we'd seen the sign and stopped. Shortly, Steve arrived leading a gentle black horse called Cuddy, who nuzzled her warm nose against my chest. Tying Cuddy to the front railings he removed his bushman's broad-brimmed hat, patted his long beard and beckoned for us to follow him inside. Whilst my parents told him our story he scurried around his small *lean to* kitchen, before serving us a banquet of tea and scones with rich clotted cream. The family from Tipperary who'd left all to start a new life in the Australian bush fascinated him, like it did most people at that time. It was the beginning of a lasting friendship.

Recently I drove from Moruya to the Araluen Valley with Rob on our way to Reidsdale, to see how it had fared over the years. Even now the road from Moruya was little more than a dusty dirt track, snaking perilously through towering mountains and hugging the side of the picturesque Deua River. At times I felt as though we were driving on the very tops of the straggly casuarinas and thick firs clinging with all their might to the steep banks. A wrong yank of the steering wheel would see us drop to the river below.

After two hours, lost in a time warp, with the farmhouses seeming much the same as they were back in the 1950s, we came to the Araluen Valley where the orange groves and apple orchards straddled both sides of the road. Now sadly the rich verdant valley I remembered from when I was seven years old was brown and bare from years of drought. Ten kilometres up the steep hill out of the valley, and after passing a herd of cattle grazing on the side of the road (the long paddock) with a modern day stockman astride a fine-looking palomino with mobile phone glued to his ear, we took the turn-off for Reidsdale. Why it is still on the map is a wonder? For there's little there to tell the traveller they've arrived; just a few houses in the middle of nowhere. Brown bare drought stricken fields on a desiccated dusty road. Not much different to when we first sighted it sixty years ago. We stopped at the entrance to what used to be the post office. On the front gate was a rusted horseshoe. Was that the one I remember helping my father nail there?

We drove up to the now deserted and derelict building and stood on the back porch looking out to the fields where I had spent so many hours watching my father digging post-holes. A place where time has stood still. Memories etched into every beam and nail. Every wooden post. Each piece of straightened wire. Every leech and yabby in the river.

And when I stood there in the silence, echoes of the past resounded through the empty rooms. I could almost smell the rich aroma coming from my mother's Irish stew bubbling in the heavy steel pressure cooker on the fuel stove, and hear the shrill whistle announcing the meal was ready. I could see my mother beckoning us to the rickety wooden table in the kitchen to sit down, my father leaning over to serve out our meal and then saying grace before we started.

As if only yesterday I could hear Viv's incredulous voice when she came across something new that no-one else had seen. 'Teeny, come quickly. See what I've found! Don't tell anyone else.'

It might just have been a rabbit hole…a footprint from some unknown animal, or what she thought was the wriggly line left behind by a snake.

I could see Peter Bopping riding up the gravel road. Bush hat on his head. Whip in hand. Cigarette hanging out of his mouth.

I could hear the excitement in Gill's voice. 'Here comes Mr Bopping. Saddle up everyone. Have you got your tin mugs?'

Heading up the hill we passed the wooden bridge where Dibs and Gill had crashed their bikes, scaring us witless.

I heard Eugene's strangled voice as he rushed in to tell my mother what had happened. 'I think they're okay,' he had tried to assure her, his voice quivering. 'I can see them moving.'

On the way back to Canberra we stopped at the Shoalhaven River, where we'd often gone to cook bacon and eggs on a campfire under a towering weeping willow on the sandy beach after Sunday Mass. I could see my father, legs sprawled, plate on his knee, swiping at the flies. My mother in her pink and white floral dress splayed over her slim legs and her high heels next to her on the sand. I could hear our laughter as we jumped from one rock to another and splashed in the clear water. Picking up a stone I skimmed it across the smooth surface of the river. I watched it jump five times out of the water before it reached the other side.

'A *record*,' I could hear my seven-year-old self scream out in joy.

Last week Dibs and Gill also returned to Reidsdale and Braidwood and met many of the people who remembered us from the 50s. They even went to St Bedes, which looks much the same.

CHAPTER 13

Moving to the National Capital

Our time at Reidsdale was soon to come to an end when my father secured a job with the Courts and Titles Office of the Attorney General's Department in Canberra. He and Eugene spent the weekdays boarding there, returning to the post office at Reidsdale on weekends. Eugene had been accepted into the first intake of students at the Christian Brothers College, St Edmunds, in Kingston. He left us one early morning looking very much the young gentleman in his grey uniform with straw boater hat perched on his proud head. With no house available in Canberra, we girls kept the home fires burning at the post office. We spent many hours on our knees saying the rosary and copious novenas asking for a house to become available. But it took time. Obviously God had more pressing matters on hand.

This was also the year of the 'big floods' so he'd quite a lot of protecting to do as well. With the creek having broken its banks we evacuated from the house, under strict instructions from my father and Eugene, who were comfortably ensconced in Canberra.

At least the 'grass was greener' when the rains finally ceased.

As you can see the Catholic Church was very much part of my early life. Having been born a Catholic, in those days to have any thoughts of being anything else was touted as 'definitely likely to end up with one's soul burning in the roaring fires of hell'. I was not going to contest this belief. And apart from anything else the Esmondes had been Catholics since the Crusades. They'd even been hanged, from O'Connell's Bridge in Dublin, for their religion. In the 1950s I never thought of being anything else, although today I've seen enough bigotry, abuse, sorrow and death in the name of religion to make me rethink.

Like most Catholics, much of my young life was spent in guilt. I fully appreciate those people that still have the faith. Both my parents had enormous faith and at times it has been of great comfort to them. It was particularly to my father during his life and impending death, and to my mother through trying times and in coping with the loss of my father.

Back in 1954 I was praying along with the rest of the family for a home to become available in Canberra. In fact Eugene had been sent up the road and across country to collect a set of holy scapulars that a friend, Billy Maher gave us for that very purpose.

'On the way back he got slightly waylaid, stopping by the river for a spot of fishing and to check his rabbit traps,' my mother told me with a smile. 'He left the scapulars in the bushes whilst he had a swim. When he got home to the post office empty handed I'm afraid I was furious and sent him back to find them, which he eventually did, after hours of searching.'

Needless to say the prayers that went with these holy pieces of cloth were added to our rosary each night. The time on our knees was now getting longer and longer. Today my knees are not as good as they should be. I've no doubt that the endless hours of praying in my youth contributed to this greatly.

However, God must have heard our prayers. For before too

long a house became available in Condamine Street in the suburb of Turner in Canberra's northern suburbs, belonging to fervent Catholics who were going overseas on a diplomatic posting. Fortunately for us they'd told their kindly Irish parish priest, Father Lynch, to find a deserving Catholic family to fill this house in their absence. We were the deserving Catholic family and a very grateful one at that. It seemed to me at the time that the only real estate agents in Australia were the priests. After all, had they not found us the last two homes to live in?

Before moving to Canberra, we undertook the long journey back to Morriset to have Christmas with the Frosts. Again we children were packed into the back of the Holden, together with Porky and Viv's cat. For some reason only known to Viv she stuck her head in the pressure cooker we were taking to the Frosts and it took forever to get it out. When we returned to Reidsdale we borrowed an old truck, packed all our belongings (which was not much) and moved lock stock and barrel to Condamine Street, a castle compared to our two other houses in Australia, but still a long way removed from Drominagh or Clonmoylan. Built of red bricks it had three bedrooms, a small living room, a minute kitchen, and one tiny bathroom. Sitting on a green mowed lawn, amidst a thick row of tall fir trees, it positively gleamed compared to the ramshackle post office at Reidsdale. Needless to say it wasn't long before my father started a vegetable garden and built a chicken run out of wire meshing, making it feel more like home.

Although it sat slap bang next to the Baptist church we, of course, went to the Catholic church up in Braddon, where we were all paraded in our Sunday best, Eugene in long socks and shorts and the mandatory tie, my father in his best attire, my mother dressed to the nines with her green hat and donkey brooch.

Our friend Vince Thompson, who was an altar boy with Eugene, remembers, 'Your parents always paraded you right up to the very front seat. I used to get the giggles watching you.'

I can still remember the embarrassment of that long walk to the front. Was it because the nearer to the altar we were, the closer to God we'd be?

Across the road from our house was the Turner Primary School. Father Bateman, a gentle Australian priest, whose job was to go into the public schools to coax Catholics back into the fold, roped my mother into teaching catechism to classes of unruly students here.

'They had little interest in what I was teaching them,' my mother said, 'but if you were a Catholic, classes were compulsory.'

Dibs didn't spend much time at Condamine Street, for she was now ensconced as a boarder at Rose Bay Convent in Sydney, run by the same order of nuns where my mother had gone to school, and her mother before her.

'I decided to take the bull by the horns, driving down to Sydney to talk things over with the Reverend Mother, who kindly offered Dibs a position in the school under special paying arrangements,' my mother told me. 'She was now sixteen and I felt she needed to have some sort of stability in her life.'

Sadly, Dibs packed up and left us in the last few months of living at Reidsdale for her new life in the big smoke, where she braved it out for eighteen months, but was not particularly happy. She told me that this was a traumatic time for her, trying to adjust to a new country, and coping with a totally different education system, whilst being desperately homesick at the same time. Being fifteen when we arrived in Australia, she was more affected by the cultural and emotional changes than we younger ones were.

'I remember the nuns ringing me up in a fluster,' my mother said. 'Dibs, whilst doodling in class, had drawn a pair of spectacles on a photo of the Queen on one of her exercise books. To the nuns this was no less than treason. Dibs could see no reason why the Queen shouldn't be so adorned. Eventually, the nuns decided to let things rest, but not before Dibs was given a strong reprimand and I was made to feel as though our family should be deported back to Ireland for ridiculing the Royal Family.' She laughed. 'Although I was beside myself at the time, thinking they might expel her, I must admit I thought it quite humorous.'

In the meantime Eugene continued at St Edmunds. Being an Irishman, but worse still, an Irishman with an English accent, he soon developed two accents – a good Aussie twang for school and outside our home, and his normal voice for inside the door of our house to appease my parents.

One must remember this was long before the time of mass multi-culturalism and political correctness in Australia. Migrants were not as numerous as they are today.

Only recently, Eric, a great Chinese friend of ours from New Guinea,, told me that he was often referred to in the 1950s as *Ching Chong Chinaman* at his private school in the elite Eastern suburbs of Sydney, where he was brought down from New Guinea by his father to commence his education. He took it all in his stride, for he was after all the only Chinese boy in the school and as such was regarded as quite a novelty.

One day, the captain of an opposing team from another elite private school called out to his team mates on the rugby field, 'Kill the little Chinaman.'

Imagine the furore if that was said in today's society.

Gill at nearly fifteen was the fashion queen, discovering beehive hairdos, flowing floral dresses with large wire hoops, and rope skirts, which were all the rage. We couldn't pass her in the narrow hallway in one of these contraptions for fear of being entrapped. Fortunately hoops didn't stay in fashion too long, although rope skirts remained around much longer, long enough for me to inherit one from Gill, which I adored.

Socialising at this stage was mostly at parties in peoples' homes or the local church hall where the girls sat around the walls hoping to be asked to dance and feeling humiliated if they were left a wallflower. It was even worse for a pimply faced youth rejected when he'd taken an age to work up the courage to walk across the acres of floor to ask a girl to dance in the first place. There were also 'barn dances', held in farmers' shearing sheds or hay barns. Little alcohol was served and many of the Catholics of the day had taken what was called 'the pledge', meaning they didn't have a drink until they turned twenty-one. A few years later at one of these dances I won my first kiss. We were playing the heady game of the time 'spin the bottle' and the bottle ended up pointing at me. I must say, not only was he extremely easy on the eye, he was a darn good kisser.

It was difficult for Dibs and Gill. My parents expected that they should not go out with anyone who wasn't a Catholic. Unfortunately this was a belief held not only by my parents. Social intermixing between religions was still frowned upon, particularly on behalf of the Catholic Church, though other churches could be just as biased. They were also not supposed to go out with anyone who 'wasn't of our class'…slightly difficult when we were living in one of the less affluent areas of Canberra. An Aussie twang was also a 'no no'.

This caused us all to lament, 'Why on earth did they bring us to Australia if that's what they insist on?'

Now my mother can see the unreasonableness of such requests. 'I think we were trying to hold on to what we had left behind,' she said remorsefully. 'In hindsight this was ridiculous and very hard on Dibs and Gill.'

This attitude of my parents limited Dibs and Gill's scope of boyfriends considerably, becoming an awful bone of contention within the family. There were many heated arguments with raised voices, which I tried to avoid by hiding in my bedroom. Today Dibs and Gill tell me it was indeed a traumatic time for them both as they tried to come to terms with our parents' demands. Many a boyfriend was given short shrift and hearts were broken.

By the time I started dating, my parents realised that raising teenagers in Australia, where Catholics were far from the majority, was a different kettle of fish to Catholic Ireland and they became more lenient.

Canberra was established in the early part of the twentieth century. Hence even in the 1950s it was still relatively small with a population of only about 40,000. Being the planned capital of Australia from the very beginning, the first Parliament house was built there in 1910. Designed by Sir Walter Burley Griffin, Canberra was really only accessible by motor car, train or aeroplane. There were two distinct areas in Canberra at this time: North and South.

South was definitely the side to be on if you wanted to be part of the social set. For here the embassies, large homes and 'old money' were to be found amidst the wide tree-lined streets and avenues of Yarralumla, Deakin, Forest and Red Hill. There was no Lake Burley Griffin then, just the meandering Murrumbidgee River flowing under Commonwealth Bridge and forming a definite border between the southern suburbs and the less fashionable northern suburbs where we lived. The Capital is set bang in the middle of hundreds of acres of sprawling sheep country, nestled into a stunning mountain range, known as the Brindabellas. Dry and incredibly hot in the summer, it becomes icy cold with heavy frosts in the winter. Running along the horizon, the rolling hills of the Brindabellas are an artist's palette of ever-changing colours, with the spectacular evening sunset disappearing behind the peaks in a crimson blaze, as if it is a glow from a monstrous bushfire. Forward thinkers planted every variety of deciduous tree throughout the city, making autumn a sight to behold, as the brittle leaves turn a burnished gold before covering the ground in a luxurious carpet.

Long before Lake Burley Griffin became a reality, my parents took us on picnics to the small rivers and streams that originated from the mountains and snowfields. The Cotter Dam, where we often swam, was the collection spot for the Murrumbidgee after it joined the Murray River system. A popular spot with swimmers and sunbakers, it had a number of shaded river beaches ideal for setting up camp. As this was virtually the only swimming hole within close proximity of the Capital it was the 'place to be seen' and definitely a meeting spot for the young of the time, where lithe brown teenage girls would parade in itsy bitsy bikinis trying to outdo each other, and the young men would leap off overhanging branches into the gushing river, trying to impress.

Wood collecting in the 1950s was an essential pastime, but one I enjoyed. Often we made a day of it, packing a picnic lunch to devour hungrily as we sat on a log in an isolated paddock where a farmer was pleased to have the fallen branches from his hordes of gumtrees carted away. One of the best spots for wood collecting was near the small village of Collector on the way to Lake George, at that stage full of water, unlike today. Sadly a number of Duntroon cadets drowned in the lake in the mid-fifties and I remember my father and Eugene joining in the fruitless search.

John and Betty Collins, retired rubber planters from Malaya, had a sprawling homestead, Euralie, outside Yass, with hundreds of acres leading down to the picturesque Murrumbidgee River where we often went to picnic and water ski. Betty, (who later changed her name to Liza as it had far more class to it) whose family came from Ireland, knew of the Esmonde family and she and John were a wonderful source of inspiration for my parents, introducing them to many of their friends. For quite a few years we had memorable school holidays at their rambling beach house at Whale Beach, north of Sydney. Situated on the lower side of the road, just near the small corner store, it had a steep access down a rough track and onto a sandy beach where we all learned how to surf in the tumbling waves and fished off the rocks. For hours we'd sit playing cards on the deep verandah at the front of the house, with a bird's eye view of the ocean, or otherwise muck around in the courtyard to the rear – where I've a photo of us all holding the fish we'd caught that day. I've never been an avid surfer, yet I love the beach. My husband, Rob, having been brought up at Manly in the northern suburbs of Sydney, where surfing was a religion, adores it. If the surf was up, classes at Manly Boys High were given a miss. In fact, he and his friend, Max, assure me that during their last summer at school they quite often only attended classes on a Friday, but both managed to pass the Leaving Certificate with flying colours.

Back in Condamine Street, we were rarely short of friends, for, within a short distance of our house, at least ten children were going to the same schools as us. (In Gill's case St Christopher's Good Samaritan Convent in Manuka, Eugene St Edmunds, and Viv and I at Our Lady of Mercy in Braddon). I sometimes excelled in drama and Viv was captain of everything imaginable, including the softball team. At an eisteddfod at the Albert Hall, I recited 'The Man from Snowy River' where to my amazement I won first prize.

These were the days when a bottle of milk was compulsory. It was warm as it was delivered to the school grounds and left in the sun until lunchtime. It was also when we had to line up for hours waiting to receive the painful jab of a polio needle, which put the fear of God in us all.

The Sisters of Mercy were a kind and down-to-earth lot. On many occasions they'd roll up their flowing habits, take off their shoes and enjoy a game of softball…unlike the strict Sacré Coeur order I went to later on. It was a great honour to be asked to ring the school bell for recess and I must have done the posting of letters at some stage, for just last week Gill sent me a holy card she'd found from Mother Ignatius, the kindly headmistress, dated 1957, thanking me for 'being her little helper posting the mail'.

With the holes in my cast-off shoes filled in with cardboard, I remember the bitter cold of the classroom with no heating whatsoever – bad enough for those of us who could move around, but unbearable for a sweet girl, Clare, confined to a wheelchair after suffering a horrendous bout of polio. However, on the whole, life was simple. We played with our hoopla rings, threw coins in hopscotch squares, flicked marbles across the street, sucked the fizz from sherbet bags, licked sticky toffee apples or ate soggy tomato sandwiches. If we were lucky we were allowed to order sausage rolls and fairy bread from the canteen as a treat. We entered announcing competitions on

2CA, the local radio station, where Steve Liebmann, who years later was to become the anchor for the national *Today* show, judged me as the winner one week, with the grand prize of a bottle of Coca Cola and a new yo-yo. But best of all we discovered Mrs Lew's riding school at Acton, a tranquil refuge, where we spent most of the next years of our life in a horsey heaven.

Mrs Lew was, in fact, Bobby Llewellyn, a tiny formidable lady, who was always immaculately turned out in cream jodhpurs, a sparkling white shirt with a bright tie adorned with horses' heads, and highly polished riding boots, her neatly tended blonde hair encased within a hairnet. With her kindly face always beautifully made up, she was never less than spectacular and she had a heart of gold. Being so short, but, it seemed, always riding the largest horse in the stables, she'd carry a heavy metal bucket or a stump of wood to the side of the horse, using it to mount and dismount.

Mrs Lew had the best riding school in all the world as far as we were concerned, the horses' paddocks being under the weeping willows below Commonwealth Avenue Bridge right in the very core of what is now Lake Burley Griffin. The actual stables were situated between the Australian National University and the Canberra Hospital amidst groves of thick pine trees, where the heady aroma of chaff, saddle soap, horse sweat and fresh manure filed the air. The quaint timber cottages fronting the stables sat in a neat row, all built well before the war, with small porches to the front and rear and narrow gardens leading down to the yards. No one house seemed more glamorous than the next, although some gardens were tended better than others. None of the inhabitants seemed to complain about the flies or the smell of horse manure, or if they did, they never managed to change things. In fact many of the residents became our friends, often enticing us to pull up on our horses at their back door for a yarn, where they'd give us a cool drink and a piece of cake. The stables remained in that spot until they were relocated adjacent to the pine forest on the Cotter Road when Lake Burley Griffin was about to become a reality.

We usually walked to Mrs Lew's and back, some two miles from Condamine Street, stopping in Civic Centre for fish and chips wrapped in newspaper at the Seven Seas or for a milk shake at the Blue Moon Café. If it was very hot we'd drop off at the new Olympic swimming pool complex where Viv and I often competed in races or lay on the hot cement with our bodies covered in coconut oil, trying to develop suntans like the Aussies, much to my mother's horror, who assured us we would live to regret it – which of course we have.

Mrs Lew kindly allowed us to ride whatever horses were free if we helped with the catching, grooming, and saddling for lessons. My favourite was Goldie, a fourteen-hand gelding. I just adored him, dreaming of his white splashed face day and night. Viv, had Danny Boy, a small black pony, lent to her by Dib's boyfriend at the time, Kelvin. Viv and Danny Boy managed to win most of the cross-country and show jumping events at the time.

'One day,' my mother told me,' I remember coming to watch. I didn't go often, as I got too nervous in case you fell off. This time I was horrified to see Danny Boy caught on the top of a monstrous high jump he was attempting to clear, swinging backwards and forward with Viv's legs dangling in mid-air, before, much to my relief, they were both rescued.'

Well after Viv had given up riding him because she became too tall, Danny Boy and I won the ACT Cross Country Event, riding up scrubby dales and down steep glens in the basin of what is now the lake. There have been few achievements in my life that have surpassed this moment of glory, particularly as I tended to live in the shadow of my older sisters in the riding world.

When we first moved to Tasmania some twenty-five years later, I took part in the Taranna Gymkhana on the Tasman Peninsula and again won a first prize – mainly due to the fact that my horse, Devil, was the only horse who could be persuaded to go backwards when asked. Or, as Rob unkindly suggested, the ruddy-faced judge was Irish and possibly took a fancy to me, being the only woman in the event.

Back in Canberra, Dibs had Kinsale, a 16-hand bay that she won many events with. Gill did much the same on Aaron, a stunning white Arab, not the easiest horse to handle, bolting once through the streets of Canberra with Gill on board. Often Viv and I would ride our horses home, tying them up in the back garden, where we'd have lunch. Then we'd ride back to the stables again in the afternoon before walking home through the paddocks and suburbs, often in the dark. It never crossed our minds that our parents should pick us up, or if it did, they would have been far too busy to be able to do so. Other times we'd ride over to ICEM, the immigration government office where Gill worked and have lunch with her or visit Dibs at St Peter Channel's Primary School in Yarralumla where she taught a lively class of kindergarten children. Occasionally we'd persuade Eugene to come riding, but on the whole he was more interested in playing rugby or competing in athletic competitions, where he excelled at hurdles.

Gill also met her future husband, Colin, a crack show jumper in Canberra at the time. Over fifty years later he's as divine as ever.

They first met when Gill was trying to put the bridle on Aaron and he was refusing to co-operate.

'I wouldn't be doing it like that,' Colin said in his wonderful long Australian drawl, walking up and taking over.

Now they live in Tamworth in New South Wales where they're both involved in the Riding for the Disabled, after retiring from managing a Santa Gertrudis cattle stud, Hardigreen Park at Wallabadah, during which time Colin became President of the Santa Gertrudis Association of New South Wales. Last time I was in Tamworth with them we went to the magnificent new Equestrian Centre where we watched the Australian show jumping trials. I've never seen such an impressive array of riders and horses in one venue before. Gill and Colin went on to have four beautiful children, Andrew, Allison, Mia and Liam. Like Rob and I, they have five grandchildren. Colin is the only member of our family who refuses to call me Teeny.

'You were given a perfectly good name, Rosemary, so I'm going to use it.'

After breaking the heart of a few Canberra fellows, Dibs married Peter, an archaeologist and moved to Dunedin in New Zealand, where she joined him on isolated digs. It was such an adventure that her photo made the front pages of the *Women's Weekly*. Not long after leaving school (where she'd be the first to say she didn't excel) she discovered teaching was her calling. For over thirty years she was a marvellous success (particularly with gifted children for which she did a thesis and won a number of awards), until she retired to Gippsland in Victoria where she runs a highly successful business, Glendalough Park Cattery and Kennels with her gorgeous second husband, Kevin. For years she was on the local council and is still on the tourist board for the area.

Back in Canberra in the 1950s, school holidays were often spent on droving and camping treks. Mrs Lew would load up a Clydesdale horse with billy cans, swags and tins of food and take paying guests on a trek through the mountain ranges. Often the paying guests were children of overseas ambassadors who wanted their children to experience life in the Australian bush before returning to the confines of their concrete jungles.

Somehow Mrs Lew always managed to find a spare horse for the Esmondes, at little cost if we would pitch in and help. We'd make up our own swags with our clothes and sleeping bags (lovingly made by my mother out of old army surplus), which we'd carry on our horses, together with leather saddle-bags filled to the brim with our own tin plates, knives and forks and a steel water bottle.

We were an impressive sight, riding through the streets of the classier suburbs of Canberra, Mrs Lew to the front on her seventeen-hand grey gelding, her daughter, Jan, not far behind, leading the pack horses. Then all of us would be bringing up the rear, with our saddle-bags and water cans dangling off our newly polished saddles. We wore large brimmed felt hats with corks, just like Peter Bopping in Reidsdale, to ward off the flies. Quite often people came out to their front gardens to wave us off, even as we rode through Mugga Way, brimming with large mansions and embassies, down Mugga Lane and out into the sunburnt countryside towards the small village of Tharwa and up to the Goodradigbee mountain ranges.

Most of the nights, were spent in various shearers' quarters, like those at the historic Lanyon Station, which was first occupied following white settlement by the ex-convict, Timothy Beard, who was transported to Australia for life in 1806. After Beard was evicted, James Wright and his friend John Lanyon also settled as squatters. When Lanyon returned to England, Wright stayed on with his large family and a workforce of convicts before he got into financial difficulties and was forced to sell Lanyon and move to the nearby station of Cupacumbalong, where we also camped.

Lanyon, now owned by the government, was, for many years, the Sidney Nolan Gallery and is a tranquil haven on the perimeter of the Canberra suburbs.

In the 1950s we had gymkhanas involving the local children in barrel and flag races. We'd help with mustering or shearing sometimes. At night, singsongs were held around a huge campfire on a riverbank with the sound of a lone guitar and our young voices rising upwards to the spectacular Brindabella Ranges, as though we were in a huge amphitheatre.

Often I watched in awe as romances took place. One of these was between the beautiful blonde daughter of one of the more prominent ambassadors to Australia and a good-looking rough and tumble shearer working on one of the sheep stations we'd camped on down by the river. It was quite a 'hot affair', often conducted behind the bushes in the dark of night and out of Mrs Lew's sight and hearing. Not ours, however. Needless to say, after the illicit romance was discovered, the poor girl was immediately plucked from our midst, never to join the riding treks again. She was shipped back to her home country to continue her education in a style more suited to her background.

In the mornings we'd get up early and light a fire to cook breakfast and boil the billy on a wood fire. At night it could be a walloping stew, or if we'd been lucky enough to score meat from one of the sheep stations it might be a barbeque on a grate over the fire. I remember we drank tinned pineapple juice and large quantities of sweetened condensed or powdered milk and lunch was often cracker biscuits smothered with Vegemite or cream cheese. One of the boys got bitten on the behind by a snake when squatting with the call of nature, but after a hasty trip to the Canberra Hospital he survived. I fell in love with a young fellow with a great singing voice, who serenaded us with bush ballads, and owned a large black horse, although in hindsight I think it may have been the large black horse I fancied most. Not true!

Endless hot summer days ran blissfully into each other as we galloped over rocky streams, through acres of parched overgrazed paddocks, climbed steep stony mountains; scrambling down the other side, with our hair streaming in the hot wind; our bush hats flapping up and down on our fly-covered backs. And then all too soon it was time to head home. Reluctantly we would trek back along the dusty roads, through Naas and Tharwa, finally clattering into Acton where we'd stop at the hospital canteen and gulp a freezing cold 'spider' down in seconds, relishing the tangy taste of lemonade and ice cream sliding down our parched throats. After a final wash and rub down of the horses, we'd lead them across the road, letting them loose under the towering weeping willows on the banks of the Murrumbidgee River, before stopping to gorge ourselves with luscious ripe mulberries off the ancient tree near the gate.

Bobby Llewellyn was later rewarded in the Queen's Birthday Honours for her service to the equestrian industry and the youth of Canberra. I can think of a no more deserving person to be so honoured. When she died we all mourned her loss, but particularly Gill, who'd kept in constant contact.

My father made ends meet with his job in the public service, plus a milk run in the morning, (which we often helped with) and overtime at night. Later he became a proofreader with the *Canberra Times* and then the *Australian* newspaper when it first started. At weekends he delivered bread. This was all a long way from being 'the squire' at Drominagh.

At Christmas time on the milk run, most of the customers would leave my father a present: chocolates, bottles of whisky, or other alcoholic offerings (which, if I was helping, I'd have to immediately confiscate in case they were a temptation) to put under the Christmas tree. In the winter it was pitch dark and freezing cold. Morning after morning my father hauled himself out of bed at four-thirty and started his run, pulling his wooden trolley from one house to the next.

'He used to carry a ruler to fight off the dogs,' my mother recalled with a laugh.

At first my mother managed to get a job as a cleaner at the Australian National University at night. I know how humbling this was for her, but both my parents worked without complaint, bringing much needed money home. There were, after all, seven mouths to be fed.

For a short period my father tried his hand at being a Massy Ferguson tractor salesman out at Yarralumla. He ended up working at the Department of External Affairs as his day job, which he had for many years, before retiring and starting his own business, Braddon Flyscreens, having realised flies were a 'darn nuisance' and no-one in Canberra seemed to have come up with a satisfactory solution. It was a roaring success, bringing him enormous satisfaction and some well-earned rewards. Mind you it should have, for it was incredibly hard work. Particularly in the summer months, when he'd start at the crack of dawn and finish late into the evening, making and fitting each and every fly screen window and door himself, working out of the garage of our then-home in Ijong Street. Soon, to his great satisfaction, he was earning more than the Department Head at his old public service job and had opened a small factory in the industrial area of Fyshwick.

After the cleaning jobs – and later as a proofreader with the Attorney General's Department – my mother secured a job as a casual at David Jones Department Store, working in different sections and enjoying it on the whole.

'Except when I was in the bakery section and had to wear a white starched baker's hat,' she told me recently with a wry chuckle. 'I found this a bit humiliating.'

Looking back, I've the greatest admiration for them both.

Steve Forsant came to stay in his covered wagon pulled by his ever-patient horse, Cuddy. He set up camp on the government nature strip across the road from Condamine Street. Each night he built a roaring campfire, which we all crouched around as he told us yarns of his past. Amazingly no-one asked him not to light the fire or to move on.

After a few months he did move on – to Hall, a small village just north of Canberra, where we visited him often at his makeshift campsite. Then he and Cuddy wandered further north. He was not an old man, but with his long grey beard and rotund build, he seemed ancient to us children. Years later he reappeared, asking my parents for some money, which, although short themselves, they kindly gave him.

'After some rough times he made good in a new life in central New South Wales,' my mother told me, fingering a photograph of him and Cuddy in the album at Cloneen. 'A few years later he sent us money to build a roof onto the ex RAAF hut, which doubled as Eugene's bedroom. Then sadly we never heard from him again.'

Before Steve set up camp opposite our house, he took over the running of the post office at Reidsdale. Dibs on her horse, Kinsale, and Eugene on his new bike, decided to pay him a visit.

It was mid-summer, with the temperature soaring. They were to spend the night at Bungendore, a small town about halfway between Canberra and Braidwood. No-one seemed to think this was unusual – that two young teenagers should take off like this on their own, on a sixty mile journey – on one of the hottest days Canberra had experienced in years.

After the first twenty miles or so Eugene took refuge in a large clay pipe, refusing to come out till it got cooler. I don't blame him. Fortunately a neighbour from Reidsdale, Tubby Clarke, a knock-about bloke, happened to pass by in a ute. For some reason he was leading a horse from his window – a slow mode of transport. As he was also heading for Reidsdale, he suggested Eugene trade the bicycle for the horse. This Eugene did without much coaxing, for anything seemed preferable to pedalling his bike up the huge hills in temperatures like that.

Before leaving them, Tubby warned Eugene he should watch out for one of this horse's nasty habits of pigrooting. Eugene decided this was a cheap price to pay and was prepared to take the risk. On they trudged to Bungendore (Eugene surviving the odd buck from the errant horse), where they spent the night in on old barn at the back of a rambling house. Next day they limped into Braidwood after stopping at the Shoalhaven River to give the horses a swim. The day after that they followed the route our school bus used to take, arriving at Reidsdale to find Steve Forsant waiting for them at the post office.

Dibs headed home on Sunday, while Eugene stayed on for a couple of weeks with Steve. We set out to meet Dibs, finding her between Braidwood and Bungendore, with tears streaming down her face, as she was convinced we'd all perished in a car accident.

'In fact the reason we were late meeting her was that Mass had dragged on longer than usual,' my mother told me. 'I must admit if I'd known she was going to get so upset we'd have got up and left before communion, even though we were right up the front.'

I still have a vivid memory of driving towards Dibs, lumbering along on Kinsale within a thick shroud of pale dust.

'God knows why we decided to do it,' she laughed, looking back to that trip, as we sat in her living room at Glendalough Park in Gippsland, with a roaring fire in the grate where her elderly cat, Victor Hobart, (who she and Kevin acquired after a visit to us in Hobart) lolled in front of the flames. 'It probably seemed like a good idea at the time. And I don't suppose in those days it was all that unusual to ride such a long distance. But it *was* very hot.'

Later, when she finally plodded into the dusty stables at Mrs Lew's, tired and worn out, my parents decided such outings, although perhaps suited to the Irish climate, were not quite as appealing in the searing heat of an Australian summer.

Chapter 14

Ijong Street... Not Drominagh but Ours

In 1957, we moved to 5 Ijong Street in the suburb of Braddon, not far from Condamine Street. We'd been waiting for a government house that we could eventually buy to become available ever since we'd arrived in Canberra.

Ijong Street again was not Drominagh nor Clonmoylan, but it was ours.

On a large corner block, opposite an extensive break of pines, known as Haigh Park, with a huge pine tree of its own right next to the house, it was a site my father had coveted for some time. Built out of monocrete, the house comprised a large kitchen where we could all sit around the table at a squeeze, a separate living room, a dining room of sorts and three double bedrooms and one bathroom. Most importantly of all it had a sun deck at the back, making up for the fact that the small kitchen and bathroom windows faced the front, giving the house an unattractive appearance from the street. Later my father covered the front in Virginia creeper, disguising the pipes and small windows somewhat, although it would never be anyone's idea of a beautiful building.

I remember the day of the move. First of all we had to shift Eugene's bedroom – the old issue RAAF shed my father had erected in the grounds of Condamine Street. For the move it needed to be cut in half, put on a large truck, and then reassembled in the back garden of our new home. This is where Eugene and Porky slept. God help anyone of us who visited without letting Porky know. Dibs and Gill shared a bedroom and Viv and I the other.

Much later on we were to discover that Porky's greatest trick was to wait until we'd all left the house, whereupon he'd scratch the dirt under the pine tree until he had a mound to launch himself over the paling fence and disappear for the day. He would always be back behind the gate before we came home in the evening, sand hill dismantled, until the same thing happened the next day.

'It was only when I came home from work early one afternoon,' my mother laughed, 'that I discovered this happening. I watched him jump back into the garden and knock the mound down before running to the wooden gate to be there to welcome me home.' She shook her head. 'He was as cunning as a fox…but didn't realise I was already inside watching his antics.'

We set the 'hut' as it became known, down in this barren half-acre of dirt and then proceeded to bring the rest of the furniture from Condamine Street. We'd only brought small pieces from Ireland, including the broken china, silver and other odds and ends, an onyx and ivory crucifix within a glass dome and the statue of the Virgin Mary, both of which were installed on the mantelpiece beside the fuel stove. Numerous portraits of our regal ancestors were ceremoniously placed on the wall in the small hallway. Father Prendergast, a gregarious Irish priest, with an impenetrable 'west country' brogue and wit to match, helped us carry the huge fridge we'd brought from Reidsdale. The oblong cedar dining table, with an extension my father had picked up at a disposal auction, rather dwarfed the area to which it was allocated. Over the years we lived at Ijong Street, we spent many a night sitting around this table celebrating birthdays, Christmases and entertaining visitors. Later, when television arrived in our world, the TV lived on the end and was ceremoniously removed to the ground when we had visitors.

We'd also acquired a rather dilapidated lounge suite, which my father proceeded to do up and respring. But his biggest triumph of all was the hall table we called the 'invention'. This my father made in such a way as to double as an ironing board. He had removed the top of a wooden sideboard and attached an ironing board to the underside. When one wanted to iron you just had to find another member of the family to help turn the top upside down and there you had it. When one finished ironing, the idea was that it would be turned the other way round and a vase of flowers put to rest on the top to welcome visitors.

Needless to say my father was extremely proud of this invention.

Unfortunately for him, we girls quite often found it easier to iron on a towel on the floor or on the kitchen table, annoying him no end, particularly as one of us (no-one ever owned up) left a large imprint of the iron on the carpet, which had to be covered by a mat for years until it was finally replaced.

Somehow the confines of the narrow hallway in Ijong Street didn't do the ancestors within their gilded frames quite the justice that the wide corridors of Drominagh and Clonmoylan had. On occasions, when my father was feeling particularly merry, he would give a long sermon on each and every one of the ancestors, sometimes accompanied by a rendition of *The Wearing of the Green*, embarrassing us no end, but amusing our boyfriends, who actually found this most interesting. They'd no idea they were taking out such noble stock.

For hours my father foraged in Haigh Park for seedling Roman pencil pines and planted these as a screen around the barren block. Eventually it grew into a solid clipped hedge eight feet high. He also planted the land with potatoes. It was a well-known fact in Ireland that you never planted a garden until you'd prepared the soil with a crop of potatoes. This was not as widely known in Australia as one would have expected.

My classmates at school exclaimed in great glee: 'She lives in a potato patch. Ha, ha!' Children can be so cruel.

But the potatoes worked. My father turned this desolate piece of land into one of the most picturesque gardens in Canberra, later building a pergola over the rear patio where he planted the grapevine under which we took many of our meals in the hot summer months. The Virginia creeper thrived and he grew a rosemary hedge in the front, spending hours and hours trimming it to perfection, together with the pencil pines out the back – usually in the scorching heat (which never seemed to worry him), with a handkerchief tied over his face to protect him from flying branches and pollen. His array of seasonal flowers was a joy to all who walked past, and he took great delight when people stopped to exclaim and pass the time of day with him. Luckily he didn't live to see the day when the house was knocked down and a development of townhouses was callously erected upon his hard earned work, although the pencil pine hedge has survived.

Although an expert in the garden, my father was typical of his era. The cooking was left to the women. My mother managed on a meagre budget to keep us all fed, her speciality being a mean Irish stew in the pressure cooker. An Irish friend, Pat Gallagher, a long tall streak-of-fun with a mop of unruly russet hair, arrived one day on his pushbike with a couple of chickens hanging over the handlebars, handing them to my mother with much pride. I remember helping her to clean and pluck them in the laundry tub, after which she stuffed them with herbs out of my father's garden, grabbed a handful of potatoes from the front lawn, some tomatoes from the vegie patch out the back and popped them all in the oven to produce a grand meal for Pat and all of us sitting at the cedar table.

Another day Pat arrived with a grin, hastily whipping two rabbits out of a hessian bag. This time it was a tasty rabbit stew. Not bad for someone who hadn't had to cook much at all until we came to Australia. Her only stipulation was that cooking, washing up and house chores were done with a Craven A cigarette firmly placed in her mouth to get her through the task. Many a day we hid a few out of the packet to surprise her when she ran out.

Mulwala Hostel was home to many newly arrived Irish men and women. Our home became a haven for many, including the gregarious Tom Cahill and the beautiful Rose Donnelly who became a life-long friend, together with her husband Harry, an innovative engineer, who was at the forefront of Canberra's rapid progress. Rose had met Harry at Mulwala where he too was boarding when he first came to Australia.

In 1957 my father's mother Eily sadly passed away in the nursing home in Dublin. Needless to say this caused my father great grief. I'd like to say I was overcome with immense sadness also, but I'd known my grandmother for such a short time that after three years in Australia she'd sadly become a distant memory. In the back of his mind I'm sure my father had held onto the faint hope that he'd somehow get back to Ireland before she left this world. For months he was guilt ridden, going into a slight decline. However, one consolation was that the small amount of money she left him in her will helped us pay some outstanding bills, although it took forever to get to Australia.

Everything we needed was always explained by: 'When the money comes from Ireland.' Yet when it did eventually get here it was well and truly spent.

In 1958 we also exchanged the Holden for a highly unreliable pale-green Armstrong Siddeley with a wide stepping-board, one of the first automatic drives and governed by a fluid clutch. My father adored it, no doubt thinking back to the fancy cars of his youth, so overlooked the odd problem he had with her.

My mother was not quite so forgiving, as time after time she and the rest of us were left stranded somewhere when the car refused to go. Yet, sitting proudly in the driveway, it added a bit of glamour to the street, until a Volkswagen Beetle eventually replaced it, lowering the tone somewhat

Chapter 15

The Reluctant Student, Rose Bay

In 1959, Viv, like Dibs, went to boarding school at Rose Bay Sacré Coeur Convent. For the first time in our lives I was on my own, so to speak. I left our primary school in Braddon and started as one of the first intake of students at the new Braddon Catholic Girls High School (now Merici College) adjoining our local church in Braddon. Here, amongst other things, I played hockey for the first time. Much to my amazement, I became quite good and made the first team in the initial few months of being there. Pulling up a good four inches shorter than most on the team, this was of great surprise to everyone, most of all to me. I'd eventually found something at which I excelled. Sadly this was not to last long. For in 1959 I was sent to Rose Bay, where hockey was frowned upon as being unladylike, meaning I had to give up my short career.

Viv was a great success at Rose Bay; I not quite so.

I was desperately homesick, spending most of my first term in tears, demanding to be sent home, much to Viv's utter humiliation. I never really overcame this homesickness, hence my memories of my four years there are not as happy as they might have been.

Rose Bay Convent, now known as Kincoppel Rose Bay, is

a stately stone building set on acres of prime real estate in the Eastern suburbs of Sydney. Sitting proudly on the hill, before the road branches down to Vaucluse, it boasts wide uninterrupted views of the harbour on three sides. Why I didn't just enjoy the view, I don't know. Set around a central courtyard to the front, it boasts a glorious chapel with an ornate marble altar and dark wooden pews, where the nuns (dressed in black habits with ruffled frills surrounding their demure faces), and we girls, seemed to spend a great deal of each day praying. Or so it seemed at the time, although we did have many picnics in the extensive grounds rambling down to the water, or if we were lucky, on Shark Island in the middle of the harbour. Most of the students of these days were from large farming families from around New South Wales where I spent a number of school holidays. My most memorable one was in Orange when I stayed with my best friend of the time, another Rosemary, on her parents' extensive sheep station where we rode horses, swam in the dam and played tennis on the grass court down by the river.

This was the time when a pound of wool was worth a pound and sheep stations were literally rolling in it, so perhaps in hindsight my father should have hocked everything to the bank (or at the very least us children) and bought a farm at Reidsdale to stock up with sheep.

Viv became a 'blue ribbon'– the equivalent of a prefect, allowing her to walk around elegantly with a satin blue ribbon draped over her shoulder. I didn't get this honour, but was more than proud when Viv did.

We were somewhat short of male company, not being allowed to fraternise with any, not even with Riverview, the school across the harbour, which was our 'brother' school so to speak. In fact if a boy happened to come to Mass in the side chapel adjoining our main chapel, it was a great occasion. His parents hauled one poor fellow, the brother of a classmate of mine, there each morning where he'd endeavour to position himself out of sight of all of us desperate girls. Fortunately for us this was extremely difficult to do. I don't think he was particularly good looking, but at least he was a male. Kambala Girls College adjoined our convent on the bottom side, but as it was not a Catholic school we weren't allowed to mix with them either. We swam in a small seawater pool cut into the rocks where a couple of the students excelled to such an extent that they were regarded much like pop stars of the day.

One evening after supper, with all the students gathered in the long study as usual, Viv and I were highly embarrassed, yet somewhat proud, when a chapter of *Channel Dash*, a book just released about Eugene Esmonde VC was read to the entire school.

I hated Latin, ancient history and needlework, but loved English literature, public speaking, drama and geography. I also adored the library where I spent many happy hours, particularly if we weren't going out to visit the Duncans (he went to school with my father at Downside) at their delightful waterfront home in Camp Cove at Watson Bay. Music practice was held in tiny cells down in the school's dungeons, which were so dark and eerie that I soon decided the piano was not for me. The rec room was down there too, where one of the more talented girls reproduced the latest hit songs on the piano and we'd dress up and dance with each other on the odd Saturday night. We had The Art of Gracious Living classes given by Mary Rossi, one of the better-known Sydney identities of the time, where we'd learn how to walk in high heels, talk with the right pronunciation, eat with good table manners, and generally behave like a lady.

On the whole the nuns were kind and gentle, some stricter than others, some more patient teachers, but it seemed as though they all had our well-being utmost in their minds. One was so beautiful that even the workmen's eyes would pop out of their heads when they saw her. She sang like an angel, unbelievably passing up a career in Hollywood to become a nun.

Arriving to pick us up one afternoon at the front door of the convent for a week of school holidays at Whale Beach in the Armstrong Siddeley, my father could hardly contain his admiration when he met her for the first time, and Viv and I had to hurriedly move him on.

I have to say that my days at Rose Bay on the whole were spent in counting the moments until school holidays arrived so that I could be back in Canberra and riding at Mrs Lew's, or cuddling the new addition to our family, Trudy, a satiny black Dachshund (who Porky only just tolerated), rather than putting my head down and getting on with my studies. To this day I can recall that sick feeling in my stomach when holidays came to an end and we had to return to school for another long term.

Having completed her Leaving Certificate, followed by a stint at nursing and being an air hostess with Ansett, Viv eventually returned to Canberra to work at a number of jobs in order to save up for 'overseas', which was the aim of all young girls in the 1960s. She left in 1967 with a friend from her Ansett days, and after a time in the Greek Islands, with work on enchanting Mykonos, she toured Europe, ending up getting a holiday job in a small café in Spain. With her black hair, nutbrown eyes, and her skin now tanned by the hot sun, she was frequently mistaken for a Spaniard. Eventually she ended up in Ireland, working in Dublin where she modelled, subsidising that with waitressing and secretarial work.

Married to Tim Cresswell, a dashing Welshman she met in London, she now runs a great tourist operation at their farm, Cilwych, which has been in the Cresswell family for generations, on the banks of the picturesque River Usk in South Wales. Here their two lovely daughters, Laragh and Dominie, were born, and I often visit. Only recently I took two of my grandsons now living in France, Hubie and Ru, to stay with Viv and Tim on Cilwych where the boys rode horses amongst the green rolling hills, fed the pheasants and played on the grassy banks of the River Usk. The lovely and talented Laragh was home from the far north of Scotland where she was working as a production manager on the television series, *Monarch of the Glen*, so with her tantalising tales of what it was like working on a TV show she was a great hit with the boys, as she let them help her muck out the stalls and watch her exercise the horses in the field adjoining the stables.

Unfortunately for all of her siblings in Australia, Viv is a long way away. Sadly it is close to fifty years since we've all been together in the one room. Each of us has been with her separately at Cilwych or in Ireland, but we've never been together all at once. And as Viv hates flying she has never made the long trip back to Australia.

CHAPTER 16

A Fortunate Meeting

Eugene was accepted into Duntroon Royal Military College in 1962. I remember vividly taking him out there on his first day and leaving him with the other cadets in the grounds of the College. He was understandably nervous and looked very alone. He won a boxing competition in his first term, which gave him a good start in his new life. What I didn't realise then was that in a different weight section was my future husband, Rob, a delicious tall blond fellow with startling blue eyes. He won his section also.

'Due mainly,' he told me, 'to the times I had to protect myself as a surfer on Manly beach, once for chatting up someone else's girlfriend.'

Well, a bloke has to learn somewhere.

In 1963 I left Rose Bay, returning to Canberra to work at the jewellers, Angus and Coote, where Viv had worked for a short time. I also commenced a business course at the Metropolitan Business College. In my spare time I joined a Repertory Society, starring in some rather obscure productions. I played the wife in *The Importance of Being Earnest* and had a short romance with Earnest. I also did a spot of modelling; mainly in fashion parades, where I wore Angus and Coote jewellery. One outfit I modelled I was allowed to keep. I remember it well: a grey linen suit with a silk polka dotted blouse. An invaluable outfit as I mixed and matched it a hundred different ways, for wages were not what they are today, my salary at Angus and Coote being a mere fourteen pounds a week.

During this time I dated a few fellows, including the genial Peter with tight curly blond hair and a wicked sense of humour, whose friend Richard took Viv out. Richard owned a small white Triumph sports car, in which he transported us everywhere, including to Manly Beach in Sydney one weekend where Viv and I shared a room overlooking the Corso. After swimming on the beach and sunbaking for hours on the scorching sand we then went to Bondi Surf Club where we stomped to Col Joye and Little Pattie. Other times we'd drive down the long winding road to Bateman's Bay on the south coast of New South Wales to brave the surf, before undertaking the long trip back up the Clyde Mountain where we'd stop every hour or so to fill the radiator up to stop it overheating. Other times we'd go up to Perisher and toboggan in the snow or ride through the pine forests out near Mrs Lew's new riding school.

My father's half-sister, my godmother, Aunt Rosemary, joined us in Canberra from Ireland. At this stage she was well into her 70s and was having her first trip to Australia. Peter and Richard adored her, rushing her from one tourist spot to the other, quite often carrying her tiny frame on their burly shoulders or in the back of Richard's sports car; her long grey spider web hair billowing in the wind, a radiant smile from ear to ear. She said it was the best holiday she'd ever had, particularly as Dibs had arranged an interview with the *Canberra Times*. Gracing Saturday's front page, she was described as this 'distinguished visitor from Dublin', which tickled her fancy no end. She went off with Dibs to board her P&O liner in Sydney, clutching the article under her arm to show everyone back in Ireland. I'm not sure what her reaction was to her brother's new life, a life so different from at Drominagh, where she'd spent much of her youth. For although our house at Ijong Street was now a rich oasis of tall firs, colourful flowers, shrubs and green lawns, it certainly was far removed, not just in distance, from Drominagh or Clonmoylan, where she'd last visited us.

Canberra now had a number of coffee lounges we patronised regularly. After work on a Friday night we'd head to Lumleys to linger over cappuccinos and raisin toast. It was a smoky atmosphere, underground, with no ventilation, adding enormously to the feel of the place. In the corner, a pianist or a lone trumpeter played soulfully until the wee hours. We wore twin sets and pearls, before mini-skirts became fashionable and I remember fondly a pair of shiny pink pedal pushers that I almost wore out. We tied our hair back in high ponytails and painted our lips luscious pink. However, each Sunday we still dressed demurely for Mass, after having been to the mandatory confession the day before, despite the fact I was having more and more doubts about the wisdom of a priest hiding behind a dark screen listening intently to a young girl's bad thoughts, which I'm sure would arouse even the holiest of men.

With one of those 'mother me' faces and cocker spaniel brown eyes, my next serious boyfriend, Phillip, had a Peugeot car, which could only be started by using a heavy handle to crank the shaft. This was particularly embarrassing after a night at the drive-in theatre when we'd be the last car left in the lot. Yet, despite this, and his penchant for being at least an hour late for dates, we went out off and on for over a year until I received an invitation I couldn't refuse.

'Do you think it'd be okay if I asked Ro to come with me?'

Rob Peterswald probed Eugene, after Rob's date for the Queen's Birthday Ball at Duntroon couldn't go at the last minute. I remember Eugene asking me if I'd mind Rob ringing. I gather there were certain formalities that needed to be adhered to, one of them being to get the brother's permission.

Rob Peterswald, or Bob as he was then mostly known as, was one of the cadets who had left his car at Ijong Street for us to look after the year before, as cadets weren't allowed to keep one out at Duntroon until their last year. I think leaving his car with us was more that he, as well as Eugene, fancied the rather striking Indian university student, Leila, living next door and Rob could visit her at the same time as his Renault Floride. I was often sunbaking in the back garden when he came, but being much younger at that time (in your teens three years was quite a difference in those days) had not made much of an impression. Or so I thought.

We'd also had Rob's twenty-first-birthday party at Ijong Street the year before he'd asked me to the Queen's Birthday Ball. Parties at Ijong Street are fondly remembered – we'd cram into the small living room with music blaring; cheap wine and beer, sausage rolls and chipolatas being our main sustenance. Sometimes my parents huddled in their bedroom, or, if forewarned far enough in advance, took themselves off to a country hotel. On thinking back, they were more than understanding. Somehow or other we managed not to destroy the house and a quick clean up the next day usually put things in order.

Many romances commenced at the parties in Ijong Street. Many have survived to this day, including a few couples that have recently visited us on *Sea Dreams* in the Mediterranean.

A photo that sits on our bookcase shows me with Rob at his 21st, standing under the haughty ancestors in the small hallway – with me dressed in the trusty grey linen suit with polka-dotted silk blouse. However, that was in October '64. It would be June '65 before we had our first real date, as we were both going out with other partners and I was going away.

At the beginning of '65, Viv and I went to Cairns in far north Queensland. For some reason we made the front page of the *Canberra Times* as we set off.

First we flew to Sydney, then on to Brisbane, where we caught the train the rest of the way. The only problem was that the train we caught was also the mail train, so it took an eternally long time to get to Cairns, as it stopped at every mail-box along the endless stretch. I remember the dry and parched Queensland landscape scorching in the blazing sun; how dilapidated the farms were as we chugged through the middle of cane fields; the old Queenslanders built on stilts with huge verandahs and corrugated iron roofs and falling down outhouses; the dusty gardens; the sound of cane toads; the deeply lined burnt faces of the farmers; Aboriginal children with trousers held up with string playing in the dirt; mangy dogs lolling under the tiniest piece of shade; and the smell of burning cane and spirals of thick smoke rising to hide the tree-covered mountains in the distance.

Not much has changed over the years I've driven that stretch of road since.

Finally arriving at our destination in Cairns it appeared not to be what the brochures proclaimed it to be. For across from the esplanade, where we were staying in a rambling Federation bungalow, there was little more than a mud swamp when we woke the next morning with the tide out. Later, when the tide came in, it was better, but nothing like the Cairns of today with its fancy boardwalk, magnificent pools and huge marina where we've stayed on our yachts a couple of times. I have to say that in '65 the coral reef was more spectacular than it is today, as it struggles to survive the onslaught of tourists and the dreaded crown-of-thorns starfish. I remember looking at the coral though my mask as if it was a magical window to another world where I'd been given the keys to a supernatural city of millions of different shapes and textures, with the enchanting residents being one of the most astonishing communities on this planet.

When we'd first arrived in Cairns, Viv and I were feeling a little down at mouth after the long journey until we'd the good fortune to meet a group of fun fellows in the flat next door who proceeded to show us the sights and give us a grand time, or a bit of *craic* as they say in Ireland. As we'd no car they drove us everywhere, including up the winding hill through the thick rainforest with crystal clear waterfalls, small creeks that sparkled like diamonds and green satin ponds surrounded by tropical flowers with petals as thick as a sow's ear, until we reached the Atherton Tableland. Another day they drove us along the spectacular coastal road to the sleepy village of Port Douglas, a far different place to the tourist mecca it is today after the renowned developer, Christopher Skase, moved in. Another day we ventured inland to the country town of Mareeba, where groups of Aborigines squatted by the side of the road and huge anthills sprouted from arid fields.

As we'd arrived in Cairns on the off-season, jobs were almost impossible to obtain – something we'd overlooked in the planning of this 'working' holiday. So after Viv had a stint as a housemaid on Green Island (where a Texan with a girth like a whale asked her what a gorgeous girl like Viv was doing cleaning his room and she agreed, leaving that day) we stayed for another few weeks before boarding the plane south.

When we came back to Canberra, I started the course at

the Metropolitan Business College for Ladies, where I was supposed to become an efficient short hand typist. I mastered the typing in a fashion, but I certainly never managed to master the shorthand.

Chapter 17

Falling in Love

Dressed to the nines in a blue taffeta dress with matching shoes and handbag and my hair in a new bob, I waited in the hallway at Ijong Street for Rob to arrive to take me to the Queens' Birthday Ball in June, 1965.

Resplendent in a dark-blue dress uniform with a patrol neck collar, gold buttons on the jacket and red stripes down the side of his immaculately creased trousers, he carried a bunch of red roses. I thanked him profusely for the carnations, gushing they were my favourite. My mother, mortified, was trying to gesture they were roses. I was so nervous I couldn't tell the difference.

The ironing board was up the right way, a vase of fresh flowers from my father's garden in pride of place on the top. Rob was not sat down for a lengthy dissertation on the ancestors hanging in the hallway; however, my mother, being somewhat smitten herself, spent far too long chatting him up in the kitchen before we got away, telling him roses were in fact her very favourite flower of all time.

'It was then,' she told me fondly not long ago, 'that I decided Rob reminded me of my beloved brother-in-law, Phillip.'

The ball was held in the function hall at Duntroon, which doubled as the instruction room during the day, where huge sand models of battlefields predominated. We danced to Hang on Sloopy, The Lion Sleeps Tonight and Under the Boardwalk. Despite the fact that alcohol was limited, it stopped no-one from enjoying themselves. Mind you I feel sure some of the soft drinks had a touch of illicit liquor added.

All in all our date was a huge success. Rob decided I was worth asking out further, and I was certain at the ripe old age of eighteen that I'd fallen blissfully in love.

Rob still tells the story how a few months after that first date, at a party in Torrens Street in Braddon, he asked me to dance. After a moment I gave him a huge smile and said: 'Yes… of course I'll marry you.'

The music was loud and he assures me I misheard. That is not true, but it makes for a good story. I think after fifty years he actually believes it now and almost has me believing it too.

Rob was born in Taree, New South Wales. A long time further back his family came from Europe. A number of years ago we discovered the Peterswald castle in Poland, which was Silesia, and have visited it twice. We have now also found the Peterswald Chateau in Buchlovich in the Czech Republic, a magnificent estate on acres of manicured grounds, miraculously surviving world wars, communism, and depression.

Recently Rob has written an historical novel, *The Castle at Peters Forrest*, depicting his family's history.

After Europe, one of his ancestors went to England as Master of the King's Horse. Eventually his great-great-grandfather, William John Peterswald, arrived in Adelaide, where he became the third Police Commissioner of South Australia. It would appear he was regarded as a somewhat controversial character, but one to be revered. Only last year we purchased the plot of land in the Adelaide cemetery, where he's buried in good company – between the hugely ornate graves of the noted Downer and Ayers of Ayers Rock families. There is even a mountain, Peterswald Mountain, in the Northern Territory called after him.

Rob's family moved to Sydney in the 1950s and Rob went to school at Manly Boys High where he and his friend Max Doerner, not only played truant if the surf was up, but also tennis and squash together, Rob becoming the New South Wales Schoolboys Squash Champion in 1960. During the course of the six months since I had my first date with him and leading up to his graduation in December, I often watched him play rugby, tennis and squash. Rob was the only cadet in Duntroon's history to win both the squash and tennis championships for four years in a row, getting a full colour in rugby as well and a half colour in athletics.

Years later I met General Cosgrove, the Chief of the Australian Defence Forces and future Governor General, at a function in Hobart. He was a few years behind Rob at Duntroon.

He told me: 'You realise your husband's a legend…one of the best athletes to ever go through Duntroon.'

To say I was proud is an understatement.

I also went to Avalon in Sydney to meet Rob's family, where thankfully I seemed to pass muster. I'd previously met his brother, Dick, a lawyer in Goulburn, a rural town not far from Canberra. Rob and he often played in opposing rugby teams and we'd spent a few evenings together celebrating their various wins or commiserating a loss. Sometimes the headlines in the sporting pages of the *Canberra Times* would herald: *Peterswald outclasses Peterswald*.

I learned early on that Rob's family, his father John, mother Hazel, sister Wendy and Dick were very dear to him.

Graduation Day at Duntroon was quite an occasion,

comprising a Passing Out Parade, morning tea in the lush grounds of Duntroon House and a great gala ball at night to pin the pips on the graduating cadets' epaulettes. This job of pinning on Eugene's pips was to fall on my mother, together with Allison Griggs, my great friend whom I'd met at business college and whom I'd introduced to Eugene. For over two years they went out together, until it petered out. Eugene met someone else, and Allison met Fred Lewis, who ended up an Admiral in the American Navy in Washington where they still live and we visit.

Rob's mother proudly helped me pin Rob's pips on, and an honoured guest was his Uncle Keith, who played a central part in Rob's life, together with his wife, Winsome. Keith had been a Rat of Tobruk, also slogging it out on the notorious Kokoda Track. Despite this arduous ordeal the army became a great love of his. He was overjoyed when his nephew was accepted into Duntroon – even more so to be at his graduation. Dick had newly married during the year, to Fran Wilson, a lovely dark-haired girl, whose family was well-known and respected in the Goulburn district, where they lived until recently when they moved to Murrumbateman, the picturesque wine district north of Canberra, close to where their daughter, Joanna, lives with her husband, Tim, and their three children. Nearby in Canberra, their son, James, lives with his wife, Marianne, and their two children.

Mid-morning we were on the front steps of Ijong Street ready to go to the Passing Out Parade. I wore a pink checked suit with a short skirt and an Audrey Hepburn style hat. Standing beside me, my mother appeared regal in a floaty floral dress with a matching hat of silk flowers and Dibs shone in black and white. Waiting for us anxiously in the car, my father looked debonair in his dark pinstriped suit brought out of mothballs especially for the occasion.

Despite the searing heat, Rob, Eugene, and the rest of the cadets looked resplendent marching on the parade ground in full dress uniform. Jim Connelly was presented with the Sword of Honour and went on to become a Major General in the Australian Army, as did three others from that class.

Years later, a TV series based on the class of 1965, called the 'Sword of Honour' was produced with a well-known actor playing the part of Jim. Loosely based on the cadets' experiences, it was difficult to identify individuals.

Watching Eugene march and receive his commission from Lord Casey, the Australian Governor General, my mother and father were seeing their dream come true. The grass was definitely looking greener now. Here was their beloved son carrying on the great tradition of the Esmonde family in the military forces. Suddenly all the struggling seemed as though it was worthwhile and I felt enormously proud of him, Rob, and the other cadets, many of whom have remained our greatest friends and allies over the years since.

After the parade we had morning tea under a thick arbour of trees on the lawns of Duntroon House, built by Robert Campbell in 1870. Every time I go there I admire the beauty of the building, which boasts wide verandahs with stone pillars covered in vines. In this grandiose setting the graduating cadets were treated as officers for the first time and we all felt a part of a special happening.

However, my trip to the hairdresser later in the day in preparation for the ball was anything other than a special happening. I returned home with an unbecoming heavily lacquered beehive. Dear Eugene helped me wash it out and style it into a smooth bob. His kindness is something I've remembered fondly all my life. I wore a white sequined slinky evening dress with a split up the side and a deep v to the front. By far the most sophisticated item I'd ever owned. Later I dyed it black and wore it for years.

Rob had now graduated to the position of 1st lieutenant in the Royal Australian Infantry. Eugene was a 1st lieutenant in the Royal Australian Artillery. I remember watching my parents elegantly and happily dance the night away to the Royal Military College Band. It was ages since I'd seen them waltzing together. A picture of hunt balls, elaborate parties in Dublin and Drominagh flitted through my mind. With all the hard work in keeping the wolf from the door over the past eleven years they'd not had much time for relaxing. Let alone dancing.

And I, of course, was in heaven in Rob's arms.

The highlight of the evening was the parading of Casey, an authentic complete human skeleton, mounted on the skeleton of a horse, accompanied by enormous cheers and catcalls. The story goes that Casey, fed up with his miserable life as a first year cadet at Duntroon, where bastardisation was the norm, retired to a remote cupboard. Here he remained until some years later the door was opened, whereupon he fell out in his present skeletal condition. How the horse got in the cupboard with him remains a mystery. Not enough of a mystery, however, to spoil a good yarn and tradition.

Over the next few years many of those cadets, including Eugene, went to the battlefields of Vietnam. Some went to Malaya; others, like Rob, were posted to Papua New Guinea or to various postings around Australia and the globe.

As a forward observer it was a dangerous job in Vietnam for Eugene, causing us deep concern. He managed to return safely, much to the family's relief, although he'd lost a lot of weight. Yet he soon put it on again, making his way to Brisbane to GOC Northern Command as ADC to General Hassett, where he spent two years. This is where he first set eyes on his wife to be, Jenny Sharpe.

His second trip to Vietnam was in 1971, after which he returned to Australia and married Jenny, whom we all thought extremely glamorous. He eventually retired from the army in the early 1980s as a Lieutenant Colonel. With Jenny he then took over the Sharpe family business, from Jenny's father, Sir Frank Sharpe, who unfortunately had become seriously ill. Sir Franke had received a knighthood for his services to the Queensland community, in particular being the first to introduce avocado farming and commercial radio to the state. For many years he also had the Bells helicopter franchise and held a pilot's licence well into his seventies. He was an amazingly talented man.

As well as the family business, Eugene and Jenny now have a development company and have three lovely children, Godfrey, Eugene and Grania, all enjoying careers of their own: Eugene in China and Godfrey and Grania in Brisbane.

After graduation, Rob returned to Mona Vale with his parents. I joined him in January, when we announced our engagement. That summer in Sydney seemed to go on forever. We were young, happy and carefree, despite the Vietnam War hanging over our heads. Rob and I shopped for an engagement ring on the Corso at Manly and celebrated our announcement at the Music Hall at Neutral Bay, with Dick and Fran. For hours we sat in the hot sun, turning ourselves brown as hazelnuts in the wonderful beer garden at the Newport Arms, watching the yachts tugging at their moorings in front of the Royal Prince Alfred Yacht Club in the blue waters of Pittwater, where thirty seven years later we anchored our own yacht,

Oceania, as we sailed north, compiling our photographic book *Beyond the Shore*. We met up with many of the class of '65, as they flitted in and out with old and new girlfriends. We devoured delicious seafood at the Spit or at the famous Doyle's Restaurant at Watsons Bay (which we featured in *Beyond the Shore*), and swam at Manly and Bondi, where I burned my feet to blisters on the searing sand. We partied at friends' houses and in discos and surf clubs, often rolling home in the wee hours of the morning. A few hours' sleep and it started all over again, but not before Rob's mother had insisted on bringing me a huge cooked breakfast in bed.

It was a wonderful *long hot summer* in more ways than one.

However, all good things come to an end. Soon Rob had to head north to his new posting as an Infantry Officer with the 1st Pacific Islands Regiment in Port Moresby. I had to go back to Canberra and my job as a less than enthusiastic secretary at a solicitor's office.

It was sad saying goodbye, but Rob was excited to be taking up his first posting. As there were a few of his class going with him to New Guinea, he'd not be altogether amongst strangers. The idea was that Rob would come back on leave from Moresby at the end of the year, whereupon we'd get married in Canberra. Then I'd join him. At just nineteen, I was regarded as far too young to set off with him to New Guinea. Also, where would I live? Rob would need to reside in the Officers' Mess, and housing was impossible to find. Most importantly I had no money and needed to save. So I worked at my secretarial job during the days. At nights I worked as a waitress in a new atmospheric jazz club come Italian restaurant, in Garema Place in Civic Centre. The ferocious chef only turned up when in a good mood, so a lot of the time I was the chef as well – trying to placate a room full of disgruntled patrons. But I saved a handy bit of cash and wrote to Rob most days, waiting anxiously for his return letters. Yet I couldn't wait for the year to pass, so that we could get married and I'd join him in New Guinea.

Chapter 18

Leaving the Nest for Papua New Guinea

A few months after Rob left for Port Moresby things changed dramatically. Suddenly I was on my way to his side. After one too many drinks at the Officers' Mess bar at Taurama Barracks, Rob had made a rash promise that he could break the Papua New Guinea triple jump record. In attempting to do so he had broken his leg. One evening he made a frantic and persuasive phone call to my parents, assuring them he couldn't live without me.

Exaggerating somewhat, he convinced them that he was almost wheelchair bound and desperately needed me there to drive him around. He forgot to mention the mere fact he had a Pacific Islands soldier quite willing and able to do this job for him. He seemed to have also forgotten that I was unable to drive myself, despite some valiant efforts from both my father and him. I could, in fact drive, but had been unable to find a policeman or driving inspector to agree with me.

Days of persuasive arguments, standoffs and numerous phone calls took place. Eventually, my parents, worn down by it all, gave in and I found myself winging my way to my new life in the *wilds* of Papua New Guinea, where Michael Rockefeller, son of the American tycoon, Nelson, had disappeared not long before. It was rumoured that he had been eaten by cannibals, as had a patrol officer in the highlands. Yet cannibals were the least of my parents' worries. Where I was going to live before marriage was much more on their minds. Young Catholic girls of nineteen didn't live with their fiancés before marriage in those days. Certainly not young Irish Catholic girls. Eventually we sorted this out by organising that I would share a room with Diana McCarthy (the fiancée of Mike Battle, a fellow classmate of Rob's) in a house belonging to Jan, a family friend of the Peterswalds from their Taree days. Jan was now married with two young children and living in the Moresby suburb of Boroko.

After a sad farewell to my family (little did I know it would be thirteen years before I would see Viv again), I set off on the long journey. I stopped off in Brisbane to catch up with Eugene and stayed at the Salvation Army Hostel in the centre of the city. Eugene was stationed at the army barracks at Wacol preparing for his first trip to Vietnam. After buying some new dresses suitable for the tropics in the sales in Fortitude Valley, I flew on to Townsville, then Cairns and eventually Port Moresby.

I was somewhat nervous and a bit apprehensive. After all this was only a short time since I'd been incredibly homesick boarding at Rose Bay, and here I was, off to the unknown to meet up with a man I'd only really known in depth for six months.

Although we were engaged, it was a different matter to leave the bosom of one's family and the security of things familiar, to start a totally different phase of life in a strange country, particularly for a fairly naive nineteen year old. I had long, brown hair with a fringe, which I'd had cut too short in Brisbane, so looked even younger than what one would have thought.

I wore one of my new purchases – a yellow floral dress with cut away shoulders and falling well above the knee. I'd no idea what the army wives and girlfriends in Moresby would be wearing at the time; however, I soon discovered that my dresses were shorter than most, causing me a few anxious moments when Rob introduced me to the Commanding Officer at the Mess and I realised I should perhaps have worn something more staid.

Jackson International Airport at Port Moresby was a series of long low-line iron and tin buildings in fairly barren land, nestled amongst rolling khaki hills, not dissimilar to Canberra in the dry season. In the distance the magnificent Owen Stanley Ranges rose majestically, the tips of the tallest mountains disappearing into the wispy clouds. The approach to the airport was over clear blue waters dotted with miniature islands surrounded by tantalising turquoise and ochre coral. On a number of reefs fishing boats trawled, and heading to the port were a couple of huge tankers. From the air, Moresby looked dismal, cold and overcast; however, on stepping out of the plane it was as if I was in the midst of a steaming sauna. I'd never experienced such heat and humidity before. By the time I walked down the stairs of the plane and squelched onto the scorching tar of the runway, much to my horror my hair had dissolved into a mass of lank tangles, much like a string mop, and my newly applied makeup ran as if a muddy river down my sweat soaked cheeks. I soon learned that limp hair and melting makeup would be the norm in the tropics. It wasn't long before I gave up wearing makeup at all, apart from a dash of mascara and lipstick.

For a moment I was rooted to the ground, my mind a rope of tangled emotions. Excitement rippled through my sweltering body. Yet what if I was a disappointment? Why had I got my fringe cut so short? What if after all this time apart, Rob didn't have the same feelings for me that he'd had before? And I for him. Had we rushed into an engagement too quickly? What if I hated living in this strange land? These were all thoughts I'd had before, particularly on the long flight up. But now, standing on the tarmac at Port Moresby, they appeared even more real.

However, the moment I saw Rob behind the wire mesh of the terminal, all my fears disappeared. Soon I was inside and amidst a noisy crowd of Pacific Islanders jostling and shoving each other. Runny-nosed glistening *pikininis* scampered across the cement floor or clung tightly to their parents' bare legs. There was the smell of unwashed bodies and heat and dust, mingled with cigarette smoke.

Somehow it all seemed so familiar. As if I had come home.

With his hair even blonder from the sun, Rob was now deeply tanned. This, of course, made his blue eyes stand out even more. His leg in plaster made it difficult for him to move quickly, but I more than compensated for this by rushing through the crowd and almost jumping into his outstretched arms. For a moment we clung to each other and I scolded myself for having any doubts. Of his love. And mine.

When he went to collect my luggage, I looked around at the mass of brown sweaty bodies in all forms of dress. Some looked as though they'd wandered straight in from their villages with spears in one hand and jagged bones through their ears and noses. Clinging to the wire netting, dozens stared in awe at the passengers still disembarking off the huge *balus*. In one corner a *meri* squatted on the dusty cement floor, feeding a small baby on one breast and a piglet on the other. (In a critique of my novel, *Bird of Paradise*, it was suggested this was unlikely. I assure you it wasn't.) A mangy dog lolled lazily beside them.

Rusty steel benches overflowed with passengers waiting to return to their villages or with those who'd just come to the airport to make a day of watching the *balus* drop out of the sky.

Most of the men had alarmingly red teeth from the *betel nut* they chewed constantly. Others smoked roll your owns wrapped in newspaper. And in contrast to all this there was a group of neatly dressed expats drinking champagne, obviously farewelling a family back to Australia, whilst others talked animatedly to newly arrived passengers.

Rob's role in New Guinea was to help build an independent viable country: to endeavour to throw off colonialism and create a vibrant nation that would be capable of looking after itself without the help of Australia. Years before, when he was in high school, he'd applied for a cadetship as a patrol officer in the New Guinea Highlands; however, it hadn't come off. Now he was here. To be sent to Papua New Guinea as a young Lieutenant was one of the best postings an infantry officer could hope for. To Rob, it was a chance to make his own mark. A chance for him to be independent himself; to be patrolling in the high mountains and impenetrable jungles for months on end, the only white man with his Pacific Islands soldiers, making his own decisions and having to survive on those decisions.

It was an exciting time in the history of Papua New Guinea, a time, long before Independence was granted, when we were all filled with optimism. In hindsight we may have had the sanguinity of youth, but we definitely felt that we were going to make a difference.

During the early 1960s, Indonesia's campaign against the Dutch in what was then Dutch New Guinea (now the Indonesian province of Irian Jaya) and its confrontation with Malaysia, sparked fears of possible Indonesian expansionism towards Papua New Guinea. It promoted a surge of activity on Australia's behalf to expand the military in PNG and to strengthen security infrastructure along the Indonesian-Papua New Guinea border. Within the space of a few years the Pacific Islands Regiment was increased from about 700 native soldiers to a force of over 3000, including Australian officers.

By the mid-1960s, with the perceived threat from Indonesia diminishing, the military build-up levelled off, though Papua New Guinea continued to occupy a significant place in Australian strategic planning.

It was into these changing times that I arrived.

Rob's driver, a soldier from Buka Island, drove us from the airport. He seemed almost as excited as Rob on my arrival. Being from Buka he was blacker than other Pacific Islanders.

Outside the Holden's window my first glimpse of Moresby flashed before my eyes. I saw frangipani trees lining the streets, pandanus and coconut palms, hibiscus bushes, houses built on stilts with bougainvillea and jasmine draping from verandah posts onto parched lawns and garden beds. Most of all I was amazed by the number of Pacific Islanders ambling along with seemingly all the time in the world. The women wore a mixture of native and European dress. Some were in grass skirts made of pandanus or banana fibre, two tiered with a bustle effect, others wore *meri* dresses, consisting of a free flowing Mother Hubbard with puff sleeves. The men either wore *lap laps, calicoes* or shorts and T-shirts; hair styles varied according to where the people originated, either closely cropped tight or massive fuzzy affairs; occasionally almost straight. Ears were usually highly decorated with dangly ornate objects hanging from large holes in their elongated lobes. The women carried heavily laden string bags *(bilums)* over their heads; others had baskets with fruit and vegetables balanced precariously on their foreheads or arms full of firewood.

When the first Europeans arrived in Port Moresby there were two main groups of natives. The Motu and the Koitabu, the Motu being sea-going people with a language closely associated with other Melanesian and Polynesian languages, the Koitabu people speaking an inland non-Austronesian dialect. A great proportion of the population in the 1960s was of similar makeup, with a large group of squatters from the highlands and other areas. The Police and armed forces were made up of tribal groups throughout Papua New Guinea and the outlying islands. The first European to visit the island, in 1873, was Captain John Moresby, whom the town of Port Moresby is called after.

As it turned out it wasn't a great time for my arrival, for a strict curfew had been placed on the soldiers of Taurama Barracks, after a sit-down strike, as the police were getting higher pay than they were.

'I'm sorry, darling, but you'll be on your own tonight,' Rob informed me, driving into Moresby.'

I looked at him in alarm. This is not what I'd envisaged.

'I'm afraid I'm duty officer,' he explained, 'and couldn't get out of it. I've got to ensure there aren't any troops found out drinking after curfew. If I find any they'll be arrested by the Military Police, thrown in a paddy wagon and taken back to barracks, later to be charged.'

This meant that I was to spend my first night in Port Moresby with my hosts and Diana, minus Rob. This was the first indication I had that no matter what the circumstances, a PIR Officer's job came first.

Positioned in a flat dry and dusty street in Boroko, a suburb at the intersection of Waigani Drive and Sir Hubert Murray

Highway, my host's bungalow sat amongst others of similar style. Built of timber on high stilts, to catch any slight breeze, it had the laundry and drying area with table and chairs underneath. Upstairs was an open plan living and dining room with timber floors and louvre windows, again to catch the breeze. In the centre of each room was a large ceiling fan. Furniture was typical of most houses in the tropics: cane chairs, bright floral cushions, beanbags from a Chinese store, and the odd nick knack brought up from Australia. Most of the houses occupied by expats, including in the army barracks, were built after the war, the majority in the nineteen fifties or sixties. Most had a T-shaped floor plan.

Jan was a pleasant woman with a no-nonsense air about her in both dress and demeanour. Later, when I met her husband, a tall thin guy, and quite a smooth talker, I felt he and Jan weren't really suited, although it would be years later before they divorced.

After a quick cup of tea, Rob left to go back to Taurama Barracks and I explored my new home. Peering into the cupboards in my bedroom I was to share with Diana, I tried to form an image of what she'd be like. After a short nap in the oppressive heat, I was to find out, for suddenly I was awoken by the clip clop of her high heels on the wooden floor.

Mike had met Diana on a holiday to Surfers Paradise some years before, when she and her parents were living in a beach house in the popular suburb of Mermaid Beach. In fact it was Rob who had introduced them, as he'd met her on the beach the day before through a friend. I could see why both boys were so taken with her. With her tanned olive skin, (a feature far more suited to the tropics than my Celtic covering) luminous dark brown eyes and divine figure she was eye-catching to say the least. But she was more than that. She was also great fun.

Over the next months we had some marvellous times, as we still do to this day.

Diana and I didn't last long in this household. We seemed to be forever blotting our copy book: overflowing the shower, late for breakfasts, not on time for their very early dinners and in hindsight causing more havoc than the mere amount of money we were paying each week was worth. So, in the end, it was mutually agreed that we should look for somewhere else. No doubt Jan and her husband heaved a sigh of relief when we packed our bags and moved out. With two young children and a fairly demanding husband I feel that the poor woman was more than generous to offer to have us in the first place.

Yet the problem in moving from this abode was that accommodation in Moresby then was still practically non-existent. This meant that Diana and I were constantly on the move. The only places available to rent were when expats went back to Australia for holidays and their homes or flats became available. With much hunting and scrounging we found some of the funniest and scariest places to live in, the most notorious being over the markets at Koki above a Government truck storage area. Coming and going was negotiated through dozens of front-end loaders, lorries and bulldozers. This was even more testing for Diana at night when she returned from her job as a waitress at a small café in Boroko, a job she took to subsidise her daytime job as a secretary with the Government, which didn't pay all that much. Mind you, being left on my own when she was out at work, and Rob away on patrol, was just as scary. The flat adjoined a native stilt village of dilapidated corrugated iron and cement sheet shanties built on wooden stilts over the water, the original timber thatched buildings having been burned during the war.

Although smaller than the largest stilt village in Moresby,

Hanuabada, an original Motuan village, the one next to us, still housed hundreds of Pacific Islanders (these days referred to as Nationals), scores of little *pikininis,* not to mention dozens of starving dogs, scrounging pigs, hordes of chickens and numerous cats.

Koki Market was where we bought most of our fruit and vegetables from villagers squatting on straw mats or behind rickety trestle tables set out in the centre. Here, amidst a mass of throinging people, both local and European, with the smell of mud on low tide, seafood, wood smoke and human sweat still engraved in my senses, I'd pile my cane basket full to the brim in order to last the coming week. In the sixties, Koki was relatively safe, with the tranquil sight of islanders' fishing boats pulled up to the shore and most people more than friendly. Recently I read that several tourists were robbed at gunpoint with everyone else looking on with interest, but doing nothing.

In our flat at Koki, up a flight of long stairs, there was only one bedroom and one bed too, fortunately double, which Diana and I shared. In the corner we placed a tree branch to hang our clothes on. One dark night, with Diana at work, I lay cowering under the sheets thinking I was being attacked by a mass of spear wielding natives, only to discover when I eventually ventured outside, carrying a steel machete in my hand, it was a family of cats from the village next door prowling on the roof, the same roof over which we clambered to hang our washing on the makeshift clothes-line spanning two poles.

Diana, Mike, Rob and I had great fun at this flat. We threw copious dinner parties with a few disasters on my behalf, as I tried my limited cooking skills on the unsuspecting. Apart from my lack of cooking skills, trying to follow a recipe was somewhat difficult, for few of the ingredients were available in the Moresby stores. Yet the quality of food made little difference as we consumed glasses of Chianti around the small table with a red checked tablecloth under the window and threw numerous shindigs. Mind you, when I was talking to Diana recently she assured me we could only afford water a lot of the time.

'You make it sound as though we were forever drinking plonk,' she laughed. 'Don't you remember how much we scrounged and saved for a bottle?'

One bash the four of us organised was at the old ruins at Idler's Bay on the Napa Napa Peninsula, east of Port Moresby. After setting up trestle tables with more red and white checked tablecloths and candles in Chianti bottles, Diana, I and the other women, ran down the crumbling stairs and changed into long dresses. With tropical flowers placed behind our ears and colourful necklaces dangling around our necks, we re-emerged barefooted to a blood red sunset across the sparkling bay and a night of Rolling Stones, Dusty Springfield, the Beatles, too much wine (definitely not water this time) and later a sleepover within the stone fort, awakening to a magnificent golden sunrise emerging over the hills.

In a moment of grog fuelled enlightenment, the boys talked of throwing the army in and turning the ruins into an international hotel. As far as I know it still remains as a ruin.

Often a group of us would hire a boat and head out to Fisherman's Island, not far off the coast of Moresby, where we'd picnic on the soft white sand and swim in the luminous turquoise waters off the beach, returning home late in the afternoon, windblown and sunburnt, despite the gallons of white zinc cream we covered our faces in.

At other times I went horse riding at the Koitaki Country club at Sorgeri, past the Laloki River gorge, a popular spot for those wanting to escape the heat of Moresby. I remember Rob sitting on the deck at the clubhouse enjoying a cool South Pacific Lager, as I rode a chestnut Galloway in the paddock below. Afterwards we sat on the verandah watching the last of the hot sun settling down behind the rubber plantation in the valley below.

Further on from the turn off to the Varirata National Park, was a lookout for the spectacular Rouna Falls, and just before reaching Sogeri is the Kokoda Track junction. In the 50s and 60s those that mostly walked the Kokoda Track were the army on an exercise, or patrol officers. Today it's a great achievement for people from all walks of life to have walked and survived the track, and many do. In fact on our last visit back to New Guinea, Rob and I appeared to be the only Australians on the Air Nui Guinea flight arriving into Moresby that weren't there to walk the track.

Despite my fears, right from the moment I arrived in Moresby, Rob and I fell into step as though we'd never been apart. Of course, like all couples, we had our disagreements, but most of the time we were blissfully happy and I was falling more and more in love with both him and this strange country and its enigmatic people.

Often a Saturday morning was spent shopping in Burns Phillip, Steamships and the other shops in the main drag, followed by a long lunch at the Top Pub, otherwise known as the Moresby Hotel. The Papuan Hotel, known as the Bottom Pub, where Errol Flynn once drank and brawled, was another popular haunt, or it might be the Boroko Hotel beer garden. Evenings were frequently lazed away at the drive-in theatre where you could get a glass of wine and sit in deck chairs under the stars. We also spent many an hour on the verandah of the Hibiscus Room, or Biccy Room as we called it; a rustic café-come-restaurant, nestled up a side street, with a verandah overhung with tangled jasmine and bougainvillea vines hidden behind a huge hibiscus bush. One evening, enjoying a meal on the verandah here, Rob had to rescue the cook from a local scoundrel, who had a knife held to the unfortunate man's throat. For what seemed like a lifetime, I sat at the table with my spaghetti bolognaise getting colder, with Rob holding the attacker in a neck hold until a policeman arrived, and took over. I was amazed how calmly Rob sat down afterwards and finished his meal.

Although the food at the Biccy Room was fairly basic, which a lot of food of the sixties was: frozen prawns in a cocktail sauce, (we even had frozen oysters in Moresby) chicken Maryland, Hawaiian, or in the basket, spaghetti bolognaise, Vienna schnitzel or curried sausages, the atmosphere more than made up for the food's shortcomings.

The new restaurant, Tabu, at the bottom of Badili, was much more adventuresome. Coquilles St Jacques and superb reef fish being their specialty. The Yacht and Aviat Clubs, or the huge verandah at the pub in Konedobu, where most of the government offices were sited, and where Diana worked during the day, were also popular haunts for lunch, with the long sandy stretch of Ela Beach a great spot for lazing by the water and sunbaking, but not for swimming, due to the weeds at low tide and the dreaded black sea urchins.

Rob had bought a white TR4, commonly called Flying Bricks, known as such for the speed at which they hurtled along. Yet they were pretty ordinary on corners, with more than a few crashing. Fortunately, after a few more driving lessons, and a test going up and down the hills around Moresby, a terrified policeman told me I'd passed the dreaded driving examination, probably scared out of his wits he'd have to go through it all again. A licence was duly handed over in grand style, whereupon I was able to whiz around Moresby and out to Taurama Barracks on my own. Unfortunately, a few months later, the car's lack of performance on corners was put to the test when Rob was involved in an incident with a hire car going around a steep bend, with the hire car winning. Both Rob and TR4 were nearly wiped out.

Eventually we got the car back, this time painted bright red, a colour taking our fancy. Unfortunately they neglected to paint the inside, including the doors, under the bonnet and boot, so it looked rather odd for the rest of its life. And, in any case, red was a particularly stupid colour for a hot climate.

It was difficult to get good cars in Moresby, as rust was a problem and many were less than roadworthy. Yet a reliable car was essential, for the drive on the dusty road to the barracks at Taurama, out past Korobosea, was long and remote. Once I broke down on the way to collect Rob, but fortunately an hour or so later an army patrol truck came past and rescued me. A mobile phone would have been handy, but in those days we didn't even have a phone in the flat, let alone the car.

Diana and I spent many months on our own, as Rob and Mike, both platoon commanders, were away on army exercises for lengthy periods. It was a changing time for the army then. Rob enjoyed his patrols in the vast and barely explored mountains and jungles, particularly his interaction with the colourful and enthusiastic soldiers in his platoon. From different tribal regions around the country, many left stone-age villages to join the army, exchanging *penis gourds* or *lap laps* for jungle greens. Each had his own unique personality, some more outgoing than others, but on the whole they were a happy lot with the odd bout of sullenness, which usually meant trouble approaching.

For long periods Rob trekked the arduous interior; the Hindenburg Wall, the Southern Highlands and along the Ok Tedi River from Mendi to Tari by way of Lake Kutubu, a seemingly bottomless crater, where ancient skeletons and shrunken skulls hung from caves along the mountainous shoreline. In places, the locals had never seen a white person before, and even the modest equipment carried by the soldiers was the source of never-ceasing curiosity. Radio schedules and airdrops were unexplainable mysteries, feeding the latent cargo cults. And a *balus* was often regarded as a huge strange bird dropping out of the sky. Some even strung enormous nets between trees, hoping to catch this unique bird carrying gifts of western civilisation.

Rob and his platoon spent weeks at Telafomin, Manus Island and Rabaul. They paddled in the searing muggy heat in dug-out canoes on the Fly River and built rafts to traverse swollen rivers. Everything he needed he carried in his heavy pack on his back, with Caribous and Hercules flying in now and then to resupply. For hours we'd sit on the living-room floor going through his rations, either preparing for a patrol or unpacking when he came home. The bars of chocolate were the best. Heaps of curry powder was essential, as the provisions, particularly the bully beef and endless rice portions, were pretty bland. Paladin for malaria and water purifier tablets were essential. Unfortunately the latter didn't always work and dysentery from polluted water and other tropical diseases was often a problem on patrol.

They slogged along the Kokoda Track on training exercises, sometimes against an SAS regiment from Australia. He told me of the rotting relics of World War II, not yet swallowed by the encroaching jungle, the fox holes and trenches, rifles and helmets, all a reminder of the bitter battles fought there during the war.

When we were in Moresby in 1966, the Second World War seemed like an age away. Yet in reality it was only just over twenty years since those brave Aussie troops had slogged through this hell-on-earth, holding back the Japanese whilst General McArthur languished back in Australia in the comfort of a hotel in Brisbane.

Rob spoke Pidgin English; often this wasn't enough, for if the soldiers had been recruited from a particularly remote tribe, they were sometimes more fluent in their local dialect. Yet language was not necessarily a barrier.

A few Pacific Islanders, including Ted Diro, Ken Noga and Patterson Lowa, had been selected to train at Portsea Military College in Victoria to become officers in the Pacific Islands Regiments. Over the years there has appeared to be much competition between these three, who've had their fair share of controversy within the politics of Papua New Guinea. I knew Patterson Lowa the best; a fine-looking guy with much charm, particularly where the women were concerned. First I met him in Moresby when he was a platoon commander and then later when we were in Wewak, where I became friendly with his Australian wife who was finding it difficult adjusting to life married to a Pacific Islander, with all the ancient customs, not to mention his copious *wantoks* (relations) demanding a part of him. I have a lovely picture of Charlotte sitting on Patterson's knee under a coconut tree on the beach at Moem Barracks.

A fellow officer at the time at Taurama Barracks was Michael Jeffries, past-Governor General of Australia. Later, when we were to finally find a house at the Barracks, he and his glamorous new bride, Marlena, were to become our neighbours and only recently we danced the New Year in together. Another neighbour was Caroline Cotter, head prefect from when I was at Rose Bay. She was now married to a Scotsman, Ian, who'd transferred to the Australian Army. She'd terrified me at school, but here in Moresby we became firm friends.

All in all there was a tremendous group of people living this fascinating existence, many of whom we've kept in touch with over the years. Others sadly have died or we've lost touch with.

Within the first two days of my arrival in Moresby I was lucky enough to find a job as secretary to Ron Firns, the Managing Director of a small airline company, STOL (Short Take Off and Landing). I was not the greatest typist in the world and my shorthand was sketchy to say the least. Whether it was the short skirt I was wearing, or that his trusted secretary of many years, Lois White, had returned to Australia, leaving him with a huge chasm to fill, I was employed on the spot.

STOL was one of a number of small airline companies operating in Papua New Guinea at the time, PATAIR being its main competitor. Ron, with his thinning sandy hair and mass of cornflake freckles, was an amiable boss (until someone upset him and all hell broke loose). When I first met him he was smoking a cigar and dressed in pretty much the expat uniform of the time: shorts, long socks, lace-up shoes and open-neck shirt, though his shorts seemed shorter and tighter than most.

Taking up my position behind a small desk in the front room of STOL's headquarters, a ramshackle building at the bottom of Lawes Road, opposite the Steamships Trading Company, I started my new job with some trepidation. My office, with rough cement floors covered in seagrass matting, whitewashed walls and the lavatory positioned outside next to a small native settlement where tribesmen often sat on the dusty ground smoking or chewing betel nut, was different to any office I'd worked in before. It was more fun too. Our only form of cooling was a small fan in the corner, so most of the time I worked in a lather of sweat, not just because of the intense heat, but also due to the huge amount of tapes Ron hurled on my desk as he careered past to his office at the rear. Deciphering his voice, as he spoke into a tape recorder when flying one of his Cessnas or Aztecs around remote parts of Papua and New Guinea, was somewhat tricky to say the least. It didn't take me long to realise that Lois had been much better at interpreting his jangled terminology than I ever would be. And he certainly wasn't backward in telling me so, which I'm sure I deserved.

Ron had retired a number of years before from the Department of Civil Aviation and founded STOL, together with his Aerial Mapping Business run from the same office at Lawes Road. Out at Jackson Airport was the cargo and maintenance division.

Ron Firn's contribution to the airline and mapping industries in Papua New Guinea is legendary. Looking back it was a privilege to have worked at STOL, if at times it was somewhat chaotic trying to juggle the books to find enough money to stay in business. Yet one thing it never could claim to be was boring.

John Kaputin, now Sir John Kaputin, was one of the air traffic controllers at the airport. I had a bit to do with him in the running of STOL's schedules and a number of functions we had out at the strip. Like most girls of the time I was rather enamoured with this stylish Papuan. I even based my character, Ted, in my novel *Bird of Paradise* loosely on him. For many years after Independence he served as the Foreign Minister for Papua New Guinea. In 1994 he was knighted. Then he took office as Secretary General of the African, Caribbean, and Pacific group of states. His flourishing career was not without the odd bit of scandal.

Wearing a uniform of an incredibly short blue linen dress with red and white braiding around the neck and arm-holes, I found life at my desk at Lawes Road was not all typing and paper work. The odd distraction took place. One morning a local fellow walked into my office, planted himself in the cane chair in the corner, opened his zipper and waved his most private of parts in my direction, all the time sporting a huge scarlet betel-nut grin. With the naivety of youth, I screeched, retracting in a huddle to the rear office to be comforted by the rest of the staff; whereupon the culprit got up and walked outside, never to be seen again.

Incidents of this nature were quite common, particularly while driving on the country roads. It wasn't long before I learned to ignore such behaviour. Unfortunately, if you lived in Port Moresby now, there'd be much more than a waving penis to contend with. A hatchet or rifle is more likely to be waved in your direction.

Another part of my job was helping to run the Hertz Hire Car business, which Ron also owned. In fact the car, which had the run-in with Rob in his TR4, was one of our cars, causing me more than a spot of embarrassment at the time.

Liz Brown, a gorgeous blonde with super long legs, which most of the men admired more than they should have, managed this part of the business. We became firm friends, and many an evening after work, with Rob away on patrol, we'd sit on her verandah in deep wickerwork chairs gazing out over a fading sunset across Fairfax Harbour, drinking the odd Bundy and Coke with her four blonde, sun burnished children squealing with delight in the makeshift swimming pool in the garden below. Even to this day, whenever I have a Bundy, I'm reminded of that tranquil scene.

Chapter 19

A Tropical Wedding

With accommodation so sought after in Moresby when a bungalow became available in Boroko for a couple of months, Rob and I decided to take the plunge and get married. Now we'd have somewhere to live together, even if it was only for a short time before hopefully a more permanent house became available. Marrying in such haste caused a bit of a stir, with many an eye cast in the direction of my stomach. They were to be disappointed, for I wasn't in the family way, nor would I be for over a year.

There was only one dress shop in the whole of Moresby with anything that slightly resembled what a bride could wear for a wedding.

Rushing in, I said to the flamboyant lady behind the glass counter, 'I need a wedding dress urgently? I'm getting married in the morning?'

'Tomorrow?' she exclaimed, raising her more than ample frame from behind the counter. 'Haven't you left it a bit late to find a dress?'

I hastily explained the wedding was to take place in the morning, but not for a few weeks down the track. Finally we settled on a short white dress, (which my mother later made me lengthen before she'd allow me to walk down the aisle and I later shortened again to use as a tennis dress). The kind, but confused lady, with a clutter of coloured bangles jangling on her sunburnt arms, placed on my head a Brigitte Bardot style white cloth flower. Rather fancy we both thought. Together with matching shoes, hurriedly sent up from Brisbane, I was ready for the big occasion. Fortunately we found Diana a blue dress from the same shop, for I'd asked her to be my bridesmaid. Mike was to be best man. Sadly, my mother was the only member of either of our families able to fly up for the occasion.

'Of course I'll come,' she told me over the phone from Ijong Street. 'No matter how much it costs.'

And, true to her word, on the twenty-eighth of November she arrived early one morning, clutching presents from all the family. We were married at the sac sac church at Taurama Barracks – our romantic lovers' dream. Built in the old tradition, with woven cane and palm thatched walls and ceilings, it had all the character, charm and exotic feel of the Pacific Islands. In the absence of my father, Tom Medson, the burly and kindly Quartermaster at Taurama Barracks, walked me down the aisle – under a roof of tropical flowers, lovingly arranged by Rob's soldiers. In front of me, Diana looked divine in her blue dress. Our entrance was heralded by a rendition of the Hawaiian Wedding song, which we'd convinced the Padre, Father Ray Quirke, to allow us to play. I'm sure he thought it was a hymn he hadn't come across during his long and noble priesthood. By the altar, Rob stood resplendent in his uniform of green shirt and knee length shorts, starched to the hilt by his faithful batman, Wafiaga, as they always were. If the uniform couldn't stand up on its own it meant there wasn't enough starch and more needed to be added. Years later I stood at the laundry tub in our house near Holsworthy in Sydney before Rob went to Vietnam, with tears streaming down my cheeks, trying to get his jungle greens to stand up just right; not something I was good at.

At the altar, Mike stood by Rob's side, the two of them with gleaming swords and polished leather Sam Brownes. Later I was to discover that the grins they sported were more a result of a few whiskies they'd shared with Padre Quirke before the service than the actual joy of seeing Diana and I walk up the aisle. In fact Rob had shared quite a few whiskies with this garrulous and amiable priest over the previous weeks, for in those days, to marry a Catholic meant hours of tutoring beforehand in the ways of the Church. Fortunately in this case, Father Ray was far more interested in sharing an odd tipple with his pupil, rather than lecturing about the Catholic faith and the future of its children.

After the ceremony we dipped our heads through a guard of honour of Rob's fellow officers and soon afterwards, ensconced in a green army Holden, the Pipes and Drums of the 1st Pacific Islands Regiment escorted us up the dry parched hill to the Officers' Mess, a low-line vine covered structure with louvred windows and doors, set in a midst of dense greenery. Here my mother, dressed to the nines in a regal floral dress and matching hat, together with Tom Medson, Colonel Hearn, the Commanding Officer of Taurama Barracks and his wife, Jenny, plus Rob and I, greeted the guests at the front door. I've a lovely photo of our friends Colin and Marilyn Hicton shaking my mother's hand. It's hard to work out whose flamboyant hat sported the most flowers – my mother's or Marilyn's.

The Mess stewards had done us proud. Taking pride of place at the head of our table was a lavish two-tiered wedding cake one of the army chefs had spent hours decorating, a somewhat gaudy bride and groom perched proudly on the top. Above our heads a huge portrait of the Queen lauded it over the happy scene; an amusing backdrop for the controversial Irish poem my father had telegraphed through, much to the consternation of my mother and me, who knew what this meant.

Back in Ijong Street my father was enjoying a drink for the occasion.

A couple of hours later, Rob and I were scooting out the door under a shower of confetti to our honeymoon in Tapini in the southern highlands, a gift from Ron Firns at STOL.

My mother was to stay on her own in our bungalow at Boroko, taking over the TR4 and Snoopy our dog. I was terrified of leaving her by herself, but she assured me she'd be fine. And fine she was as she whizzed around Moresby with the car roof off, wind blowing through her blue rinsed hair, before hopping on a small plane to visit the outlying Trobriand Islands, which she just adored, coming back laden with a bundle of ebony carvings and walking sticks that these celebrated islands are so famous for.

'It reminded me so much of my times in India,' she told me nostalgically as we reminisced in Ireland. 'I adored it.'

When the time came for her to head back to Canberra, where my father was waiting anxiously at Ijong Street, she was devastated to be parting from us and leaving behind this weird and wonderful country with its fascinating and mysterious people.

CHAPTER 20

Tapini...and Life as a PIR Officer's Wife

Leaving for our honeymoon was tricky. First we had to find the pilot to fly the small plane taking us to Tapini. After finally tracking him down in the pub at Boroko we took off in trepidation, particularly after he told us his scarred and battered face was the result of a flying accident a few years ago in America. In those days, after the war and in the fifties, sixties and seventies, pilots would come from all over the world to get their flying hours up in Papua New Guinea. He was one of these. For a moment I thought of refusing to go with him. Surely he was breaking the law by drinking before flying. Yet this was Moresby, not Canberra. And after all, he assured us he'd only had a couple of beers. Even so I was doubtful. Yet to give him his due he flew the plane without a hitch.

With the dry arid plains of Moresby behind us, we were soon soaring high above green ribbons of rainforest and over the majestic Owen Stanleys, following narrow water courses, and drifting into white, floaty clouds. An hour or so later the pilot took a stiff left turn, flying on top of a deep ravine with a crashed Caribou in its depths and brought the plane down into Tapini, where a few of the locals rushed out and shoved wooden chocks behind the wheels to stop the plane running backwards.

Chapter 20 Tapini...and Life as a PIR Officer's Wife

Tapini is one of the most difficult strips to fly in and out of in New Guinea. When you take off it's like jumping off the end of a cliff, the wreck of the Caribou at the bottom of the chasm reminding you grimly of what can happen if the pilot misjudges.

If by chance you've read my novel, *Bird of Paradise*, you'll recognise Tapini and the lodge where we stayed. In real life, our host was Andy Anderson. In my novel it was Ernie Morris. There is only a slight resemblance between the two, but the guesthouse is much the same. A long low-line timber bungalow, it boasted a Somerset Maugham verandah to the front, looking out over the village and beyond to the lush Loloipa River valley stretching to the high savannah mountains on the skyline. Where Moresby was dry, Tapini basked in thick lush greenery, dotted with red hibiscus bushes, bougainvillea, poinsettias, cassias and wonderful creeping passion fruit vines. To me it was one of the most romantic honeymoon spots in the world. Unfortunately we've only one Polaroid photo to show for our time there, as our film was ruined on returning to Moresby when I opened the camera accidentally. Amazingly, fourteen years later when we moved to Tasmania we met Sue and Donald Clark at Koonya. They too had spent their honeymoon at Andy Anderson's guesthouse in Tapini, three months before we did. I've heard of few other people who've been to Tapini for a holiday, let alone a honeymoon, for it wasn't as though it was well-known.

We spent the week horse riding, bush-walking, enjoying sundowners on the verandah and dining with Andy in the wood-panelled dining room. (I had to take to my bed one evening feigning sickness, in order not to have to try and do justice to another of his huge generous portions of kindly prepared dishes served in style by his houseboy with the wonderful name of Ajax.)

Andy, a retired patrol officer, had many stories to tell as we sat on the deep verandah in wickerwork chairs talking till late at night, listening to the sounds of the tropics or watching the rain fall onto the lush greenery. If only I could remember some of those stories. One day we attempted to go for a helicopter ride into the mountains. After only a few seconds in the air the sheer pin broke and we more or less plummeted to the ground, causing us both whiplash, but miraculously no other injuries. All too soon our two weeks of bliss were up and once again we were on a STOL plane heading back to Moresby and work.

Our bungalow at Boroko was not a luxurious abode, but we loved it. With a *lean-to* kitchen at the side, it had a huge central living area with bedrooms leading off without any doors and a pretty decrepit bathroom out the back, which from memory we shared with another army couple. We'd found a wonderful houseboy, Ben, a solidly built fellow from Hanuabada, with a huge betel nut grin, who was extremely kind to the new *missus* of the house, helping me with chores and cleaning up after some disastrous cooking escapades in the kitchen.

With the lease at Boroko sadly at an end we were on the move again. Once we baby-sat a married quarter out at Taurama Barracks for a couple when they went home to Australia on leave. One evening Rob arrived home with a huge wild cockatoo he'd found on patrol, sitting it proudly in the corner of the sitting room on a tree stump – where it scared the living daylights out of me. When he finally realised it was the cockatoo or me that would have to go he took it down to the company headquarters to make it their mascot.

After that we rented a flat up the top of Paga Point, reached by a steep winding dirt road – or otherwise accessed by 500 steps from the centre of town. It had the most magnificent view of the endless ocean dotted with islands on one side and Fairfax Harbour and Moresby town on the other. Most of the time I stayed there on my own as Rob was away on patrol. I was quite often terrified, even though I had a machete under my bed and Snoopy, who looked as if he was a gentle cross between a dingo and a fox, to protect me. But Snoopy wasn't much interested in being a protector, having neither the cunning nor the bravery of his look-alikes. His greatest occupation was to chase the TR4 down to town, where he'd proceed to terrify the poor policeman dressed in a stifling blue uniform with long white gloves who was directing the traffic from a podium in the centre of the main street. Having done that successfully, Snoopy would then return to Paga to loiter the day away under the huge hibiscus bush by the back door. At night times he refused to sleep outside, instead cowering under the bed and declining to come out no matter what the emergency may have been.

Our bungalow's wide shady verandah, swathed in purple bougainvillea and snow-white frangipani, was where I first fell in love with the astonishing butterflies of New Guinea. Some were the size of a fist, ranging in colour from the most startling blues to daffodil yellows; others wore delicate silk gowns woven in the finest textures of blood reds, blacks, browns, and ochres. For hours I'd watch them playing within the flower petals or dancing on the lawn in the bright sunlight; nature providing a paintbox far more vivid than any human could possibly produce. The only other time I've seen such a stage show, although not as many varieties (New Guinea has more varieties of butterflies than anywhere else in the world), was amongst the orange, tangerine, olive and fig groves on the island of Corfu in the Greek Islands. We were anchored on *Sea Dreams* in the sapphire horseshoe bay of Kalami and swam ashore to walk along a shady path to the next cove of Agni – with dozens of tiny butterflies flitting from branch to branch around us, and often landing on our heads.

One balmy evening at Paga we had a *mu mu* on the front lawn, with hurricane lanterns lighting up the trees, and a long trestle table laden with tropical fruits and salads. A bottomless bowl of potent punch soon had us all singing loudly and dancing to the Rolling Stones and Bob Dylan blasting from the record player we'd bought that morning from one of the Chinese trade stores.

However, before too long we were on the move again, for another married quarter became available at Taurama Barracks. Soon we packed our belongings, plus Snoopy, into the back of an army Land Rover and moved in.

Taurama Barracks was a mini-village with its own doctor and dentist and small supermarket. The married quarters were divided into three sections. One for the officers, another for other ranks (ORs) and at the far end was where the Pacific Islanders lived. The Officers' Mess was the centre of our life in most respects, much like a country club with the officers expected to retreat there after work each afternoon for a drink, and on Fridays for *happy hour* when the beer was half price. There were many single officers living in the mess and of course this was their home so to speak. Not to turn up for a beer after work was frowned upon by the hierarchy. To stay too long was frowned upon by us wives. There was a fine line between the two.

On the whole the Mess was a male domain. Sometimes we women were invited. Functions were a mixture of formal and informal affairs. We had theme nights, cocktail parties, lunches and formal mixed *dining-in* nights where the men dressed in full mess kit, even in that heat, and the dress I wore to Rob's graduation, now dyed black, had many outings.

One *dining-in* night, the officers had, was for Malcolm Fraser, the then Minister for the Army. The next morning there were many sore heads, Rob's being amongst the worst. One of the rituals of a *dining-in* night is the subalterns' court, usually taking place at the end of the evening when everyone is somewhat merry, or pissed to be more precise. Here a mock judge and jury summon a person before the court to be tried. That person could be the Commanding Officer or any other officer or visiting dignitary. In this case it was Malcolm Fraser, who was fined seven ports. I don't think it had to be any great offence to be fined, probably that he was too tall, or had his tie at half-mast. He refused to down the seven ports unless the subalterns kept him company, which most of them did. Mr Fraser was notorious for the amount of alcohol he could consume in one sitting. Years later, when he was in the news for losing his trousers after some function overseas, I thought of that night back in Moresby when Rob arrived home three sheets to the wind.

Tropical storms can be terrifying in New Guinea. It's as though the whole sky is alight with orange and yellow strobes, splitting the trees and shooting through the windows. On a few occasions, with Rob away, I'd huddle in the lavatory as it was the only place the lightning didn't penetrate. A couple of nights I took my mattress and a terrified Snoopy in there too.

Yet, when the worst of the storm had passed, I'd love to sit on the wooden steps leading down from the living room to the garden, watching the rain falling through the dense tropical foliage onto the lawns. And then when the sun broke through, the raindrops on the thick frangipani leaves would shimmer and sparkle in the sunlight as if they were clusters of polished diamonds. After the long months of the dry, the rain was a pleasant relief. Needless to say, after months of the wet season, one desperately wished for the dry again.

It was quite an odd feeling living in someone else's shoes for three or four months, and then moving on into someone else's, which is what we were doing as we moved from one house to the next with people away on leave. We bought ourselves a carved wooden anchor, ceremoniously placing it up on the wall as soon as we arrived at each new place, right up to the home we live in now.

The army quarters at Taurama were pretty much all the same, with the area under the house a great spot to suspend a cane hanging-basket chair amongst the lush greenery, where we could enjoy a drink in the cool of the evening. Sometimes it was not long before the neighbours, hearing the clink of glasses would amble over to join us. All the houses were built closely together, making it virtually impossible to have a party without the whole street knowing, so it was best to invite everyone (within hearing distance at least), lest people felt left out.

Farewelling or welcoming a family into the barracks was a ritual, sometimes starting off with a weekend brunch and often turning into a whole day affair. Everyone would bring a dish and for hours we'd sit out under the huge pandanus or frangipani trees, with children playing in makeshift rubber pools nearby, the sound of their laughter filling the air.

Under the house was ideal for long hot evenings; rickety trestle tables were set up with white tablecloths and hurricane lanterns casting a spectral glow onto the dense greenery. Quite often we'd have three or four fondues going, (with bowls of hot spicy sauces to dip our meat or cheese into) and mosquito coils curling languid spirals of grey smoke into the warm evening air. We had no television, so entertainment was our own making, with music forming an essential part of our lives, as it still does. We wore long flowing dresses, one-piece culottes or short mini-skirts with flowers in our hair, and danced barefoot on the lawns. Rob even had a bright cotton caftan he'd throw on at night, or if we were going out it might be a beige safari suit. At times, particularly in Wewak later on, we occasionally ended the night with a motor-scooter ride around the barracks or through the football fields down to the beach where we'd skinny dip in the ocean. The main mode of transport for the officers within the barracks was small scooters and since there was no real restriction on riding these (or if there was we disregarded it), it was a fun, if not a foolhardy sport when we challenged each other to a race.

Cards, particularly Poker and 500, until they were banned a few years later, also played a major role in our lives. After the ban, we still continued to play, but needed a sentry on the front door. One evening in Wewak the adjutant was walking past and heard someone shout out *'Full house'* in excitement. On enquiring what was going on, he was told by the fellow on the front door that the loo was full. To give him his due he took it no further.

Many a day at Taurama we were treated to the evocative sound of the pipes and drums being practised by the soldiers, with the poignant notes wafting over the trees to where we enjoyed our *happy hour*. Often they marched through the barracks, either first thing in the morning or just on dusk. And every night a truck would come through the barracks spraying for mosquitoes. I think it was DDT or some such dreadful poison, but it kept the mosquitoes at bay and hence the cases of malaria. So far I'm still alive, but I hate to think what it did to our systems, not to mention the many children who played out in the gardens as they were sprayed. Each morning Paladin parades were compulsory for the soldiers, where they were handed out Paladin anti-malarial tablets. Should they not show up, they were charged.

When Rob was away, I spent most of the time sleeping with the machete under my bed, for even in the sixties there were quite a few break-ins and attempted rapes. The barracks was not immune. In one incidence, a young wife, living across the road from us in Taurama, woke up to find an indigenous fellow in her bedroom wielding a huge carving knife. I awoke to sickening screams. Alarmed, I shook Rob, who, in half a daze, leaped from the bed, taking off in the direction of the screams.

Suddenly it dawned on me he was stark naked. 'My God… come back and put some clothes on,' I yelled, as I ran after him with his shorts.

Stopping to put them on gave the attacker time to escape. Fortunately he was arrested the next day, confessing to what had happened, the story being, that he was a *wontok* of a 'houseboy' newly arrived in the barracks. He'd evidently hidden in the bushes near the Mess, where the woman had gone to watch a movie with a girlfriend, whose husband was also away on patrol, and followed them home. As they sat under the house drinking coffee and strumming a guitar, the fellow crept up the back stairs to the kitchen, where he got the carving knife, then hid in the bedroom cupboard. Only when the woman was asleep did he come out and attempt to attack her. Scared off by her screams and then Rob's shouting as he rushed towards the house, he dropped the knife, peed in the corner, and scurried down the back stairs. Unfortunately Rob had taken to the front stairs, missing him as he went.

A few weeks later, I was looking after a friend's albino bull terrier, Timmy. With Rob away on patrol again I was on my own, apart from Snoopy and Timmy. Snoopy didn't think much of Timmy (certainly no prize to look at), putting up with him in a bored sort of way. One night, with Snoopy asleep under my bed, Timmy wanted to relieve himself outside. After going through the front door to let him out I heard with alarm it slam behind me in the wind. Here I was, starkers (with no air-conditioning and the overhead fan giving little relief from the oppressive heat, we mostly slept in the nude) on the front steps with all the doors and windows locked.

After initially sitting staring into the blackness, with tears of frustration falling down my cheeks, I resolved the situation by finding a sheet in the laundry down below and wrapping it around me. Still I couldn't get back inside as all windows and doors were locked from the inside. Snoopy, I might add was still asleep. It was only 2am. After ten minutes or so, with Timmy now back from his walk, I decided to scurry through the shrubbery to Mike and Diana's house in the next block, where I knocked on the door.

'I can still remember opening the door to this demented figure wrapped in a white sheet,' Mike recalls with a laugh. 'And that dog…well, it must've been the ugliest mutt alive.'

After that I made Timmy sleep in the laundry below, whilst Snoopy continued to languish under the bed.

I spent my 21st birthday on my own. Not that we planned it that way. Rob was somewhere far up in the mountains on patrol and due back that day.

'Book a table at the Biccy Room,' he told me, before he went away the week before, knowing this was my favourite haunt.

Even though he wasn't back by seven, I dolled myself up in anticipation, thinking he'd arrive any minute. I can even remember the dress I wore. White with a silver band around the neck and cut away at the shoulders. Rob had bought it for me when he went on a trip to Canungra in Queensland for a training stint. He'd won some money at the picnic races at Beaudesert and had splashed out on this dress when down at the Gold Coast before coming back to Moresby. I adored it and had it for many, many years.

At about seven-thirty there was a knock on the door. Outside stood a young single second lieutenant I'd met a few times at the mess, who was obviously the Duty Officer come to give me some news. He looked me up and down, noticing how I was dressed up to the nines, and probably thought: Don't like the look of this. What I'm about to tell her may not go down so well.

'There's been a health scare amongst your husband's platoon and no-one's allowed to fly out of the camp,' he told me apologetically with a look of genuine distress in his grey eyes.

I stared at him in horror. 'But it's my twenty-first birthday. We were going out to the Biccy Room.'

He seemed so sorry for me that I thought he was going to offer to take me out himself when he came off duty. And I must admit, being all dressed up and with a dinner booking made, for a brief moment I thought I'd have accepted. But, after shifting from one leg to the other, and running his hand through his mop of dark hair, he obviously thought that taking the wife of a fellow officer out on the town for her 21st birthday wasn't such a good idea after all. Once again he apologised profusely and left me standing there.

I was not impressed to be stood up (even it was unavoidable), collapsing into tears and suddenly feeling very alone. It wasn't as though I could even pick up the phone and ring my family in Canberra. We didn't have one. Eventually I got undressed and spent the evening painting my nails. It would be another week before the platoon was given the all-clear and Rob came home, whereupon we celebrated my coming of age at a candlelight table at the Hibiscus Room and I wore the same dress.

Shortly after this episode we acquired a small motor-boat painted in army green. One day Rob and I decided to move it from one side of the Peninsula, Bootless Bay, to the other side at Moresby Harbour. We were on our way for about two hours when the motor conked out.

'The bloody sheer pins broken,' Rob told me a few minutes later, looking worried.

I looked around the boat. 'And we've only got one oar!'

My memory fails me as to why we were on this expedition with only one oar. I suspect one had fallen overboard earlier on and we couldn't retrieve it.

As it was, there was nothing for it other than to beach the boat and take to the land, or rather the swamps. What seemed like hours later we were still wallowing in mud up to our necks, with spiders and all the other delights of a tropical quagmire surrounding us. Now Rob had a mutiny on his hands. I still remember his encouragement, assuring me he could see light and hear cars…a ploy to keep me going.

'Come on darling…we're nearly there,' he coaxed time and time again.

Since then it's taken me a long time to believe him when he says: 'We're nearly there'. No matter what trip we're on.

Eventually we found our way to the open spaces and hitch-hiked to the Mess. As I wasn't allowed inside (women being *persona non grata* unless invited to a function) I had to remain in the scorching heat, with Rob bringing me out a lemon squash. He and one of his platoon soldiers returned the next day with a new sheer pin (and another oar) to take the boat the rest of the way to Moresby Harbour where they put it on a mooring. The following week Rob went out on patrol again. When he came back, the boat had sunk to the deep, dark chasms of the ocean, where I presume it still sits today. Fortunately we've had more success with the many other boats we've owned since.

A few months later Rob won the Papua New Guinea squash championships in Lae. When we returned home in a tiny plane to Moresby, we were greeted by flashing bulbs and a gaggle of reporters. In the next day's *South Pacific Post* he made the front page. He even made the back page of *Nui Gini Tok Tok*, the newspaper for the Pacific Islanders. Squash was like a religion in Moresby at the time, squash possibly being too fine a word for it, as like in most squash courts in those days, squash was only a minor part of the evening's competition. Celebrating or commiserating afterwards, whilst downing copious bottles of South Pacific lagers, was the chief activity of the night.

With Rob away on patrol once more, I flew with a couple of girlfriends to the Trobriand Islands to the north of the D'Entrecastreaux group, where my mother had previously visited. Totally different to the rest of the Province, the Trobriand Islands are flat, low lying coral atolls with Kiriwina Island being a popular 'get a way' of the day. Much of the weekend we rattled around in the back of a rusty beat-up truck, visiting serene villages, and admiring the unique and elaborate carvings and ebony walking sticks the islanders had on display. Long tranquil twilights were spent talking, and devouring sumptuous local chow, on the huge verandah of Tim and Beverly Ward's wonderful hotel, which was decorated with wooden carvings, colourful shells, and covered in hibiscus and frangipani. Later, when dusk had fallen, we'd listen to a *sing*

sing put on by the villagers dressed in intricately crafted tribal costumes, elaborate head-gear and painted and greased bodies. In the morning, the sound of a cockerel crowing, children playing and the cheerful chatter of the villagers tending their yam gardens below our verandah gently woke us up.

The Trobriand Islanders have strong Polynesian characteristics. The women, with their light-brown skin and often long straight hair, are generally a more attractive race than the rest of the New Guineans. The villagers' lovingly tended yam gardens provided a staple food, some of which we enjoyed the night before in the hotel. On the whole the villages were set out much the same, with the yam houses forming an inner ring surrounded by *sleeping* houses built of timber and woven palm. All this was encircled by a ring of palm trees with neatly trimmed hedges, washing lines strung between wooden poles, gardens of bright flowers and bursting bushes of native plants. A great sight from the air.

The Trobriands' most notorious white resident was Cyril B Cameron, otherwise known as King Cam or King of Kitava. A more than colourful character, he died in 1966 after almost half a century of reigning over Kitava, at the same time maintaining a harem of young girls he'd offer with great delight to special visitors. You can still see where the villagers buried him on a hillside overlooking the lagoon with a raised cairn of coral rocks over the grave. In this day and age I'm not so sure he'd have been so revered by the villagers, yet back in the first part of last century, such dallying with the local girls seemed to be acceptable. Often white men had two or three native wives, or in some cases had a white wife and numerous native mistresses, leading to a mixture of white, black and coffee coloured children.

When I boarded the plane to go back to Moresby I was sad

to leave. But I had many reminders of my time there, including a rare copy of the best-selling book in the Trobriands for many years, *The Sexual Life of Savages in North-Western Melanesia*, written two centuries before by the anthropologist, Bronislaw Malinowski.

A few months later, with Rob once again away on patrol, I started to feel nauseous in the mornings. At first I put it down to a tropical bug; however, it wasn't long before I discovered that I was pregnant. When I picked Rob up from the airport I gave him the good news. Although we hadn't actually planned it we were both delighted. Fortunately I soon got over morning sickness and sailed through the first three months without anyone at work noticing I was pregnant.

When I did pluck up the courage to tell Ron Firns, he said with a grin, 'I should have known you wouldn't be around for long.'

But it wasn't my pregnancy that forced me to resign from STOL. It was another posting for Rob.

CHAPTER 21

A Settler's Wife... Lae

'How would you like to go to Lae?' Rob asked me one evening when sitting in our wicker hanging-basket chairs under the house in Taurama, with the rain thrashing the tall ferns and flooding the ground, causing tiny rivulets to cascade into the garden.

Asking me this was a mere formality, for in reality we had little choice.

We started our posting outside this sprawling township in the Province of Morobe when I was four months pregnant. Lae is built on a headland, turning its back to the sea, losing the benefit of the beautiful view of the Huon Gulf. A pity, as before the war the town was better orientated. Looming mountains rather than the sea grab your attention.

In our day, Lae was a mass of fumy streets, clamouring traffic and laid-back Pacific Islanders. Although most of our time was spent out at Igam Barracks, the Hotel Cecil and the Lae Club in town were good places to meet for a sundowner and a slap-up meal.

Near the Botanical Gardens is a sombre war cemetery with the graves of thousands of allied servicemen, mainly Australian and Indian, who perished there during the Second World War. There are 2808 graves, 2363 of which are Australian. Many with everyday Australian names. Most so very young. In the centre of Lae, Mt Lunaman was used by the Germans and the Japanese as a lookout point. The Germans called it Burgberg, meaning Fortress Hill. It is also known as Hospital Hill.

Rob went to Lae first to assume his position as temporary captain, second in command at Igam Barracks, where he was to take possession of our brand-new house in this newly established remote army settlement. Snoopy and I flew in a few weeks later in an army Hercules to the airstrip just outside Lae, where Rob and his army driver, a happy mischievous fellow from Mount Hagen, met us. After a hot dusty drive along a dirt road we arrived at our new home, a bat-winged house set on stilts in the midst of a tsunami of brown dust. It seemed to be in the middle of nowhere. It was.

Snoopy proved to be a problem. We were told by Rob's company commander that we should probably not bring him with us. Unfortunately for Rob, my Irish stubborn streak came to the fore and Snoopy was delighted to accompany me on the trip and was over the moon to see Rob. I don't think either of us was ever forgiven by the company commander, a small stocky man not given to much grace and charm. Needless to say, this didn't herald a good start in our new posting. But what was I supposed to do? Leave Snoopy behind in Moresby? He was now very much part of the family, keeping me company during the many months I spent on my own. As it was, I had to part with him a few months later when I returned to Australia and Rob went to live in the Officers' Mess. But when it came to that time, we found him a good home with one of the other army couples, who were to be there for the next eighteen months. After that, he went to another couple, where he lived to a ripe old age. Yet I was devastated to leave him behind in Lae when the time came.

Chapter 21 A Settler's Wife... Lae

Igam was indeed a barren camp. There were no gardens, apart from a few shrubs around the Officers' and Sergeants' Messes. Our job, together with the few other families, was to establish the area. From the neighbouring jungle we dug tropical plants, shrubs and bamboo, planting madly, trying our hardest to turn this desolate terrain into something that resembled a garden and home. Fortunately the wet season was just around the corner so most things thrived.

At first I was pretty lonely, as I wasn't working and none of our friends from Moresby were around. Rob was at work all day or away on patrol. For the first time since coming to New Guinea I was homesick. Maybe being pregnant, my hormones were playing havoc, for on a number of occasions I burst into tears for no apparent reason or got myself in a state about entertaining official guests, including generals, politicians or anyone else sent to Igam to parade the Aussie flag or have a jaunt to the tropics. As the Commanding Officer wasn't married, a lot of the entertaining fell on our shoulders.

One day I removed the best steak available in Lae from the freezer, placing it on the bench to defrost. I told Lani, my young houseboy, to leave it there to thaw out while I lay my sweltering pregnant body down for a rest under the ceiling fan in the bedroom, before preparing a meal for a visiting dignitary, General Daley.

I arose at five to prepare the meal. No meat. The General was coming at seven.

'*Lani!*' I shouted (screamed actually) from the door. '*Kai Kai, it go* **where**?'

With a large grin from ear to ear, Lani sauntered up the steps, proudly proclaiming he'd taken the *kai kai* home to his *wantoks*. '*Tenkyu*,' he said. '*Em goodpella kai kai.*'

My pidgin wasn't the best at this stage, although it was improving.

'You eatim kai kai?' I exclaimed in horror.

Lani smiled, nodding his head.

I threw my hands in the air.

Lani! *Kai kai belong General!*'

'Ah! *Kai kai belong General.*' He shook his head of tight curls and looked at me with huge soulful black eyes. '*Me sori missu… sori tu mus.*'

Obviously he'd misunderstood my instructions, for often I left him out *kai kai* to take to his *wantoks* in the small village adjacent to the barracks. Or did he get the better of me? Who knows?

Shopping wasn't a breeze at Igam at the time. Supplies were limited and hence one never set out with a menu to cook. What was available was what one used, and as a boat carrying supplies hadn't been in for a while, stewing steak was all I could find in the fridge, so hastily I made it into a curry. I always think fondly of the delightful General Daley for happily chewing his way through morsels of leather, without saying a word, as Rob's CO glared in disapproval. I received a lovely letter from the General some days later thanking me for such a lovely night but no thank-you from the CO.

The strained relationship with Rob's Commanding Officer caused Rob to rethink his army career. Maybe matters were not helped by the fact that when Rob arrived at Igam, the Commander was the army representative on the Lae Rugby Board, a post voted for by the soldiers. With Rob's arrival, the soldiers chose to vote Rob into this prestigious position and drop the Commanding Officer. Needless to say he was not impressed.

'Maybe in hindsight I should have rejected the rugby post

and relationships would have been less tense,' Rob has since told me.

Despite the shops sometimes being short on supplies, all kinds of tropical fruits, fish and vegetables were available from the local markets. We were spoilt in this regard. We could also buy what artefacts we wanted, with no restrictions on removing them from the country, as there are nowadays.

I often wonder how our garden at Igam has survived over the years. Did the trees and shrubs we spent hours planting grow? Did future soldiers and their wives enjoy the benefit of our pioneering? Or has it gone like a lot of married quarters in New Guinea today, which have fallen into disrepair. In some instances Officers' Messes and other buildings have even been burned down. The Officers' Mess in Wewak was burned during a formal function in progress a few years ago when the soldiers felt the dignitaries were being fed better *kai kai* than they were, so decided to take matters into their own hands, setting fire to the building. One of the expat women at the function described in an email to a friend of ours, how she had to leap from the table, just escaping through the door in the nick of time. For hours she wandered around the swamp and thick rainforest with the hem of her dress in one hand and her high heels in the other, before eventually fighting her way onto the beach where the police rescued her six hours later.

From Lae, we took a number of trips into the mountains. On one occasion, friends came up from Port Moresby. We spent the weekend in a guest house at the highland village of Wau, famous for its gold rush in the 1920s and 30s. We weren't after gold – just some cooler air and a chance to sit around an open fire once again. We drove up in our small Mini through the Wau Gorge, passing Edie Creek and then Little Wau Creek, where we stopped for a picnic and a walk through the bush. There are some thirty-eight of the world's forty species of birds of paradise in New Guinea, one of which we were lucky enough to see on this day, together with a couple of bower birds, a kingfisher, parrots and pigeons.

Both the birds of paradise and cassowaries are of great ceremonial importance to the tribal groups in New Guinea, with their feathers used to adorn their traditional tribal dress. There are also millions of species of insects, and, as I've said, copious varieties of stunning butterflies, including the largest butterfly in the world. The beetle is often used as a body ornament, in particular the brilliant green scarab beetle. New Guinea also has about two hundred species of reptiles, including two of crocodiles, thirteen turtles and about a hundred different kinds of snakes.

Most of the Pacific Islanders are absolutely terrified of snakes. Rob told me of an occasion when Patterson Lowa, the indigenous officer I mentioned earlier, literally turned white, leaped in the air and without touching the ground, levitated out of the doorway, when someone brought a rubber snake into the Officers' Mess and placed it on the table in front of him (a cruel joke in hindsight, but supposedly fun at the time).

We had a grand meal around the open fire in the hotel at Wau, afterwards watching the dancing. There was one entirely beautiful Pacific Islander dancing seductively to the loud music by herself. Tall, with tight curly hair and finer features than most Pacific Islanders; the boys were quite smitten with her, even getting up and joining her on the dance floor. From memory, Rob and I had a roaring fight as I was feeling like a fat sow about to give birth to a litter of ten and the last thing I wanted was my husband dancing with a divine-looking creature, even though I could see she merited all the attention she was getting.

The rest of our time at Igam was spent establishing this barren area, driving the long hot dirt road into Lae to shop, and meeting the boats when they came in with supplies.

In the evenings we played cards and had dinner parties with the few other couples in the barracks or dined and watched movies in the Mess. Rob had a great scam with his soldiers – slightly unorthodox, but very popular. Whoever was the best turned-out soldier for the weekly parade would be made 'fisherman of the day'. A great honour and one highly sought after, for the said soldier could take the Friday afternoon off to go fishing, meaning we had some fantastic reef fish on our table over the weekend – as did the rest of the soldiers. Sometimes they speared huge succulent lobsters that we would cook in a tin drum over a fire in the area under the house. In Vanimo, a few years later, we had some magnificent lobster bakes on the beach in front of the Officers' Mess.

Colourful tribal festivals, where the soldiers dressed up in costumes depicting their tribe and village place, were a feature I remember well. For hours they entertained us with electrifying song and dance routines. Some even looked quite terrifying with their magnificently painted and pig-greased bodies, feathered headdresses, and large spears, stomping, chanting and literally shaking the earth with thundering black feet and banging on ornate drums.

Soon, however, this weird and wonderful life of mine in New Guinea was to come to an end. For Rob had been told he was being posted to Vietnam with the 5th Battalion early in the New Year. Before I knew it, I was on my way back to Australia, to a life far removed from this great adventure.

What I didn't know then was that within a few years I'd be back again in this extraordinary country which has shaped so much of my life.

CHAPTER 22

Back Home and Off to War

My early move back to Australia was brought about by the airlines at that time not allowing women to fly when in the last trimester of pregnancy. So after a number of farewell parties and a sad goodbye to Snoopy at his new home in Igam, and then Rob out at the airstrip in Lae, I flew to Moresby and then on to Brisbane to see Eugene, now returned from Vietnam. Back in Canberra I stayed in my old bedroom with my parents at Ijong Street.

To fill in the time until Rob came down to prepare for his tour of duty in Vietnam, I secured a part-time job at David Jones department store where I worked behind the cosmetic counter selling Helena Rubenstein and Estee Lauder, dressed in a short black shift. I was soon told to lower the hemline, making me realise we were further advanced in the fashion stakes in New Guinea than they were in Canberra at the time.

When Rob returned to Australia he was stationed at Holsworthy Barracks, south of Sydney, where the 5th Battalion was preparing for Vietnam. After much searching we found a home in Illawong, with five acres of thick bushland rolling down to the Georges River, about thirty minutes' drive from the barracks and not far from where Diana and Mike Battle were now living. Mike was to go to Vietnam with the 5th Battalion also. Here we awaited the arrival of Charlotte, who was born on the 11th September, 1968, in the Sutherland District Hospital.

'The most beautiful princess in the world,' were Rob's words, as he stared at the blonde, blue-eyed vision through the glass partition. This was well before the time when husbands were allowed anywhere near the labour ward.

As the hospital was pretty crowded at the time I spent much of my labour on a trolley in a corridor. Somewhat surprised when they handed me a blue eyed blonde baby to breastfeed, I watched in horror the woman in the next bed feeding a brown eyed, dark haired one. Surely this was a mistake. Even the nurse looked a bit confused, eyeing my nut-brown eyes and long dark hair, before studying the woman's blue eyes and blonde hair in the next bed. I used to joke with Charlotte that it was only years later, when our second daughter, Georgina, was born that I realised it wasn't a mistake after all. She was just as blonde with the same blue eyes. Today Georgie's beautiful daughter, Eleanor, looks identical to them both.

Rob and I both immediately fell in love with Charlotte. Needless to say, we've been in love ever since. Unfortunately September the 11th has become notorious for the horrendous New York twin towers terrorism attacks. Not a great day to celebrate a birthday, but back in 1968 it was a joyous day for us and the rest of our families.

Gunga Din joined the three of us at this time also. A large Doberman Pincher with a will of his own, he became Charlotte's minder. In fact, on the way back from the hospital, I was somewhat put out when Charlotte and I were left in the car on a busy street in Sutherland as Rob disappeared into a pet shop to find a bed and a collar for Gunga Din.

'Well, he might feel left out,' he said, opening the car

door and dumping his new acquisitions on the seat beside Charlotte's bassinet.

Mind you, as Gunga Din sat protectively under Charlotte's bassinet out in the sunshine at Illawong, barking furiously when anyone approached, I could see Rob's reasoning.

Rob was deeply involved in pre-Vietnam training and away a lot, so Gunga Din looked after me too. As part of the battalion's preparation they went for weeks on end to Shoalwater Bay in far north Queensland to acclimatise to jungle warfare. Other times Rob was on exercises in the bush around Sydney, yet unable to come home at night. In response to a desperate plea for help, my mother came to lend a welcome hand with Charlotte, as she was spending rather a lot of time yelling and screaming (what I thought were huge obscenities she must have learned in a previous world) due to dreadful colic. No doubt this was caused by an anxious mother trying to feed an anxious baby, and not made any easier by the fact I was awaiting the departure of my husband to Vietnam. Not having a helper in the house, for the first time in a number of years, I also had to spend hours starching and ironing Rob's jungle greens till they stood up on their own accord, a job at which I was not good, as I explained earlier.

It was stinking hot, one of the most blistering summers in Sydney on record.

One day I was ironing in the laundry, with the sweat pouring down my face in rivulets. Charlotte was screaming as usual and there was only a week to go before Rob's departure for Vietnam. Kindly, Rob's mother, Hazel, staying with us at the time, came to see if she could help. Falling over Gunga Din sprawled on the ground, the poor woman broke her ankle, and I had to pack her and Charlotte into the car and make a hurried trip to the hospital where the amiable doctor put it in plaster and told her to go home and rest. Looking at my distraught baby and then at a frazzled me, he suggested we do the same, a highly stupid recommendation I thought, thinking of the army greens still in the laundry and Rob's imminent departure to defend his country from the *hordes of communists* about to arrive.

However, we did have a number of good parties around the barbeque and makeshift above-ground pool in the heat of that 1968/69 summer. There were a few of the class of '65 in Sydney at the time, either having just returned from Vietnam or Malaya, or, like Rob, preparing to go. I was envious of the ones who'd returned, although as it turned out, many of them were to go back again for a second time, including Eugene. It was a nerve-wracking time waiting for the inevitable to happen. I optimistically hoped the war would end before Rob had to leave us.

It was not to be.

We packed up the car early on the morning of his departure on HMAS Sydney. With Charlotte ensconced in her bassinet on the back seat we drove in peak-hour traffic from Illawong, down to the Woolloomooloo docks to our date with the inescapable. Not much was said on the trip in. I recall the music playing on the radio. One maudlin love song after the other did little for our morale. I looked miserably out of the window at all the other people in their cars going to work and wished I could be one of them. It seemed odd to me that life was going on around us as usual, when Rob was about to leave for the war. I'll always be grateful to the cheery Salvation Army officers down on the docks serving tea and biscuits to the soldiers, their wives, and families, doing their utmost to try and keep the morale up. A difficult job.

I desperately clung to Rob as he clasped Charlotte in his

arms for one last time. His mother sobbed when he leaned down and kissed her goodbye. When it came to my turn for a final farewell I couldn't speak, just hiding my face in the folds of his uniform before lifting my lips for a lingering kiss.

Minutes later, he and the other soldiers boarded the carrier and stood proudly on the deck. After an agonising wait, we waved a final goodbye as the huge ship drifted out to the harbour to commence her journey to Vietnam with Rob and much of the cream of Aussie youth on board. Rob was sad to leave, but also excited to be heading off to war. After all, this is what he'd been trained for. He was also anxious to get it over and done with.

Behind where I stood, the anti-Vietnam protesters waved banners high in the air, at the same time screeching anti-war chants.

'Get lost,' I wanted to shout at them. Instead I stood holding my screaming baby in one hand and clutching Rob's distraught mother with the other.

His father had decided to say his goodbyes the night before and I must admit standing there, I thought he might have made the right decision.

Drominagh on the shores of Lough Derg in Tipperary where my father and his family grew up and where I lived after my birth. The family to whom we sold it in 1949 still own it and we all often visit.

Ballynastragh Castle in County Wexford, burnt down in the Civil War of 1922/23 and since rebuilt on the same piece of land the Esmonde family has owned since the eleventh century. I spend many happy times there with my cousins.

Above: My father, Owen, with his mother, Eily, when he was about eight.

My grandfather, Dr John Esmonde, MP for Tipperary (on left) with Joe Devlin, journalist and Member for the Irish Parliamentary Party and later the Nationalist Party, in the grounds of Drominagh

My maternal grandfather, George Henry Louis Mackenzie, who spent a great deal of his life in India as a jute broker.

My maternal grandmother, Lillian Mackenzie, known as Granny Mac, who once worked for the Nizam of Hyderabad.

Coul House, Inverness, Scotland. The home of the Mackenzies, my mother's family. It is now a hotel where I love to visit and watch croquet games on the lawn.

My mother on far right end of top row at Sacré Coeur Convent, Tunbridge Wells, England.

My mother early 1930s, working at the Savoy in London where she often went dancing with the Aga Khan.

At Drominagh, 1938.

My parents on their wedding day in 1938.

Setting out for a hunt from Drominagh in 1939. My parents in foreground.

My mother's sister, Zita, and her husband, Phillip Burch, on their wedding day in Calcutta. Later Phillip, an officer with the Duke of Cornwall's Light Infantry in India, tragically died of rabies. My mother was heartbroken as she lived with them for sometime and adored Phillip.

My father's younger brother, Eugene Esmonde VC, DSO, not long before he was killed flying a Swordfish in the Channel Dash action in 1942. He was awarded the Victoria Cross posthumously.

Eugene, second from left on the aircraft carrier, Ark Royal in 1941, after the action from HMS Victorious, which saw him drop the torpedo on The Bismarck, which contributed to its sinking by the British Navy. This is the action which won Eugene the DSO, which he received from King George VI shortly before his death in the Channel Dash action, which won him a posthumous Victoria Cross. He also flew the first surcharged airmail to Australia, piloting flying-boats with Imperial Airways and Qantas Empire Airways for a number of years in the 1930's.

My father and his brother, Paddy, with their mother, after receiving the Victoria Cross from King George VI for Eugene at Buckingham Palace, 1942.

Captain Thomas Esmonde, the first Esmonde VC, who won his award in the Crimean War.

Clonmoylan on the other side of Lough Derg from Drominagh, where we moved to in 1948.

With Brownie and Peggy at Clonmoylan.

Viv on my much-loved donkey, Early Mist, at Clonmoylan.

On the bog cart on Lough Derg at Clonmoylan with my father. Dibs and Eugene in background. Such joys of childhood.

With Gill, Eugene, Dibs and Viv (I am bottom left) at Clonmoylan.

At Clonmoylan when I was six. Note the gumboots, which were rarely off my feet. Lough Derg in background.

Having fun in the snow with Peggy on the sleigh made from my mother's old skis.

At Bray outside Dublin before leaving for Australia in 1954 (we are the five on left). It was the first time Viv and I had friends nearby to play with. Eugene says we look like something out of Angela's Ashes. He's not far wrong!

Viv in front of Reidsdale Post Office sign. My mother ran the post office and my father dug post holes for the farmer who owned the land.

The house and post office at Reidsdale not far from Braidwood in NSW where we lived in 1954. A long way in more ways than one from Drominagh and Clonmoylan. It was even more derelict in 1954.

With Eugene, setting out for a day's sheep mustering with our neighbour at Reidsdale. He taught us all how to boil a billy, crack a whip and some good Aussie slang.

Eugene in front of Steve Forsant's horse-drawn caravan, which his horse, Cuddy, later pulled all the way to Canberra and parked outside our house.

Sitting on Clown with Eugene, Dibs, Viv and Gill holding Porky at Reidsdale.

With Dibs in front of my father's prized Armstrong Siddeley.

From left: Dibs, Gill, Eugene and Viv with our catch of the day at Whale Beach. I am on right.

Having fun Whale Beach, 1956. I am in the middle.

Heading off for Sunday Mass at Ijong Street. Gill, who had an even fuller rope skirt, after hoops went out of fashion, took this photo.

Braddon Catholic Girls High 1959 Hockey team in Canberra (now Merice College) I am third from right middle row.

With Viv on a working holiday in Cairns, 1964. We caught the mail train from Brisbane, a slow trip.

Dibs with our friend Father O'Brien at the Irish Embassy, Canberra.

My father in his garden at Ijong Street, which passersby would stop to admire.

At Ijong Street heading back to Rose Bay convent (now Kincoppel Rose Bay) in Sydney. Viv happier than I was with prospect of another term away.

Gill in back garden of Ijong Street. Note Eugene's bedroom – the old RAAF hut behind.

Riding with Mrs Bobby Llewellyn (Mrs Lew) in the Molonglo River, now Lake Burley Griffin, in 1958. I am front left in check shirt riding Goldie. Next to me, also in check shirt, is Viv on Danny Boy. In front of her is Gill on her white horse, Aaron. Dibs (white shirt) behind her on Kinsale. Eugene not there. Bobby Llewellyn (far left) won a Queen's Birthday award for dedication to young horse riders in Canberra and surrounds.

Eugene at Duntroon Military College, where he introduced me to Rob.

First photo with Rob. At his 21st at Ijong Street. This suit I wore often and in many combinations. I was 18.

Rob receiving the Heritage Cup from General Finlay at Duntroon. He is the only Duntroon cadet to ever win both the tennis and squash trophies every year for four years. He was also in the first XV rugby team.

Rob's father, John (Poppy), and his in-laws on New South Wales coast in 1930s. Poppy lived with us for close to 20 years later in his life when his wife Hazel died.

Rob's mother, Hazel (on right), on South Coast NSW 1930s. Love the hats.

The Peterswald Chateau (circa 1785) in Buchlovice in the Czech Republic, housing one of the best art collections in Europe. We have visited often with the family. Sadly the chateau above and castle below went out of the family many years ago.

The Peterswald Castle (circa 1208) sitting above Buchlovice in Czech Republic. It was so cold and windy each time we went there that I can quite understand why the family moved to the chateau above.

Rob's great grandfather, William John Peterswald, moved to Australia in mid 1800s, where he became the third police commissioner of South Australia in 1882.

Rob's graduation at RMC Duntroon, 1965 – a proud mother and girlfriend.

Our wedding at Taurama Barracks, Port Moresby Dec 1966. My mother, who was the only member of our families able to come to Moresby, made me drop my hemline. Later I took the hem up again and used it as a tennis dress.

Koki Market, Port Moresby, where we bought our fruit and veggies during the mid-sixties.

At our house at Boroko 1967. TR 4 before accident when we had it painted red – a particularly stupid colour for the tropics.

Rob with Bob Katter, Minister for Defence (father of present QLD politician Bob Katter), reviewing a 2nd Pacific Islands Regiment parade at Moem Barracks, Wewak.

Rob in Vietnam, 1969. This photo frightened a few of our girls' suitors away many years later.

Outside our married quarter at Moem Barracks, Wewak, 1972, where Rob served with the Second Pacific Islands Regiment.

Charlotte and Georgie at old District Commissioner's house where we lived on the hill in Vanimo in the Sepik during Rob's time with the army there in 1972.

Charlotte with our houseboy, Phillip's son, at Moem Barracks, Wewak 1972.

Charlotte with Georgie, learning to walk in front of officers' mess, Vanimo in 1972. Rob's 2PIR soldiers would often provide us with fish and lobsters from the sea.

Charlotte with friends at Moem Barracks, Wewak 1972.

Rob and soldiers from 2PIR on top of the Hindenburg Wall in Papua New Guinea. He was often away on patrol for six weeks at a time.

With new friends on Muschu Island where our friends, Eric and Eileen Tang, gifted this thatched hut for the local villagers to use as a kindergarden. We spent time on Muschu in the early 70s and also more recently when this photo was taken.

Watching a tribal dance in Wewak. The PIR soldiers often put on such displays.

Our Drominagh at Wallaroo outside Canberra – a bit different to the Irish one. We lived in a caravan while building the house in 1977. We bred Angora Goats and grew almond and walnut trees commercially. We loved to have sundowners on the verandah looking across to the Brindabellas.

My father was pleased when we called our Aussie Drominagh after his family home. Dam behind VW one of three Rob built with a bulldozer. We also erected all the fencing ourselves on weekends. This photo before we planted the almond and walnuts in early 1978.

Not sure how I didn't set the hay bales on fire.

Georgie, a reluctant chef. Hay bales were a wind break for a party.

In front of Johnstown Castle in County Wexford built by the Esmondes in the 15th century. It remained in the family until confiscated by Oliver Cromwell in his bloody rampage of Ireland. It now belongs to the Irish nation.

Viv in 1980s at her home Cilwych in Wales where we often visit.

My mother reclining in the garden at Cloneen, a 300-year-old cottage in Glendalough Co Wicklow where my parents lived after returning to Ireland in 1971.

Charlotte in front of Huntington Castle in County Carlow built by the Esmondes in 1240. It was the setting for the movie, Barry Lyndon. The ghost of Grace O'Malley, well-known in Irish folklore, appears regularly and WB Yeats and Mick Jagger have been guests.

OUR YACHTS

Prauwin *at Myall Lakes 1976 where we spent a wonderful month over Christmas.*

Charlotte Rose *at Fortescue Bay on the Tasman Peninsula with Sue and Don Clark's,* Cascades, *which Don built himself.*

Reveille *in The Whitsundays where we also sailed on* Oceania *from Tasmania, compiling our second photographic book,* Beyond the Shore.

Tasman Isle *in Norfolk Bay, which our apple orchard at Koonya overlooked.*

Oceania *in Port Davey in the South West Wilderness of Tasmania where we spent a month in 2001 taking photos for our first book,* From the Sea, on Tasmania.

Sea Dreams *at anchor in Turkey, 2014. One of our favourite cruising spots. We are presently compiling our third photographic book on the Mediterranean.*

Windermere orchard at Koonya.

The cottage we built for Rob's father at Windermere.

With my horse, Devil, outside our apple sheds. Apple pomace in bins was used to feed my pigs.

With girls and my mother at Port Arthur in 1985 on one of my parents' visits from Ireland. I used to deliver our apple juice there to the Broad Arrow Cafe and around the Tasman Peninsula with a trailer on the back of our Mini Moke.

Sitting beside Max Christmas with the other 'Leading Agents of Australia' Group, including John McGrath and Peter Blackshaw in 1992.

The Tasmanian Auctioneers and Estate Agents Board in 2005. I am at bottom right.

We started The Port Arthur Cider Company at Koonya in the early 80s. We also made fresh apple juice, processing more Tasmanian apples than Cascades or Clements and Marshall and outselling orange juice in the major supermarkets. I wrote columns for the Mercury newspaper. Suggest you try 2 onions instead of 9 in recipe!

With Charlotte and Georgie at the launch of our second photographic coffee table book, Beyond the Shore, *showcasing the sailing waters, seafood and wine on the east coast of Australia. We are presently compiling our fifth book on Australia and the Mediterranean – a new career after selling our real estate business,* Peterswalds, *and close to thirty years in the industry for me.*

Hampton (circa 1890), in Bellerive, which we renovated in 1986.

Vernon in Battery Point (circa 1878) after we painted the outside and restored the heritage listed garden. We sold when Rob had health problems.

With Dibs at Clark's, Cascades, Koonya. Cascades was the outstation for Port Arthur in penal times. Sue and Don won a national heritage award for their renovation of the convict buildings.

Our apartment in Brooke Street overlooking Hobart docks where we lived for 17 years.

View from our apartment in Canberra (where we spend part of the year) to War Memorial and RMC where Rob was a cadet with Eugene when we met.

With Eleanor and Joseph at Nidos in Turkey, Sea Dreams *in background. We love showing our grandchildren the history of the Mediterranean.*

Rob with Charlotte, Hubie, Ru, Ferdi and Stephen at their home on Lake Annecy in the French Alps where we spend time each year.

Rob with Hubie, Ru and Ferdi on Sea Dreams *in Porto Koufo in Greece.*

I have always wanted to go hot air ballooning. I finally did so above the fairy chimneys and bronze-age dwellings carved into cone-shaped rock formations in Cappadocia in central Turkey.

Georgie, Simon, Eleanor and Joseph exploring in Southern Turkey whilst sailing with us on Sea Dreams.

Ashore with Rob in Sardinia. After 50 years together we hope to have many more years of sailing ahead of us.

CHAPTER 23

Waiting for the Returning Soldier

After dropping Rob's mother off at Wollstonecraft, I returned to the house at Illawong to start packing up – for I was to spend the time Rob was away in Vietnam, with my parents in Canberra. My mother had come up to help me pack and look after Charlotte on the trip south. Later that afternoon we were confronted by a black snake slithering under the pine dresser in the kitchen. My mother, being the good Australian bush wife after her experiences in Reidsdale, tried to entice it out with a saucer of milk (she'd read this in a book). I stood nearby to knock it on the head with a spade. Needless to say the snake remained firmly where it was. Eventually a kindly neighbour came, and after discovering it was only a carpet snake and unlikely to inflict harm, removed it in a brown Hessian bag, releasing the poor creature in the bush. How long it had been living in the house watching us I'll never know. 'Days probably,' the neighbour said.

That night in bed I started to read *Death of a President*. I wondered how on earth Jackie Kennedy had got through it all and this made me think my predicament wasn't all that bad.

As I'm editing this memoir, Rob and I are at anchor on *Sea Dreams* in an enchanting bay in front of the Island of Skorpios in Greece where Jackie married Aristotle Onassis. What a magical haven it must have been back then. Although still stunning, much of the privacy they would have enjoyed has long since gone. Now yachts anchor nearby, giving a bird's eye view of the white sandy beaches and Jackie's small blue and white Cyclades bungalow on the shore where she was once photographed swimming naked. Yet the romance of this place still remains, with the melodious sound of goat bells ringing within the olive groves and just a glimpse of 'the Pink House' through the cypress trees.

I was still reading *Death of a President* when the pale dawn shone through the window-panes at Illawong and Charlotte started crying for her morning feed. Sitting in the living room with Gunga Din lolling by my feet, and Charlotte happily sucking away, I felt an ache of such loneliness that I'd never felt before or have felt since.

After a while my mother quietly came in to hand me a cup of tea.

'He'll be fine,' she said, consolingly, putting an arm around my shoulders. 'The time will fly.'

I hoped desperately that she was right.

The bushfires of 1968/69 were rife at this time, ravaging thousands of acres of New South Wales farming land, not to mention the National Parks. My mother and I spent much of that week carrying out instructions from my father in Ijong Street and the local fire brigade to keep hoses on the roof to soak the leaves in the gutter and douse any sparks or ashes. Fortunately the fire only got as far as singeing the huge gumtrees on the border of our garden before it was brought under control.

A removal truck arrived to put Rob's and my belongings into storage and my mother and I headed to Canberra, where I spent a happy, yet worried year at Ijong Street. Unsurprisingly, it wasn't long before both my parents fell totally and hopelessly in love with Charlotte, who miraculously ceased her screaming and turned into the epitome of a well-behaved baby, until she realised she had both my parents wrapped around her little finger.

In fact my mother was so distraught when Rob came home from Vietnam and we left to go to our next posting that I offered to leave Charlotte with her. 'I can always have another,' I said jokingly.

The garden in Ijong Street had matured in the fourteen years since my father had planted it in 1955, the rosemary hedge, pencil pines, and many shrubs providing a rich oasis within a suburb of fairly ordinary homes. The grapevine, covering the back patio, was a haven to sit under and enjoy endless long meals, while the garden became one huge playpen for Charlotte.

After a few weeks I managed to get a job at the local bowling alley at night, so that my mother, who worked at David Jones during the day, could look after Charlotte when I was at work. Three mornings a week I found a job massaging women's faces with a new machine just launched on the market. I also featured on the TV in their advertisements. Yet it wasn't long before I realised this wasn't the profession for me, particularly as I had to haul Charlotte around with me. I then found a temporary job as a secretary at the university, where Charlotte was able to go to the uni crèche for the hours I worked. Juggling a job and a new baby at a time when child-care centres were few and far between proved difficult, so I just had to take what jobs my mother could fit in around.

Canberra, at this time, was different to the Canberra I left behind when I went to New Guinea. Even though Lake Burley Griffin had been there since 1963, the surrounds were more established and it now formed a major part of most people's lives. We suddenly had picnic spots by the water with shady nooks; sailing boats dotting the lake around the new yacht club; islands to sail out to and barbeque on; new bridges to drive over; endless water views from Black Mountain; and walking tracks and bike trails. Where Mrs Lew used to keep her horses at Acton was now totally under water.

All in all, the lake added a novel and beautiful dimension to the Capital. When I wasn't working, I spent many an hour sitting under a huge weeping willow tree on the shore with Charlotte and Gunga Din, reading books or writing letters to Rob. Each day I waited by the mail-box for a letter or a tape in return. Charlotte got to know the sound of a man on a tape recorder, but wasn't sure who he was, even though I told her constantly it was the man in the photo – her father. Our letters and tapes were neither maudlin nor sad. They were full of love and hope for the future when this awful war would end and Rob could come home.

I became great friends with a girl whose husband was killed in action. A number of us gathered on the steps of the chapel at Duntroon to farewell his coffin, draped in the Australian flag with his cap and sword on top. It was a sad day on which we were devastated for her, yet were selfishly glad for ourselves that it wasn't one of our own loved ones who'd tragically fallen.

Once again I scrounged for wood with my father at Collector, now with Charlotte in tow. We went for drives in the country and visited the Cotter dam where Charlotte paddled in the same spot I'd swum in years before. We visited Gill, Colin and their family at the Santa Gertrudis stud they managed for a Canberra dentist – up a long and winding dirt road, past the small and decrepit mining village of Captains Flat, and into the dry hills of Beechborough – a remote property where Charlotte, and Gill's two beautiful children, Andrew and

Allison, grew to know each other. With Colin away doing a course on cattle breeding, I took Gill to the Canberra Hospital where she produced another lovely daughter, Mia. In the bed next door was the wife of my old boyfriend, Phillip. When he came in to visit her I hadn't seen him since I'd told him I was breaking off our romance to go out with Rob. As he'd got pretty upset at that time, I was relieved when he gave me a kiss and said he was glad to see me again.

Rob spent over 13 months in Vietnam, returning in the middle of his tour for his R&R leave for four days to Sydney. His only criterion was to find a hotel room with a bath. In those days that was harder than it sounded. After much searching, I finally found a reasonable motel on the north shore where we spent the four days he was home, with Charlotte staying with his parents in Wollstonecraft for some of that time. During the day we took her to the Botanical Gardens for long walks or otherwise we sat on the beach at Manly watching the waves tumble onto the shore whilst she played in the sand.

When Rob left me in my motel room at three in the morning to go back to Vietnam, the radio was playing *Leaving on a Jet Plane* by Peter Paul and Mary. Every time I hear this song I think of him clutching me in his arms as he gave me a final kiss before heading out the door to another seven months of the unknown.

Rob doesn't talk much about Vietnam, except to say: 'It was a war that had to be fought and I'd no regrets about going.'

Serving as a company second in command with the 5th Battalion he was mostly stationed at the Australian army base at Nui Dat from where they set out to fight the Viet Cong in the dense jungle.

It's not for me to tell his story. I'll leave it for him to do so if he wishes.

I'd like to say I gave the morality of the war a lot of thought, but I didn't. As far as I was concerned, if Rob thought it was worth fighting for, so did I. My main concern was that my husband, the father of my daughter, should get home safely. Looking back now, I can see why it was a war that caused so much controversy and I wonder at Australia's involvement. Yet I realise that at the time it was probably necessary.

But how can war be necessary? When Rob and I were anchored on our yacht, *Sea Dreams* in Split in Croatia we ventured through the mountains to the tragic city of Sarajevo in Bosnia. We stood on the bridge where Crown Prince Ferdinand was assassinated, starting the First World War, one of the most important events in our history. Later, we wandered amidst the market stalls set up in the remains of the Old Town, which was mostly destroyed during the endless siege of the 1990s' war. Seeing the utter destruction and ruination of that city, and so much of Bosnia and Croatia ravaged by snipers and bombs, made me realise how destructive war is. How incredibly cruel people can be to each other. In so many cases it's religious beliefs that are the cause of friction. Surely, if there is a God, that's not what He would have in mind: that neighbours should massacre each other, slaughter each other's children and rape the women because one family is Christian, the other Muslim.

Vera Toll, whose husband, Colin, was in Vietnam with Rob, spent the year in Canberra, when she wasn't working, keeping me company and waiting for the big return. Vera, a divine-looking brunette with the greatest sense of humour, kept me going. She was wonderful with Charlotte, who adored her, not to mention my mother, who found Vera's cheerful company a breath of fresh air, at a time when fresh air was what we needed more than anything else to get us through each day of waiting.

Chapter 23   Waiting for the Returning Soldier

On the night the boys finally came home from Vietnam, Vera and I dolled ourselves up to the nines to meet them off the plane landing at Mascot Airport in Sydney round midnight. Out at the airport, we put a dent in the mudguard of my car as we nervously parked in the jammed car park.

Colin arrived staggering off the plane first and told me with misplaced humour and slightly slurred words: 'So sorry, Ro. The bastard was late and missed the plane in Saigon. I tried to stop it, but couldn't. Reckon he'll have to wait for the next one.'

As you can imagine this freaked me out somewhat and I collapsed into tears, only to look up a few minutes later to see Rob rolling off the back of the plane. It took me quite a while to forgive Colin.

Rob assures me that waiting in line to get off the plane he knew nothing of this. But he had in fact nearly missed the connection in Saigon, due to a mechanical problem on the plane from Nui Dat, only leaping on to it at the last minute.

What was blatantly obvious was they'd had a riotous trip home to celebrate the end of their tour of duty. And why not?

We spent a few days in Sydney for Rob to catch up with his family, before heading off to Wangi on Lake Macquarie for a month's leave. This was not far from the Esmondes' first Australian house at Bonells Bay in 1954. We visited the tiny matchstick bungalow and felt amazed we'd all survived there those years ago. From memory it looked much the same as it did in 1954, although even smaller than I had envisaged. One evening we met William Dobell, the famous artist, at the local RSL Club, where he'd sit for hours at a table in the corner wearing a black beret.

Our little cottage at Wangi was right on the shores of the lake. I found it through an advertisement in the *Sydney*

Morning Herald. It proved to be what the advertisement described: quaint, remote and right on the water. Just what we wanted.

The owner of the cottage, a spritely lady, with a mass of floaty grey hair and wearing a green woollen twin set, a tweed skirt and a set of shining white pearls, alarmed us somewhat one sunny morning when she arrived at the front door to announce: 'I've come to collect my husband.'

Rob and I looked at each other in consternation. 'Your husband?'

'Yes. My husband. I left him behind.'

Rob shook his head and cast his eyes into the house and then back to the lady. 'I'm afraid we haven't seen him. Where's he likely to be?'

'On top of the cupboard in the bedroom.'

'In the bedroom we're sleeping in?' I exclaimed in horror.

'Yes, the room overlooking the lake.'

With this startling piece of news she rushed inside, whipped a chair from the kitchen, carried it to the bedroom and removed a cardboard box full of ashes from on top of the cupboard. After a cup of tea, during which time she told us the poor man had fallen out of a tree in their daughter's back garden and broken his neck, she bade us farewell and left with her husband safely tucked under her arm.

After a few days in Port Macquarie, Vera and Colin came back down to stay with us. We enjoyed a couple of weeks' swimming, fishing, cooking up feasts and playing cards, with the odd vino and beer to keep us lubricated. At the bottom of the garden we had a small wooden rowboat we'd take out on the lake. One day we caught the largest crab anyone had ever seen, later cooking it over a makeshift fire by the water's edge. Charlotte spent hours feeding the ducks and swans scavenging within the tall rushes, and there was a huge weeping willow to swing off at the end of the garden and a leafy gumtree to picnic beneath. We had meals at the Wangi pub and I went to the Wangi church for mass on Sunday, almost feeling part of the local congregation.

Like Cloneen, this cottage was what people hope to find at the end of a journey. Or could it have been that it was the beginning of our journey together as a family after Vietnam that made it so special?

Yet it wasn't all roses. Charlotte was taking time to get to know Rob. She was often furious to find I had this strange man in my bed and refused to believe he *was* her father. Up until then, she'd understandably thought my father was hers too. But after a few weeks, things settled down as they got to know each other and became the apple of each other's eye.

Only recently Rob and I returned to Wangi where we spent the night in the Wangi Pub, not much changed over the years. The beds we slept in were definitely from a time gone by: lumpy mattresses and rickety legs. There was even a 1950s' walnut dressing table and wardrobe ensemble with a tarnished oval mirror and an orange chenille bedspread. Before driving on to Gill and Colin at Tamworth, we searched for our little cottage on the shores of the lake. We thought we found it. One of the few still remaining much the same as it was in the sixties. Or were we romanticising? Maybe it had long since gone the way of others and been replaced by the smart new lakeside mansions. We also hunted for the house I'd lived in as a child in Bonells Bay, but alas it was not where I remembered it. Stopping to change a flat tyre, we chatted with a couple of locals who told us the new high school was built on the same site as the one-teacher school I went to all those years ago and that the St John of God Brothers' home for the disadvantaged boys was now an upmarket housing estate.

As with most things in life, time moves on and waits for no-one.

CHAPTER 24

Adjusting Again... Kapooka

Our first posting after Rob returned from Vietnam, was to Kapooka Army Camp ten miles from the town of Wagga Wagga in the Riverina district of New South Wales. Kapooka was expanded during the Vietnam War to be able to give initial military training to all regular soldiers and national servicemen before continuing to their corps training.

Rob was happy to secure a position as Major Training, soon becoming involved in his job, preparing the new recruits for Vietnam. After the initial euphoria of having Rob home, I felt at a bit of a loss. I was left on my own with Charlotte and without a car for hours on end in our tiny fibro married quarter amidst rows of identical quarters sitting side by side with little privacy, about two miles before one reached the barracks. It was an odd set up, as most army camps were in those days. It seemed to be government policy to isolate defence personnel in settlements on the outside of towns, making mixing or socialising with the local community difficult. Now the government tries to integrate everyone within the community. As in New Guinea, the officers at Kapooka lived up one end and the other ranks down the other. In the middle was the inevitable canteen. Unlike New Guinea, we went into the town of Wagga to the doctor and dentist.

During the time Rob was in Vietnam I'd become more

independent. And now suddenly to be stuck at home was depressing. Being brutally honest I was jealous of Rob. He was able to go off to work, have a drink at the Mess with his fellow officers, and arrive home in time for dinner, whilst I had many hours to fill in on my own with Charlotte. There were other wives of course, but many of them didn't have children and worked during the day as well.

There was also a dreadful drought, causing the worst mouse plague in the Riverina's history. If one opened the knife and fork drawer the blighters ran up your arm. They'd also play the fiddle on the end of the bed, eat their way through the linen and frighten Charlotte out of her wits in her cot, even nibbling on her toes. Nothing could be done to stop them coming in droves from the parched fields looking for water.

Mere mousetraps were not up to the job. So Rob set up an ingenious trap. To a chair in the kitchen he attached a broom with a piece of cheese at the end, under which he placed a bucket of water. The mice, and sometimes the odd rat, would run up the broom handle to get the cheese and fall into the bucket. We caught hundreds this way, yet there seemed to be thousands more. It was probably rather cruel but we were desperate.

In the summer it was stinking hot; in the winter freezing cold. Yet it wasn't all doom and gloom. We made good friends and played lots of golf. Rob broke his wrist when playing rugby and had to play golf one handed. He even became quite good. When he got his second hand back in use, his game never recovered, his balance being all out of kilter.

Our house was a typical army married quarter with a small living room to the front, basic kitchen with lino on the floor at the rear, three tiny bedrooms and a bathroom and laundry.

Chapter 24 Adjusting Again...Kapooka

The floorboards were bare, with the inevitable boot polish mark around previous inhabitants' carpet squares. Worst of all it stank. One day, when I was entertaining a girlfriend in the living room, I pointed with a broom to where I felt the smell was coming from in the corner and accidentally tapped the ceiling. In a second it collapsed down around us with many of the dead mice from the plague falling into our laps.

At weekends we went for long walks and drives into the countryside. As usual we had numerous dinner parties (after we were moved to another house) and functions at the Officers' Mess, where, I believe, Susan Peacock, the wife of Andrew Peacock, our then Defence Minister, did a famous dance on the table. The Mess here didn't have the character of the one in Port Moresby, but it was a good place to have a party or a barbeque in the grounds. I also found a horse to ride on a sheep station nearby and after a couple of months Charlotte had a few little friends to play with. One, unfortunately, slammed the door on her finger, cutting the top off, whereupon we rushed her to the doctor with the missing bit on ice. However, there was nothing he could do, apart from watch her father, the brave Vietnam vet, nearly faint on the floor. Fortunately it's hardly noticeable today, although she's had to adjust to using another finger for writing.

One scorching day I arrived home to see all the rubber hoses we owned on the roof, sprouting water in all directions, Rob's new 'air conditioner' at work. Not popular with the army, but it gave us slight relief. In winter we huddled around the small open fire, our only form of heating. Colonel East, a small, genial, dapper gentleman with a great sense of humour was Rob's Commanding Officer. For some reason he made rather a fuss of me. One evening at the mess, as I performed my officer's wife's duty and enthusiastically welcomed the new

Commanding Officer to replace him, Colonel East pulled me over and said, 'The king is dead, Rosemary. Long live the king'.

I was mortified, missing him enormously when he went.

The Catholic padre was also an interesting character. I believe he's now back in Ireland married. I'm glad about this, as we spent many a night around our fire at Kapooka discussing the lonely plight of the Catholic priest. Being Irish he was a great party man, enjoying the odd tipple. He was also rather a hit with the ladies, so I'm sure he leads a much happier life these days.

It was fascinating watching the new National Service recruits arriving at the barracks with long shaggy 1970s' hair, and then to sit at Mass on Sunday and see them walk up the aisle with basin cuts, having been to the barber the day before. I felt sorry for them on the whole, for they seemed so young to be going off to the war. Yet a lot of them were looking forward to the challenge, in some cases even getting quite excited. And a number who I've since met up with have told me they enjoyed the comradeship of the other recruits and still do, although I know there are many who were irreparably damaged.

I used to get rather distracted at Mass on Sundays, watching the new recruits taking communion, and wondering how the padre was managing to conduct the service without some obvious discomfort, after such a party in the mess or one of our houses the night before. I can only imagine the altar wine was a good 'hair of the dog'.

The National Service recruits were not there by choice. They were there purely because their date of birth came up in the draw. Rob's job was to turn them from soft civilians into hardy soldiers in an obscenely short space of time. It was not an easy job, but one he enjoyed and was good at.

It was a long drive from Wagga to Canberra and back, with

Charlotte usually dreadfully car sick and Gunga Din sitting up in the back slopping everywhere. We passed the Dog on the Tucker Box at Gundagai umpteen times on the way to visit my parents and catch up with friends back in the Capital. Often my mother hopped on an alarmingly small airplane to visit us, a couple of times with Gill's Andrew in tow. I remember feeling so lonely when they went home. Rob was studying, finishing his degree by correspondence, so spent a fair bit of time with his head in books. In those days one didn't graduate from Duntroon with a degree, as one does these days. I desperately wanted to get a job. Yet with Charlotte at such a young age, and being so far out of town, it was difficult to think of anything I could do, so instead I immersed myself in the garden and started a correspondence course in creative writing.

One morning, when I went to get Charlotte from her bed she had disappeared; Gunga Din too. After much panic, we discovered them both ambling along the road about four blocks away, Gunga Din in front, Charlotte attached to his lead at the rear. He was so gentle with her, but terrified the milkman, postman and anyone else who called.

Anzac Days are of utmost importance in Australian country towns. It was Rob's job to speak at remembrance services around the Riverina area. I accompanied him, helping the Country Women's Association afterwards with lunch. Later, Rob would play *two-up* with the men and I gossiped with the ladies, discovering what life was like living in a country town or on remote sheep stations, for some of the women had travelled many miles to proudly watch *their* returned soldiers march.

Yet one of the things that irked both Rob and me was that although he'd just returned from Vietnam he wasn't welcomed into a Returned Soldiers Club, a dreadful insult to all those who served in Vietnam. I remember the indignity when we were refused entry to one RSL club down the south coast.

'Sorry mate, you've got to be a member,' a smart-looking fellow wearing a tweed coat and sporting a neat moustache informed him.

Rob gave him a generous smile. 'I've just come back from Vietnam. Could someone sign me in perhaps?'

'I'm afraid not.'

Oh boy! Did I feel like giving him a piece of my mind! Instead we left meekly.

The RSL had been less than welcoming to any Vietnam Veterans – a bone of contention for many years. Now, of course, many of the RSL clubs are full of them, which is a good thing as many of the older veterans have sadly passed away.

Two things happened during our time at Kapooka. I fell pregnant with our second daughter, Georgina, and my parents dropped a bombshell by announcing they were returning to Ireland to live. We were over the moon with the forthcoming arrival of our new addition to the family, but were sad to be losing my parents.

For many years my father had had a hankering to return to his beloved Ireland. Now the opportunity had arisen. He loved Australia and had built himself up a good business in Canberra with his Braddon Flyscreens. Yet he assured us all that unless he died on Irish soil it was unlikely the Good Lord would find him and welcome him through the gates of Heaven. We all believed him and my mother certainly wasn't going to be the one to put it to the test. After all, my father had been over fifty when we came to Australia so most of his life had been spent in Ireland. We were all settled in Australia, or New Zealand, apart from Viv, who was now married to Tim in Wales. Gill and Colin were still at Beechborough. Dibs was living with Peter on the remote archaeological dig on the south island of New Zealand, and Eugene had finished his second tour to Vietnam and was living in Brisbane.

As I mentioned before, my father's brother, Jimmy, who had run the gift shop in Glendalough in Co Wicklow, had died. Wheelchair bound for many years, he'd managed to run the shop during the Irish summer, and holiday in Spain during the Irish winter. This sounded perfect for my parents when the opportunity was put to them to take over the shop. They could live in Glendalough for the Irish summer and come to Canberra every second Christmas to look after my father's business when it was at its busiest in the summer months. (He took on a partner to run it when he wasn't there). It would also give them plenty of time to keep in touch with their grandchildren, who they were sad to leave. If it had been left to my mother I don't think she would have gone at that time.

So with mixed feelings one early autumn morning we saw them off at Canberra Airport, bound for the Western Provinces of Kenya to catch up with my father's brother Donal still a missionary there. It was seventeen years since they'd seen each other. Flying via Mauritius and Nairobi they were met by Donal at Kisumu beside Lake Victoria. Later Donal took them on to his mission at Eregi amongst the Balluylia people, who'd accepted him as their *Mukhulundu mukhali Muno* (clan leader), where they viewed the Church of Pius X he'd had built and dedicated to his brother, Eugene Esmonde, VC, DSO. In 1957, he saw the need for a new church in Muloli to cater for the fast growing Catholic community. He laboured tirelessly, writing letters of appeal for funds from his large group of friends and benefactors in Europe and America. My parents spent a couple of weeks helping Donal in the mission and visiting outlying villages where he was erecting small brick buildings to serve as meeting places and schools. Donal's mission covered about 10,000 square miles, so as you can imagine he was constantly on the go.

Leaving him at the airport at Kisumu, my parents hopped on the same tiny Cessna that had brought them in, flying to Nairobi and on to London and eventually Dublin. When they arrived in Ireland my father knelt down and kissed the ground.

He wrote: *…it proved to this exile at any rate, what the poet, Goldsmith, meant when he wrote: 'Lives there a man with soul so dead who never to himself has said "this is my own, my native land."'*

When I next saw my mother it was in the far top corner of Papua New Guinea in the Sepik, where we were stationed at Moem Barracks outside Wewak.

Chapter 25

Wewak in the Sepik

'We'll have a holiday when we get there, and I can be with you for the birth,' Rob said.

I should have known better.

The idea was that we'd arrive in our new posting before Rob started work as a Company Commander with the 2nd Pacific Islands Regiment at Moem Barracks. I could have the baby, with Rob there to help look after Charlotte.

When we arrived at Moem Barracks, Rob was soon sent on patrol near the Indonesian Border, leaving Charlotte and me on our own to cope with the arrival of Georgie. This I did some six weeks later in the Wewak General Hospital set on the peninsula of Cape Boram.

Rob didn't set eyes on her until she was nearly three months old.

On the 21st March I awoke in the middle of the night, knowing I was in labour. Shoving Charlotte in the car I drove to some friends' married quarter up the road at Moem.

'I need to go NOW,' I exclaimed to a startled Kate when she opened the front door in response to my frantic banging.

Without wasting a minute I bundled Charlotte inside the door for Kate to look after and Jim, her husband, kindly drove me into the hospital at Boram, driving off hurriedly after dropping my suitcase inside the front door.

In those days men were still not involved in the birthing ritual, and certainly not with someone else's wife. I stood forlornly in the corridor before a pretty young nurse bustled out from a back room, and took me to a ward overlooking the beach. Fortunately at this stage I'd made friends with a number of other army wives as well, who took it in turns to sit with me during the labour. The doctor, later to become a friend of ours, took it all a bit too casually, eventually ambling in from the beach, wearing a pair of shorts, T-shirt and rubber thongs, to do the final delivery after I'd been in labour for some sixteen hours.

Georgina Anne Peterswald made her way joyfully into this world on the 22nd of March, 1972. I was ecstatic with my gorgeous new addition, if somewhat exhausted and lonely without Rob. Once she'd been washed and weighed she was placed inside a meat-safe on castors.

The next morning, a nurse with a mass of steel wool hair and a no-nonsense manner arrived in a flurry. 'Here,' she said airily, handing me a sheet and a pair of scissors, 'I'm afraid we've run out of nappies and we're short staffed.' Somewhat startled I took the sheet and started cutting.

Bronwyn Walkem, who, with her husband, Graeme, are fellow Tasmanians and great friends of ours from our Wewak days, also had her daughter in the same hospital, just six months later.

'Opposite me was a Sepik woman. She had her *pikinini* with her all the time, mostly attached to her breast,' Bronwyn said, as we sat on the verandah of their home looking across Coles Bay on Tasmania's east coast, to the spectacular rock formations that form The Hazards. We were sipping a Tasmanian Pinot, whilst devouring flathead Graeme had caught that morning off the Fisheries. 'That *pikinini* never cried,' Bronwyn laughed, 'whilst Simone screamed non-stop from her meat-safe. For some reason the Sepik women were allowed to keep their *pikininis* with them day and night, whilst ours had to be kept in another room unless we were feeding them.'

She was right, for the woman opposite me had also kept her baby with her all the time. And what's more she had the help of many enthusiastic *wontoks,* making me wish dreadfully for a relation of my own.

Early the next morning, I returned to Moem Barracks with my new baby. I decided that even though the overworked staff were kind, one day in the hospital was enough. I could survive at home just as well.

Georgie was the only white baby in the hospital, so caused quite a stir. Not only were the other babies black, Georgie, like Charlotte, was the palest blonde with vivid blue eyes. As I waited to be picked up outside the hospital the next morning, a group of *wantoks* hovering out front waiting to visit their relations in the hospital, came up to me and pointed wondrously at her white skin and fairy floss hair.

I only became slightly nervous when a tribesman, wearing nothing other than a tattered loin-cloth, with a huge carved bone through his nose and strings of heavy beads dangling from his ears, leaned his spear against the wall and asked with a scarlet *betel nut* beam, '*Mi holim?*'

I was a bit concerned he may, at the very least, want to kidnap her back to his tribe. Yet he was so gentle and ecstatic when he held her in his scrawny arms that I felt quite guilty for my thoughts.

Meantime, whilst on patrol near the station town of Telefomin on the border of Sandaun and Gulf Provinces, Rob was doing his utmost to survive a horrendous case of dysentery.

He assures me he was going through far worse pain than my labour could possibly have been. I have my doubts.

The Sepik region is a wonderland of islands, glorious coastlines, intricate river systems and mountain ranges. First colonised by the Germans in 1885, the area soon attracted mercenaries, explorers, traders and missionaries. Yet it is the timeless history of the Sepik people themselves that provides the mystery and exotic folklore of this fascinating area, the gem being the mighty Sepik River of some 1126 kilometres. One of the great river systems of the world, the Sepik is supposedly the largest freshwater wetland system in Asia Pacific. People living along its banks depend heavily on it for both food and transportation, with tourists finding it an unspoilt haven with labyrinthine tributaries, not unlike the Amazon, boasting remote tribal villages with some of the most unique carvings in the world being produced there.

Apart from Vanimo, near the Indonesian border, which I was to visit later, Wewak was in the prettiest setting I'd ever come across. With its iridescent turquoise water, golden sandy beaches and spectacular palm trees gently swaying in the light breeze it was a central part of our lives for those of us stationed at Moem Barracks. Situated at the foot of a headland with a marvellous view over the coast and then to the islands of Kairiru and Muschu, Wewak has a small wharf, almost to the centre of town, for local fishing boats and canoes. A longer one for bigger ships is to the east of the Windjammer Hotel along the bay formed by Wewak Point and Cape Boram. The headland where Eric and Eileen Tang, who were to become great friends of ours, lived and still do for part of the year, is a haven of bungalows nestled into the hillside amidst flourishing tropical gardens gazing out to the Bismarck sea.

Up here is the Seaview Hotel, known as the Sepik in our

day, with a heavenly outside gazebo restaurant built on poles overlooking the ocean and totally open on all sides. It was exotic and romantic. Behind the cane bar, empty wine and liquor bottles stood like a battalion of drunken soldiers on the shelves, tokens of what the patrons had consumed over the years. When we left Wewak at the end of our tour, quite a few were ours.

Covered in a maze of tangled vines with hurricane lanterns hanging from the rafters, and candles in Chianti bottles on the tables casting a spectral glow, the restaurant was an alluring place to dine. One evening I returned to the table from the loo – to Rob smoking his pipe and gazing out over the sea, contemplating, as he is inclined to do. 'This is what heaven's all about,' I said, sliding down on the wooden bench and picking up my Bundy and Coke.

The Sepik Hotel was a spot that saw many a romance begin and where the odd illicit affair was clandestinely conducted. Not that this was entirely possible in such a small community, but a couple of times it was difficult to miss a husband playing footsies under the table with another man's wife, or to be unaware of eyes locking across the table. Together with the Windjammer Hotel on the beach, it was where Rob and I celebrated anniversaries and birthdays, either on our own, at our table perched on the end of the gazebo, or with a large gathering of rowdy friends. 'Let's have a meal at the Sepik,' was all that was required to get a group together at a moment's notice.

The main street in Wewak comprised a number of trade stores, the largest and best being Tang Mow's owned by Eric Tang and his family and started years before by his industrious father. When Eric was only very young his father had made the long journey from Wewak to the eastern suburbs of Sydney where he'd deposited Eric in Trinity Grammar – neither of them speaking a word of English. This, as you can imagine, was somewhat traumatic for both father and son. Eric's father was an amazing man. Arriving in Rabaul from China when he was just thirteen he managed to secure a job as a carpenter. From there he came to Wewak where he started his trade store before going home to take a wife in his small village back in China. He brought her by boat to New Guinea and they built up Tang Mow's, still thriving to this day. During the war the Japanese took them as prisoners to Muschu Island off the coast where they were held for some years. Numerous articles have been written about the Tang family, particularly Eric's energetic and enterprising mother, who became a legend in the Wewak area.

In our day there was a small dress boutique, a coffee shop and a chemist of sorts. There was even a travel agent, where the gorgeous Eileen worked. For those of us at Moem it was the 'thing to do' to head into town on a Saturday morning to shop, have a coffee, or browse the colourful markets where we bought our weekly supply of fruit and vegetables. Later we'd stop off for lunch at either the Windjammer Hotel or golf club on the way back to Moem.

We celebrated my sixtieth birthday at the Windjammer with Eric and Eileen; our first visit to Wewak since we left in 1973.

'Where would you like to have your birthday?' Rob asked one freezing cold evening in Hobart, knowing I've a hatred for huge celebration parties for milestone birthdays, particularly ones for as ancient an age as this.

I'd always had a hankering to go back to New Guinea. This was the opportunity to do so. I remembered the Windjammer as being perched on the edge of the beach, nestled within swaying palms – huge verandahs opening languidly to the breeze, the sweet smell of jasmine and honeysuckle mingling with mosquito coils and the tangy salt air; frangipani and bougainvillea flowers covering the sandy beach; gorgeous multi-coloured butterflies playing in the trees alive with birdsong; children with glistening ebony skins digging for cockles and hunting for shells, and others frolicking in the surf. This is where I wanted my birthday celebration to be.

I was not disappointed.

It was almost as I remembered though possibly a little fancier today – with magnificent artefacts, native paintings and gigantic carved stools around the outside bar on the back verandah overlooking the beach. Sir Hugo, boasting a Jimmy Edwards handlebar moustache – and the presence to go with it – was now the proud owner. He was a friend of Ron Firns, who I worked for in Moresby. Sadly he told me Ron had died only the year before.

The stunning young waitresses, who were possibly from the Trobriands, were great hostesses. The Chinese banquet of seaweed soup, coral trout, chilli prawns, oysters mornay, barbequed pork and village greens was mouth-watering; although I could have done without the blaring TV in the corner, not an asset to this setting, but a 'must have' for the Pacific Islanders these days. Even one hundred and twenty kenos for a fairly average bottle of wine didn't spoil my night. Sadly the Sepik Hotel has not escaped quite as easily as the Windjammer, for it has now turned into a hostel of sorts with loads of plastic and lino.

And yes Wewak had changed too. Gone are some of the buildings, others dilapidated, new ones here and there. Yet there is no taking away from Wewak's natural beauty – her endless blue waters and swaying palms; the yacht club – a romantic timber and palm *haus win* on the shores of the bay; *meris* fishing with nets, men in dugout canoes, *pikininis* playing in the mudflats or on the white sandy beaches – their mothers huddling under palms or corrugated iron humpies keeping a wary eye. Hundreds of Pacific Islanders still idle happily along the side of the road; overloaded trucks of workers, squashed in like glistening sardines, head home in the dusky twilight, while Taun market is still a thriving mass of bright umbrellas and colourful *meris* squatting in the midst of runny nosed *pikininis*, artefacts, tropical fruits and vegetables, live cockerels, baby goats and pigs. The main street is still much the same. Tang Mow's down the end, three times the size it used to be, and across the road, their massive supermarket. Recently Eileen told me that when excavating out the back – to make room for a car park– they unearthed a live bomb from the Second World War, which had to be hurriedly disposed of in the sea. Evidently there could be still quite a few such bombs buried around Wewak.

George Seeto's and other smaller trade stores are not much changed, but there's a brand spanking new bank and Guard Dog Security patrols the town. And what is a town without a huge *Haus Bet* packed with gamblers? No fancy TAB here – but hundreds clawing at the wire to throw their money on the horses back in Australia. Unlike years ago, this day we were the only Europeans to walk the streets, often being stopped by Guard Dog Security and warned of pick-pockets. Yet to me it was still the same Wewak; the unmistakable smell of dust and human sweat, mixed with the aroma of cooked fish, wood smoke and tropical flowers – with people on the whole friendly and happy to see us.

Unlike the Moresby of today, Wewak is relatively safe, although most of the expats employ security guards to patrol their homes and sleep with guns under their beds. One of the Chinese traders told us that one night, when he was having dinner with a friend above his trade store, Thugs (known as rascals) broke in and tied them all up in the bath, taking their money and threatening them with knives and guns. Another night he was getting back in his car after a game of tennis and had his throat slit. Somehow he survived, the scar still there to remind him of the horror.

'Mind you,' he told me in a matter of fact way, 'that can happen anywhere in the world today.'

In the early seventies we were given an introduction to the Tangs by mutual friends at Kapooka who'd been to Wewak previously. Many of my memories of parties in Wewak were at the Tangs' home on Seaview Road. *Mu mus* in the garden, where Eric would bury a stuffed and seasoned pig under the mango tree, cover it in banana leaves and let it steam all day. And then, when all was ready for devouring, we'd perch around white-clothed tables overlooking the ocean, kero lamps casting a warm glow, mosquito coils burning at our feet. For hours we danced under the frangipani, paw paw and mango trees on the front lawn, wearing long floral halter-necked dresses, or minis and cropped tops, our nut brown midriffs glistening in the heat. With hibiscus flowers in our hair, we sometimes partied until the sun came up over the islands, before crawling into bed exhausted. The next day we'd meet on one of the local beaches and water ski and swim under a canopy of umbrella palms with children frolicking in the sparkling sapphire water.

After a leisurely picnic we'd return home late in the afternoon with tired and happy children, or otherwise one of us would say: 'Let's have a fondue at our place,' and we'd take it in turns to have a 'do'.

When I sat on the Tangs' verandah on my birthday trip,

sipping an icy cold gin and tonic as a spectacular crimson sunset dipped below the horizon, I could almost see us then; under the paw paw tree, dancing in the cool breeze to Francoise Hardy or the Rolling Stones. And then I could see, too, the children squatting happily on the lawn, sucking the flesh of a juicy mango, drinking the milk from a coconut, and making each other flimsy necklaces from flowers from the spectacular frangipani tree.

Moem Barracks is reached along a palm-fringed road straddling a white sandy beach some ten miles out of Wewak. Our first house at Moem was at the southern end of the barracks, situated amongst the sergeants' and other ranks' quarters, where, next door, a bulky, bald headed sergeant bellowed endlessly at his unfortunate wife and children. Nowadays he may have been diagnosed with post-Vietnam Stress or post traumatic stress – such an illness not recognised in those days. Many a night I can remember cringing inside our house as he ranted, yelled and shouted, banging a stick against the wall. Every now and then I would hear his wife give a meek reply and a child would whimper. One evening the wife came over with the children and I gave them refuge.

'Why don't you leave him?' I asked.
'Where would we go?'
'Back to Australia.'
'Unless the army pays the fare I couldn't afford it.'
'Have you reported him?'
'No.'
'Should I do it for you?'
'No...it will just make it worse.'

So she stayed. And I wondered, and still wonder, how many wives with traumatised husbands did the same, until it all became too much and they finally fled. Or the husband managed to get counselling to try and put the horrors of what he went through behind him.

With Rob away on patrol, the girls and I lived here for two months waiting for our permanent house to become available up the Officers' end, where the houses were more established and closer to the Mess.

The second day I was at Moem, Colleen, slim and blonde, arrived on my doorstep, dressed superbly in a fascinating home creation of a long floral dress with splits up the side (which was to become her trademark) and with a hibiscus flower in her hair. Colleen had a knack with a sewing machine. She made us extraordinary outfits. On one occasion, when she was not sure what she should wear to a function in the Mess, she whipped a curtain off her window, turning it into a stunning gown. A few days later she returned it to the window, but not before using it as a tablecloth for a Japanese banquet. We were all in awe, particularly me, for I was not known for my sewing skills. But sewing wasn't Colleen's only skill. She also sketched an uncanny charcoal likeness of me, as she shared a glass of Chardonnay and a long dinner with Rob and me around the table in the *haus win* in the garden of our married quarter. I still have it, though, looking in the mirror, the likeness has sadly moved away somewhat.

Charlotte at age three, didn't immediately take to Georgie as one would have thought. Upsetting all the crockery and cutlery from the kitchen cupboards onto the floor, she turned around and bit one of the small girls who'd come to visit, causing a hurried trip back to Boram Hospital. Yet who could blame her for feeling neglected and jealous? With Rob still away and in a strange country, and with a new baby, I wasn't able to give her as much time as I should. I'd assured her she was getting a playmate. This tiny uninteresting bundle that took up so much of my time wasn't what she'd been promised.

With Rob still away I moved us lock stock and barrel in a Land Rover with the help of Phillip, our wonderful houseboy. Adjoining a field at the rear leading down to the beach, our new abode, like the married quarters in Moresby, sat on stilts in a lush tropical garden. Underneath, a thick mass of palms and shrubbery provided an ideal place to hang our cane basket chairs. When I went back to visit, the year of my sixtieth birthday, our house looked rather the worse for wear; borers in the walls and floor, the garden in ruins and louvres hanging in tatters from the windows, peeling paint and rubbish strewn everywhere. A sad sight all in all, yet there was no taking away from the magical position, looking across the green fields to the tall palms straddling the snow-white sandy beach.

I was lucky enough to inherit Phillip in 1972 from the previous occupants of our new married quarter. He was a total gem. A wiry Sepik, with the eyes of a cocker spaniel and a whopping big smile, he was amazing with the girls – mainly as he had five children of his own. He lived in a small fibro one-room shack at the bottom of our garden, going home to his village nearby one day a week, awful, now that I think of it. At the time it was how things were done. We were told he and the other houseboys were grateful for the money they earned (the worldly amount of about eight dollars a week), in Phillip's case allowing him to put food in the mouth of his large brood. I've never felt more at home with a babysitter in my life. When we were last at Moem I enquired if anyone knew where he was, but, sadly, no-one had any idea who Phillip was, or where to start looking.

One of Phillip's sons died when we were at Moem. Knocking on the door early one morning, he announced, 'Pikinini belong me dai pinnis.'

I looked at him in horror. 'Dai pinnis? Dead?'

He nodded his head sadly and I could see the tears in his eyes. Moving forward I put an arm around his scrunched up black shoulders. After we had both recomposed ourselves he asked for the day off to bury him. I still wonder how he came to work the next day, even though I begged him to take the week off, a month even, to recover. One of his other sons used to come to work with him often. He and Charlotte became great friends, spending hours playing under the house in a makeshift sand pit, conversing in a common language, being neither English nor pidgin. Listening to Charlotte's boys play with their school friends, when they first went to a village school at Le Chatelard in the French Alps a few years ago, I realised that children need no common language to be able to play happily for hours on end.

Rob enticed a few of the soldiers to help him build a wonderful *haus win* (a palm covered outside entertaining area) in the garden adjoining our neighbours, Dawn and Dick. Here we spent hours partying under hurricane lamps with music blaring from our new Pioneer stereo system bought from Tang Mow's. The *haus win* was particularly popular for long drawn-out fondues, Christmas lunch (as none of us had extended families at Moem we mostly joined together) and entertaining visiting dignitaries from Australia, until it sadly blew down with a huge bang one night in an horrendous electrical storm.

I'm not sure Dick has ever forgiven me for leaving the door of his car straddling a pole under his house. After borrowing it in a flurry, to rush Phillip to hospital when he cut his hand, I was backing out when disaster struck. It took three months to get a replacement door, during which time he and Dawn drove around Wewak and the barracks with a plastic covering, making me feel guilty every time I saw them. But that was Wewak for you.

One night, with Rob away on patrol, I returned from a party to find a snake on our front steps. I was proud of myself when I killed it by hurling a monstrous rock at its head. Calmly removing the slithery carcass I then proceeded upstairs, carrying Georgie in her bassinet, and holding Charlotte by the hand. The next day it was identified as a Papuan Taipan, one of the deadliest snakes in the world. Another time, when walking across to the beach through the long grass behind our house I encountered a huge python. I left it snoozing happily in the midday sun. Quite often one had to stop on the road into town to give way to these gentle beasts that were using the hot surface as a sun bed.

We purchased our seafood under the house, as a local villager would arrive most weeks with huge eskies filled to the brim with mouth-watering coral trout, Spanish mackerel or other scrumptious fish straight from the ocean. From a hessian bag, he'd drag squirming live crabs tied up with string ready for our perusal. Half an hour later the crab would be in the pot upstairs. One day a particularly gigantic one got loose. Phillip and I spent ages trying to catch it amongst the rocks and ferns before Phillip eventually cornered it, handing it back to the fishmonger none the worse for wear.

During this time, Rob spent many weeks away on patrol in areas like Telefomin, the Sepik Valley, Bewani Mountains and Milne Bay. With his company he also had numerous stints at the outstation of Vanimo, some two hundred and fifty miles up the coast towards Jayapura. From here they patrolled the border into Indonesia, stopping renegades from crossing over into New Guinea. For some reason wives and families were not allowed to visit Vanimo. This caused great contention. On one occasion, Rob's genial Company Commander from Vietnam, was flying to Vanimo the next day. After a few glasses of wine had given me a bad case of Dutch courage, I accepted his offer of a lift. All was well until a senior officer's wife arrived in a fluster on my doorstep at crack of dawn the next morning.

'My husband's furious…all hell will break loose if you dare go,' she warned me, looking as though she hadn't slept a wink, worrying about the possible horrendous repercussions of such a rash venture.

I was also told by the Commander of Papua New Guinea's Defence Force, who happened to be in Wewak at the time, that if I did go it would be the end of Rob's career.

'Your husband will never go past the rank of major if you get on that plane,' I was berated in no uncertain terms. 'What you must realise, Rosemary, is that the army comes first, family, second.'

I didn't go that time, after gentle persuasion from Michael Hughes, a charming single officer, who thought I may indeed destroy Rob's chances of promotion. But after rules were slackened, Charlotte, Georgie, and I did go a few months later, staying for many weeks. It was such a success that I was persuaded to make a return visit for a party – funded by some of Vanimo's locals kindly putting their spare change in a tin on the bar in the Officers' Mess. The tin was labelled: 'Bring Ro back for the Party.'

On my first visit to Vanimo I wore one of Colleen's creations – a two-piece yellow outfit with a bare midriff and a tiny mini skirt. As it was, Colleen and the other wives were determined I should make a good impression in Vanimo, hence doing a great deal for the cause of 'wives wishing to visit'. Rob arranged for us to stay in the old District Commissioner's residence up the top of the hill near Central Lookout, deserted some time before by the District Commissioner and his wife who'd moved to a new modern bungalow down by the beach. Built of timber and woven palms, with no doors or windows, our temporary abode had neither electricity nor running water, none of which mattered, for it sat in a glorious tropical oasis of frangipani, hibiscus, and tall pandanus with magnificent views over The Babelsberg Strait.

Here Georgie learned to walk – her stage a large open living area with rustic timber floors and gigantic knobbly poles running at intervals to hold the thatched palm roof up. With no stove (maybe the DC and his wife took it with them) we cooked all our meals by fondue or on a stone fireplace out the back. I bathed the girls in a red plastic bucket under the shade of a huge palm. They looked very lovely with their blonde hair bleached by the sun and little bodies as brown as berries despite my covering them in sunscreen. It was much warmer than my first years in Australia at Reidsdale, yet reminiscent of the times I'd bathed in the old tin bath. Mosquito nets protected us from determined insects and a gentle breeze wafted through the open windows. Overhead, a huge fan turned languidly below the rafters with mosquito coils sending spirals of soft grey smoke to linger in the humid air. For hours we watched geckos playing on the walls, having bets as to which one would get to the top first.

Vanimo is set on a picturesque harbour formed around a hill. Almost an island, it is joined to the coastline by a tongue of flat land – just the place for an airstrip. It was generally known that cars, animals and people gave way to the incoming or outgoing aircraft. A bit tricky as one got little warning of these approaching hazards.

Below the wings of the plane as I'd flown in, beautiful white sandy beaches spanned both sides of the Peninsula. The Officers' Mess was situated on the most picturesque of these. I saw the square pontoon bobbling in the sapphire water in front of the Mess and, just back from the beach, the palmed roofed *haus win*, which became the focus point for sundowners and Anzac Day's mandatory game of *two up*.

Charlotte and I, with Georgie in her pram, ambled down to the Mess most late afternoons and had a swim on the beach. In the cool of the evening, with the girls asleep in a room adjoining the Mess, we perched around the cane bar before sitting down to dinner at a long table overlooking the beach with the sound of waves gently crashing on the shore as a romantic backdrop. Enthusiastic army stewards cooked for us each night, the ingredients of many meals coming straight from the ocean out front.

Rob again had a great scam. If his soldiers worked hard he allowed them to go fishing and snorkelling amidst the miraculous coral reef some afternoons, a benefit for us all. After coffee and port we'd retire to the billiard room where we'd have a rowdy game of slosh or snooker. Or it might be a few rounds of *liar dice* on the deep verandah. Some nights we set the net off the pontoon and would come down in the morning to see what treasures we'd caught.

The Mess was a long, low-line structure, built with a combination of native and army supplies. With its many unique artefacts and rustic furniture it had great character; the bar being one of the best I've sat around. Although not fancy in any way, like Andy Anderson's guesthouse in Tapini, it too had a Somerset Maugham and John Masters feel to it.

Constantly there was a platoon from Vanimo patrolling the border to Indonesia. It was an important job that the army was carrying out at the time – stopping people from scampering over the border from Indonesian held Papua and West Irian Jaya into New Guinea. When not on patrol himself, Rob conducted training exercises in the surrounding swamps, grasslands and mountains and he and his company built a rough links golf course of sorts around the oval. Rob was a popular commander, with respect from those soldiers who served under him – an assortment of mostly happy and friendly young Pacific Islanders from every neck of the woods in both Papua New Guinea, and surrounding islands. Some continued to write to him many years after he returned to Australia.

Some evenings we played bridge with the District Commissioner and his wife, who thrashed us both. Often they whizzed us out in their speed boat to fish for Spanish mackerel or visit nearby beaches. Many a night we hiked up to John Young Whitford's (the Assistant District Commissioner) bungalow on the far hill and listened to tales of life as an ADC in New Guinea – the main criteria seeming to be the capacity to drink copious bottles of whisky. Mind you the DCs, and the young patrol officers under their command, carried out a challenging job throughout Papua New Guinea, particularly after the war when there was a lot of cleaning up to do, both physically and mentally. It was not always an easy task in this harsh country with its sweltering heat and impenetrable terrain. It was a lonely life, too. Hence the penchant for the odd drop of sustenance could be understood.

A couple of times we splashed through rivers and creeks along the coast, past surf beaches with huge waves crashing in from the ocean, mysterious waterholes, deep lagoons covered in pink and white water lilies and the picturesque villages of Lido and Waramo, until we reached our destination just over the Indonesian border. Here we stood on the headland gazing across to Jayapura in the far distance – a place out of bounds in those days. Most of the villages we drove through had immaculate gardens surrounded by borders of colourful bottles and with graves outlined with lovingly painted white stones. I can still hear the squeals of delight as children raced after our Land Rover, leaping onto the running boards, touching our white skin, with others splashing in black rubber tyres in the river or jumping with glee like cannon balls off overhanging palms into the water – a sight we saw again on our last visit, although this time we were on our way inland to Maprik and the remote village of Wasera to buy artefacts and the clay pots for which the village is so famous.

Unfortunately, I think the villagers had been told that the Queen Mary had berthed in Wewak and the entire ship's crew and passengers were coming to buy their wares. How sad we were to see their distraught faces when they realised there were only four of us. And how relieved we were to get out alive when it finally sunk in that they'd been duped, although we did our best to buy what we could, knowing our suitcases would be well over the limit and diligent custom officers back in Australia were likely to confiscate anything needed to be put in quarantine.

The trade store, opposite the beach in Vanimo, had every Indonesian spice available. It was here that I developed a taste for hot sauces, my favourite being sambal and peanut satay. A corrugated iron and fibro building, it had a rickety verandah to the front and was blazoned with garish signs for rice, Coca Cola and cigarettes. Inside, apart from the jars of delicious spices and sauces, there were canned meats and fish, tinned fruits, soft drinks, sweets for the children and the usual tobacco and cigarettes. Dried fish often hung from the ceiling, together with kerosene lamps, razor sharp bush knives and fishing nets, with a huge freezer taking up most of one wall. Above the counter, floral *meri* dresses were strung on wire lines, with lengths of bright materials and rows of the ever-popular rubber thongs and leather sandals piled up in the corner.

Most times one had to tread through a group of Sepiks squatted in the pale dust out front, often smoking tobacco rolled in newspaper or chewing on *betel nut*. Sometimes a mini-market out the back would be in full swing where bare-breasted *meris* sold bananas, mangoes, paw paws, sweet potatoes, beads, bags and carvings.

Children played together happily, with ours often joining in. The *meris* adored Charlotte and Georgie, passing Georgie from one to the other, huge beams on their fascinated faces. Mangy dogs and stray cats lolled languidly in the shade next to grey headed tribesmen holding spears, with their wispy beards wagging from side to side as they smoked, chewed *betel nut* and gossiped.

Under another tree, giggling *meris* held contented pikininis to their voluptuous breasts that shone like treacle

All in all it was a relaxing place to shop and I needed little encouragement to go in there to browse.

At times, Rob, as Company Commander, and I, hosted functions at the Mess; formal *dining in* nights, fancy dress parties, or cocktails. Vanimo was a popular place to visit, meaning Rob often entertained officers or dignitaries from Wewak, Lae, Moresby, Canberra or overseas.

Soon, however, all this came to an end and I was sitting on a single engine Aztec with Vanimo just a dot in the distance. Along the coast we landed at the small town of Aitape, later to be destroyed in a devastating tsunami, turning Father Austin Crapp, our agreeable Catholic padre at Moem, who baptised Georgie, into a local hero.

Disembarking at the airstrip in Wewak, I suddenly realised I'd left something of utmost importance behind. I grabbed

Charlotte by the hand and rushed back to see Georgie fast asleep on an elderly *meri's* knee at the rear of the plane. She too was dead to the world, snoring loudly. It was unusual for any of the Pacific Islanders to fall asleep on a plane. Most were terrified of the big *balus* falling out of the sky. For many it was their first encounter in the air. If not giving out loud curdling wails, they chewed gum or *betel nut* so ferociously that it gave me lockjaw just watching.

We women were a close-knit lot at Moem as we were often living alone. We seemed to have far too many morning and afternoon teas – welcoming or farewelling a neighbour, leading Charlotte to ask, after one of our contemporaries had tragically died: 'Did she have too many morning teas?'

To fill in the days we had flower arranging and copper beating classes, both at which I was pretty hopeless. I did another course in creative writing and we spent hours on the beach under the shade of the umbrella trees with the children playing in the sand at our feet. Charlotte, together with other children from the barracks, went to the International School in Wewak a few mornings each week and we would take it in turns to drop them off or pick them up.

Looking back I was never bored – lonely at times, but not bored.

On our last visit to Wewak I went back to the Boram Hospital. Not much had changed, although I gather the PNG Government is thinking of repossessing it to build a huge hotel. Although in a glorious spot on the beach, the neat-as-a-pin buildings are still fairly basic.

The Officers' Mess at Moem was a low-line building set amidst manicured lawns surrounded by lush trees and shrubs. Unfortunately today it's hardly recognisable as it was then, although there's a brand new Battalion Headquarters where the Commander, Colonel Mark, greeted us, before Captain Jack, a tall good-looking highlander, showed us around the compound. The Mess wasn't the only casualty over the years – many of the married quarters, not just ours, are derelict, the gardens in ruins, although now and then someone has struggled and one flourishes. The church is still there, the small army hospital too, and down on the beach there's the same white coral sand with tall umbrella palms and dugout canoes pulled up on the shore. As we got out of the car three little *pikininis* dug in the sand, whilst off the rocks their older siblings jumped and dived into the sparkling water, their mothers perched on a log – just where I have a photo of Dawn, Louise and myself sitting – with Charlotte and Georgie playing in the waves just like the *pikininis*.

I was sad about the derelict Mess, for this was where Colleen and I once danced on the table at a *dining in* night; where many a young single officer was told to take his eyes off the wife of an absent colleague; where we had fancy-dress parties, cocktail soirées and Sunday evening barbeques on the front lawn, with the children playing amidst the bushes, followed by a night at the movies, or a chess competition. Being so isolated we made our own fun with dinners or parties in each other's homes, barbeques on the beach, games of soccer or baseball and tennis tournaments. In the last year before we left we often hacked our way through the new golf course we'd all spent many sweltering hours building – between our house and the beach, long since gone. Or it might be a game of baseball. With a couple of the officers joining the women's team (and dressed as such, a couple with huge false boobs to even things up).

One evening a few of us organised a fashion parade down in the *haus win* on the beach with clothes and shoes flown in from Australia modelled by a couple of the more daring officers and a few glamorous wives. Our dressing room was a hessian sack strung between two palm trees. Not many clothes remained after the show, for the one boutique in town found it hard to cater for so many eager young women and the men had no shop at all, apart from the trade stores.

Often we played in competitions on the rugged Wewak Golf Course on the way into town, also long since gone; now replaced by a lush green course opposite Boram Prison. When we played there recently, I was amazed to see a barefooted Pacific Islander walk up to the tee and whack the ball further than I'd seen anyone hit before. In our day, it was the young local children's favourite sport to leap from the bushes claiming our golf balls in great delight – only to offer us the same ball back for a fee.

'*Yu lussem ball, missus?*' they'd ask mischievously, with a glint in their innocent looking brown eyes.

This time I had a wonderful caddy from the village down the road, who begged me in frustration after I'd mucked up another shot: '*Lukum yu ai ontap long ball, missus.*'

Taking his advice I did try and keep my eye on the ball and made the green in two shots.

Afterwards we had a drink with Eric in the clubhouse…an expansive *haus win*, the bar being a huge esky and payment by the honour system.

Back in 1972 we coaxed a couple of the other wives to baby-sit and hired a single engine Cessna to fly to Rabaul for a few of the boys to take on the legendary Jack Newton and his mate, Ian Stanley, in the Papua New Guinea Golf Championships. Our boys were unlikely contenders. Yet, seeing as it was on handicap, Mick, Rob, Eric and a couple of others thought they may have a chance. Due to bad weather we spent a night in the highland town of Goroko, famous for its tribal festivals, where we sat around a roaring fire in the hotel, a great treat after the humidity of Wewak. The local expats were more than impressed that this contingent of 'top golfers' were on their way to win the PNG golf championships, buying us copious rounds of drinks, doing little for the fitness of the golfers who were to play the next day.

Rabaul then was a spectacular harbour city on the Gazelle Peninsula. Now, of course, it's been ravaged by the Mount Tavurvur and Vulcan eruptions in September 1994 – with a new town built at Kokopo. When we arrived for the golf championships we flew in low over sparkling beaches with stilt villages perched on the edge and others nestled into lush, green, tropical rainforest. Further on, shady streets of louvred houses surrounded the awesome sight of Simpson Harbour. The Travelodge, where we stayed, sat in the midst of a rich oasis – long since gone.

Needless to say, Ian Stanley and Jack Newton took home the trophies, but not before I had a dance with both, which annoyed Rob no end as he thought they were giving me far too much attention.

On the way home to Wewak we struck bad weather again, spending two days holed up at the Smugglers Inn – nestled into the shores at Astrolabe Bay in the coastal town of Madang, known as the 'prettiest town in the Pacific.' Not a bad spot to be stranded. It wasn't difficult to fill in the time, dining on the vine-covered deck, swimming in the magnificent rock pool and snorkelling off the beach, although I did feel guilty that my kindly neighbour back in Moem had to look after the children for another two days.

Often in Wewak we piled into Eric's speed-boat for a day on the spectacular islands of Kairiru and Muschu with its cascading waterfalls, hot springs and Bali Hai huts, where we'd picnic on the beach. On our recent visit we had lunch in the Tangs' new *haus win* at Tang Bay on Muschu, which they allow the local village to use as a kindergarten. A more beautiful spot for a school would be hard to find. Gilbert, head man of the village, proudly walked me through the lovingly tended subsistence gardens, and immaculate houses on stilts, whilst delectable little *pikininis* with bottomless liquid eyes ran ahead giggling and pointing in delight. I saw where Gilbert distils beans in a steamer to make cocoa, which he sells in Wewak. Unlike many Aboriginal settlements back in Australia, New Guinea villages are often self-sufficient; eggs bartered for animal food and vegetables; chickens and pigs for *betel nut* or goods from the trade stores, fish for clothes or schoolbooks. Sadly the closer the villages are to a major town the less likely they are to be well cared for and self-sufficient, particularly in Port Moresby where the dreaded junk food has made an inroad.

An older boy padded sedately beside me, a monstrous pineapple balanced on his curly head. Wading out to Eric's banana boat later, he proudly handed it to me with a shy grin, before pushing us off the beach. Whilst waiting for us, Valentine, our trusty helmsman, had caught a huge coral trout, which was now in a bucket. That night Eileen dressed it up with fresh spices, limes, garlic, onions and tomatoes and Eric threw it on the barbeque. Once more we sat in the garden overlooking the Bismarck Sea, just as we had those years ago. All that had seemed to change was the years showing on our faces and the new swimming pool in the Tangs' front lawn.

My mother made the long trip from Ireland to Wewak to see us in 1973. After she recovered from being stranded in Singapore with the wrong visa and then a virus she caught on the plane, we enjoyed a marvellous three weeks together. She was fascinated with life at Moem, particularly the children, both black and white, who adored having a grandmother to play with on the beach and under the huge palm trees in our back garden. She loved the barbeques and dinner parties that everyone put on in her honour, and going to the Mess for a *dining in* night or the movies.

But all too soon we were out at the airport waving her off to Australia where she was to meet up with my father at Ijong Street, having put Cloneen and the gift shop to 'bed' for the winter, whilst he ran his Braddon Flyscreens in Canberra for six months.

My mother wasn't the only one we saw off at the airport. Constantly we seemed to be standing by this ramshackle building with tears in our eyes, farewelling a family back home; or it could be one of the single officers at the Mess who had become part of our extended family. If it was a senior officer leaving Moem, the soldiers would put on a farewell parade, followed by a farewell *dining in* night at the Mess – all quite a ritual.

Sadly, soon it was our time to leave. Rob had been posted to the Jungle Training Centre at Canungra in south-east Queensland.

With the peal of champagne glasses ringing in the air and amidst much hugging and kissing out at the airport we said a final goodbye to our friends. Phillip was the last one I hugged, as I brushed a tear from his eye.

'*Mi sori yu larim mi bihain long,*' he said holding my hand. '*Mi no lusim yu.*'

And we won't forget you, Phillip, I thought. But I was unable to come out with the words for the huge lump in my throat prohibited me from speaking. Leaning down, he picked Georgie up and gave her a huge hug and a kiss. Putting her on the ground he patted Charlotte on the head, before turning around and walking away to stand by the fence where he wiped his eyes with the back of his hand.

My final undoing was when the pipes and drums of the 2nd PIR escorted us to the front door of the plane through a guard of honour of Rob's soldiers. Michael Somare, the future Prime Minister of Papua New Guinea, had to be content to make his way to the back door. With a final wave from the front steps we ducked our heads and went inside to take our seats.

I didn't realise then how special my memories of this unusual place would become; how much I'd love going back, as I did for my birthday, when we were ushered up to the dais at the Garamut Tribal Festival to meet Michael Somare. Arriving at the airport the evening before – with Eric and Eileen waiting for us – there was a crowd of Sepik men, women and children clawing at the wire fence, wailing and calling out and thumping their chests in distress. It was a moment before I realised it was the body of a *wantok* brought home in the *balus* we'd just landed in that they were waiting for. Standing back we let the coffin pass to where it was lovingly placed on the back of a truck to go to a final resting place.

Before we boarded the plane in 1973 to go home to Australia, Corporal Nahshon gave Rob a *bilum* his wife had made.

He wrote: *This bilum is presented to you by us Corporal and Mrs Nahshon for the hard teaching that you have been teaching A Company as all, we hope that you will take this bilum which was made by Mrs Nahshon and put all of A Company in that bilum for sometimes before you forget all about the A Company and the Pacific Islands Regiment as well.*

Once again thank you very much for your hard work that you have done to bring us PIs to the standard where we should be and thank you for the military work that came out of your knowledge to all soldiers of A Company 2 PIR and we are very pleased that out of your knowledge we learned better ways of doing thing, such as training, work and play games.

When you finish with this bilum please leave the bilum with Mrs Peterswald and she can carry all her things from and to Canungra Barracks.

Last of all wish you all the best of luck and we hope you won't forget us A Company and 2 PIR and perhaps the all of Papua New Guinea Defence.

Even now as I write this I can see his face; the tears in his eyes as he handed this beautifully typed letter to Rob.

I hope that Wewak never goes the same way as Moresby has. Yet I know things are often not good. Unfortunately there's much government corruption, too many men beating up their wives, the spread of aids and the dreaded alcohol, *betel nut*, steam and other drugs, ruining good people. Yet, to me, no matter what happens, one can never take away Wewak's stunning beauty and the fond memories we have of our happy times there. Why else would we go back, as so many of us have?

I think of the time recently when Benny, a jovial Trobriand Islander, drove us at a hair-raising pace in the Tangs' small truck along the winding dirt road to Cape Wom War Cemetery – where we met with a Japanese family mourning their father shot down during the war. Possibly their only consolation was that he'd perished for his country in such a beautiful spot.

On the way home we passed elderly barefooted *meris*, overloaded with huge *bilums* of oysters balanced on their greying fuzzy heads. We beckoned for Benny to pull over to give them a lift and were rewarded with huge *betel nut* grins. We stopped for others, carrying sackfuls of yams, sweet potato and firewood. All were so grateful we'd picked them up in the scorching heat – for otherwise it would have taken them six hours to get back to their village. Yet Eileen told us we shouldn't have stopped. For even in the far reaches of the Sepik, insurance companies are ready to pounce. Should we have had an accident the Tangs could have been sued, or worse still our passengers' *wontoks* may have taken their revenge out on us, as happens so often in PNG.

Later we passed a gaggle of carefree, laughing school children in their bright blue uniforms waving as we drove past.

What does the future in New Guinea hold for them?

CHAPTER 26

Home to Aus and a New Career

Rob was to become Senior Instructor of Survival and Adventure Training at the Jungle Training Centre in Canungra established in World War II. Over the years, JTCC was widely regarded as the premium jungle-training centre in the world, where officers from all round the globe came to learn the skills that Australians had honed fighting in the jungles of New Guinea, Vietnam and Malaya. Having spent so many days slogging it out in Vietnam and with two postings in PNG, Rob was an apt choice for the job.

Before Canungra we visited the pretty seaside town of Kiama (the home of the author, Charmian Clift), on the South Coast of New South Wales, where Rob's parents had retired to a delightful cottage with a picturesque garden, a hop step and a jump from the beach. For many happy days we swam in the surf, walked the headlands and explored the mountains and waterfalls in the hinterland with Fran and Dick and their two children, James and Joanna, together with Rob's parents.

Rob's mother hadn't been too pleased to lose her son to New Guinea the first time, then Vietnam and New Guinea a second time, so she was more than happy to have us back in the same country and together in Kiama. Neither of his parents had seen Georgie, and of course Charlotte had grown enormously in the time we were away.

However, soon we were on our way to the small country village of Canungra situated at the foot of Tamborine Mountain, inland from the Gold Coast and nestled into a valley surrounded by the misty mountains of the McPherson Ranges. The army barracks, where our married quarter was situated, were up a hill not far out of the town. Once again we were a close-knit community. Our small weatherboard cottage, one of many in a row, overlooked the golf course on one side and a valley with a small tree-lined creek on the other. We built a tranquil arbour amongst the wattle trees and Rob planted a lush vegetable garden. Charlotte and Georgie had many young children in the barracks to play with and as the streets had little traffic they could run happily from one house to the other.

It wasn't long before we joined the riding and country club on the hill behind the golf course. Soon I had a new horse, Jolyan, a fourteen-hand black gelding (a terror to catch, a joy to ride), installed in a paddock which he escaped from twice, once causing havoc on the golf course, including the ninth green that I then had to spend hours trying to restore. Often at weekends Rob and I would take it in turns to go horse trekking with a group from the country club through the surrounding mountains. Other times we'd ride up the steep winding road to the old pub on Tamborine Mountain, where we'd hitch the horses to a fence post and have lunch on the deep verandah, with the children playing in the rambling gardens that sprawled down to the rocky stream where ducks and fish frolicked in the cool water.

During our time at Canungra I went into my first business enterprise. Rob was away quite a bit, so I felt I needed to do something worthwhile to fill in the time and bring in a bit of extra cash. Next door to the post office in the village was a deserted barn of a building. I found out who owned it and made an offer to lease. As funds were limited I drew flowers all over the floor to cover the damp stains and filled the rotting window boxes with colourful stones and rocks to make a display. Outside, I hung a sign: *This and That, which described* exactly what I was selling – bit of this and a bit of that. And one freezing cold Friday evening Rob and I served steaming mugs of gluhwein to those we'd invited for the opening.

I came to know a lot of the local craftspeople, many of them farmers' wives, by going around and introducing myself. A number of them entrusted their paintings, weaving, pottery or anything else they crafted, for me to sell on consignment, often inviting us to their wonderful homesteads for lunches and dinners, tennis parties or just for a ride around their property. Once we went to a wedding in the cutest stone church set down by a creek overhung with weeping willows, where the bride arrived in a horse and buggy. I also went down to Surfers Paradise and talked a couple of the dress shops into letting me sell their garments, also on consignment, which most of my stock was, meaning I had little outlay. It was in a good position on a tourist route up to O'Reillys' guesthouse in the Binnaburra Ranges, so I'd a constant stream of passing traffic, particularly at weekends.

Charlotte went to the local school in the village, which she loved. Georgie came with me to the shop, playing happily in a play-pen until getting bored, whereupon I'd take her to the park opposite, keeping an eye on the door of the shop for customers. At weekends I had one of the other wives working, allowing me to still ride and be with the children. I can't say it was a roaring success, but it more than paid its way. With Rob away instructing soldiers how to survive in the jungle, making fire without matches, identifying edible native plants and foods, how to kill and cook snakes and teaching escape and invasion techniques, it gave me an interest. It was also an inroad to Beaudesert where I became friends with a girl running a women's and babies' wear boutique on the main street, who supplied me with children's clothes from her shop to sell on her behalf, giving me a percentage, if in return I'd model for the fashion parades she put on in the town for charity. Even Charlotte was roped into this, proving herself a great children's model, despite hating it.

Sadly at this time Rob's mother died after a long illness and his father and his sister, Wendy, came to stay with us for some time. Rob had flown down to be with his mother, arriving moments after she passed away, leaving him devastated as she'd been a great source of love and inspiration to him over the years.

In our last year at Canungra we bought fourteen acres on Mount Tamborine, planting it out in macadamia nuts, spending hour after hour with Rob's father and Wendy helping us tend the new seedlings, carrying copious buckets of water up and down the steep tracks. Soon they were flourishing with only the odd one keeling over with not enough water. On the whole the climate was superb, with warm days but cooling off at night, when we could light a fire. We frequented a swimming pool up in the barracks often and once again the Mess became our social life. Sometimes we'd go to the Canungra Pub or the small café in the village and down the dirt road to Surfers Paradise for parties or to take the children swimming on Main Beach.

In 1974 Rob was posted to Russell Offices in Canberra, meaning I had to hurriedly find a home for Jolyan and a buyer for my shop. I was sadder to leave Jolyan than I was the shop.

Jolyan ended up returning to the farm from where I bought him, so at least I was happy to see him back with horses he knew. Fortunately one of the other army wives opted to buy the shop. Soon we'd packed up and after a round of farewell parties were heading south to the Capital once again.

We decided to become homeowners for the first time in our lives, although we'd previously owned a couple of blocks of land near Kiama, as well as the land on Mount Tamborine. After hours of searching we eventually settled for an unusual architect-designed clinker brick house, built around a central courtyard, on Herschel Circuit in the suburb of Flynn with a lovely view to the Brindabella ranges.

Yet it wasn't long before we worked out that even though we'd swapped the land in Tamborine Mountain for part of the purchase price, (about $50,000) we needed a second income to pay the mortgage. I was keen to get into something fairly quickly. What to do was the question. I wasn't thrilled with the idea of a nine-to-five office job. Besides, I'd long since decided the secretarial world was unlikely to suffer dreadfully if I never typed another letter or took shorthand again in my life. The problem was solved one morning when I was sitting at the breakfast bar in the kitchen reading the newspaper and saw an advertisement for a real estate salesman. Real estate was something that had always interested me. Something I felt I could be good at. It took me a while to work up the courage to ring the number. The ad had definitely said salesman. Not saleswoman. Or salesperson, as it would today. A kindly sounding lady put me through to a man.

'Are you interested in women?' I asked warily.

There was a slight pause; then a cough. 'Oh yes,' he said, with a chuckle down the line. 'I'm always interested in women.'

I'm sure he thought he had a total nutter on the phone and

I wasn't so sure I didn't have one also. The next day I set off nervously for an interview, after finding a friend to look after the girls. I was dressed in a smart red suit with a silk scarf tied around my head in the latest fashion.

An hour later I was sitting in a small office down a set of narrow stairs in the middle of Civic Centre. John Perryman, a delightful Englishman, with laughing brown eyes, a polished head and wearing thick black rimmed spectacles, sat opposite me. It wasn't long before I realised I'd got the job. I worked for the next five years with John and his charming wife, Pat, and his wonderful mother, Peggy (the lady I'd first spoken to), who ended up becoming great friends of ours, even coming to Tassie on a few occasions.

Although years later in Hobart I employed a staff of many women in our office, in the seventies in Canberra there were few women in the business. Lauris Andrews was a trail blazer and one of the most successful and a great source of inspiration to me as we worked together over the coming years.

Canberra at this time had changed enormously, spreading its wings to the far reaches of Belconnen to the north and the Woden Valley to the south. There were new suburbs popping up everywhere. The lake had become a haven for bird life, sailing boats and swimmers, with the Cotter and the Goodradigbee Rivers still fabulous places to go camping. With many of the Duntroon class of '65 now living back in Canberra, most with young families like ours, we frequently spent weekends on the riverbanks.

I sold a house on my first day at Perrymans', making me think: how easy is this? I was soon to realise that was a fluke. No study or examination was required for real estate in Canberra in those days. No licence required. I was given a listing book and told to go for it. The hours were long and arduous, but I'd discovered something I loved and was good at. I liked the flexibility of having time to do tuckshop at the girls' school for a few hours or take them to the doctor if needs be if I made up for it another time. I sold all across Canberra. Nothing too small. Nothing too big. Eventually I studied for my Manager's Licence, enabling me to open my own office if I so desired, yet I didn't do that until we'd been in Hobart for quite a few years.

Jim Fitzhardinge had been selling in Canberra for decades and was one of the better-known agents. Jim had been a prisoner of war at Changi, forced to work on the Burma Railway. To me he was one of life's greatest gentlemen, always arriving at work in a dapper reefer jacket, camel trousers, and sporting a different club tie each day. Sharing an office with him gave me valuable training on how to deal with people. And, as he'd an inroad to many of the embassies and huge estates in Forrest and Red Hill, I soon found I was selling many of the more expensive homes. It was a fun office with many characters. And the more I got to know John, Pat and Peggy, the more I liked them.

The girls started at St Thomas Aquinas in Charnwood, the next suburb to where we lived. I arranged for them to go to a lovely woman's house after school for a couple of hours where they played with her children until either Rob or I could pick them up after work. I must admit I agonised over this. Like all working mothers around the world, guilt plays an enormous role. When I was at work I thought I should be with the girls. When I was with the girls I thought I should be at work. Somehow we managed to compromise and I don't think they were duly stressed. Rob, appreciating the income I was bringing in, was an enormous help, cooking meals often and being with the girls if I suddenly had to head out to show a property or do open homes on a Saturday or Sunday, for unlike mine, his hours were regular.

My parents arrived in Canberra for their two-yearly visit on the same day Gough Whitlam was controversially deposed from government by the Governor General Sir John Kerr on 11th November 1975. Malcolm Fraser took over as Prime Minister with his Liberal Government in a care-taking role.

One of the most notorious days in Australian politics, it was also one of the hottest. My parents nearly expired in the heat when I picked them up from Gill and Colin's house not far from Bowral where Colin was now managing another Santa Gertrudis stud.

Georgie was not too sure about these two new arrivals, having only met my mother briefly in Wewak and my father not at all. She horrified me somewhat as I heard her tell my father: 'There's really not enough room in this car for you; maybe you should go back to where you came from.'

Fortunately this lack of manners, at age three, only lasted a few hours and it wasn't long before she didn't want to let them out of her sight. It goes without saying that we were all devastated once again when they returned to Cloneen and their shop in Glendalough after a long hot summer in Canberra, with many dinners on the back patio under the grapevines at Ijong Street or in our courtyard at Flynn. Christmas was a grand affair at our house, with Gill and her family and Dibs who'd flown up from Melbourne. Eugene was in Brisbane and Viv far away in Wales.

In the meantime Rob was working at Russell Offices, implementing the Kerr Report into pay and conditions in the services. Although he found working at Russell somewhat boring, he enjoyed having a normal life; coming home each night, being able to play squash again and take up sailing. In partnership with his brother Dick, still living in Goulburn, we bought a Boomeroo 22 sailor trailer, an ideal boat for the unpredictable conditions of Lake Burley Griffin. (Rob won our share of the cost playing in a poker school!) Many Sunday afternoons and weekday evenings were spent racing and cruising, followed by a dinner or barbeque at the yacht club on the shores of the lake afterwards – where the children could play on the sandy beach.

Adding a bolt of joy and the odd bit of naughtiness into our lives at Flynn came Gatsby, a tiny half-Labrador and half-Chow puppy. I'd spied him one afternoon when I was showing a purchaser through a house and I'd heard a commotion next door. Putting my head over the fence I saw a very noisy litter of puppies, of which Gatsby looked the cutest. Soon he was installed in a new cane basket under the breakfast bar in the kitchen where he managed to wheedle his way into all of our hearts, before he blotted his copybook time and time again by chewing anything he could lay his hands on. Even so we forgave him and he became very much part of the family for many years, though just like Porky, he'd have nothing to do with strangers. As we'd sadly had to find Gunga Din a new home when we were posted to Wewak, we were delighted to have another four-legged member of the family, even if at times he drove us all to total distraction.

Chapter 27

Our Own Drominagh

The third summer we were in Canberra we packed the Boomeroo up with supplies and towed it to the Myall Lakes north of Port Stephens, where we spent four glorious weeks meandering around this magical stretch of water. Rob's father and Wendy brought tents to camp in at night, Even so, with Gatsby on board as well, it was a tight fit to say the least.

Gatsby adored the boat and would wrap his paws about the mast with a life jacket wrapped around him. When we arrived at an anchorage he'd leap off the boat, take himself ashore; then he'd swim back, knocking his tail on the side of the hull to let us know he was home and needed to be hauled up.

There were lovely sandy beaches where the children could swim and build sandcastles, rocky islands to explore and light campfires on to cook the fish we'd catch each day. The water was as warm as a bath, often enticing us in for a swim at midnight, well after the children were tightly tucked into their tiny berths down below.

On Christmas Day we pulled into the shore and decorated a small pine tree with tin foil and flour and cooked our fish over a campfire. Even now, when I decorate the Christmas tree with my grandchildren, I think of that tree by the lake where Rob handed out presents, which we'd carefully hidden in one of the lockers. Both girls remember it as being one of the most cherished holidays of their childhood.

Shortly after this trip we decided to become farmers. I was selling a property along the Wallaroo Road on the way to the Murrumbidgee River outside Hall. Nearby I discovered forty acres with a small creek and stunning views to the Brindabellas, not far from where the Perrymans were living at Coolongolook in a long low-line Spanish Hacienda they'd built on sixty acres.

We leased the house at Flynn to an American embassy family and moved to 'Drominagh', where we lived in a caravan down by the creek, as we built our new house up on the hill. We set up a chicken run and started a vegetable garden. Sadly all the chickens were eaten by a fox, (reminding me of the slaughter at Clonmoylan, which nearly finished my father off), apart from the cowardly rooster, *Chante Clair,* who managed to escape to the roof on the partly finished house, where he crowed loudly in disgust.

We set our solar plastic shower under a gumtree and the portable loo was moved from spot to spot where Rob would dig a hole and then fill it in later. Somehow or other after a quick shower under the gumtree I managed to dress myself for work each day. With the girls in their school uniforms and Rob in his suit we'd all set off for the forty-minute drive into town. The girls at this stage had started at St Thomas Moore's in Campbell so we could drop them on the way.

It was stinking hot and the dust horrendous. At times I wondered what on earth we'd let ourselves in for, moving to this dry hot, dust bowl of a place when we'd a perfectly good house in the suburbs. The flies were horrendous, which was not surprising, as we were right in the middle of sheep country and I also suffered dreadfully from hay fever.

Chapter 27 Our Own Drominagh

But it wasn't long, despite all the drawbacks, before I loved our small farm with a passion.

My parents came back from Ireland to visit. My father helped with the supervising of our cedar house, with verandahs to the front and rear, which Rob and I paved ourselves. We also painted the house, taking many hours after work and weekends. My father was chuffed that we were calling our place Drominagh and insisted we take heaps of photos with Charlotte and Georgie leaning over the front sign on the gate.

Nearly all my family came that year to visit: firstly Dibs, then Eugene and Jenny with their two, Godfrey and Eugene and finally Gill and Colin with Andrew, Allison, Mia and Liam. There was no way we could entice Viv to make the long trip back across the world; however, it was lovely for my parents to have the rest of us there together.

To the front of the property we built a large dam, surrounding it with weeping willows and installed a flock of geese that immediately took over the farm, often preferring to perch on the house verandah. In the garden we planted just about every imaginable native bush, and many wattles and gumtrees. Rob dug out a large pond off the front verandah, which never seemed to hold water no matter how hard we tried, leaving an ideal place for snakes to sunbake, a couple of which I killed myself with a spade – once, on the way to work, with the children already sitting in the car. Rob I might add killed many, as the place seemed to be teeming with them.

Where was St Patrick when we needed him?

We were determined to make the farm work, planting the land out with a commercial crop of walnuts and almonds and going into Angora goat breeding, ending up with a sizable flock, mostly sired by Simon, a regal-looking buck. All this in our spare time, although by this stage I'd come to an agreement with John and Pat Perryman that if I didn't take a lunch hour I could knock off work early to pick up the girls from school. By now I was managing the sales part of the office and had dropped out of actually selling.

Rob's father came to live with us full time once we got the house finished, only throwing his hands up in the air once when the entire flock of goats got into his garden, devouring most of the plants. After a frantic call at work, I raced up the dirt driveway by the dam to see him in the front garden, waving his walking stick in every direction, still trying to shoo the goats out. I thought he was going to die of a heart attack right there and then in front of my eyes, for after all he was in his seventies.

'It's the worst day in my entire life,' he assured me, stuttering dreadfully, as he always did when excited.

Poor Poppy was to endure a few more 'worst days of his life' coping with our farming ventures both here and in Tassie over the next twenty years or so.

The next day the whole flock of goats disappeared, including the Saanens we'd been told to mix with the Angoras as they were more intelligent. We found them about twenty miles away, happily padding along the road, the bell on the Saanen leader goat ringing loudly. After fixing the hole in the fence where they'd disappeared, we soon learned that goats have a definite pecking order. Initially we'd put our bell on the wrong goat, which annoyed the recognised leader no end and she didn't give up until the bell was around her neck. Unlike sheep that will run in a million different directions if they think you want to do anything with them, I discovered that if I went out into the paddock and called 'Goatee Goatee', they all came running to my side.

Anchored recently off the glorious tiny island of Trizonia

Chapter 27 Our Own Drominagh

in the Gulf of Corinth on *Sea Dreams* we watched a Greek farmer herd his goats along a steep path, all the time calling out to them to keep in a straight line and not to get seduced by the enticing bushes along the way. Amazingly they seemed to do what they were told. And whilst anchored in a quiet bay off the island of Poros we watched an orderly flock of Saanen milking goats take themselves for a walk down to the shore and along a rocky path and up into the hills. When we were sitting on the deck that evening savouring an icy cool *vino* we were amazed to see the happy group return along the very same path and back up to their shed on the side of the hill. No sign of a goat herder anywhere. And just as the sun disappeared for the night a group of them posed on the crest of the hill, silhouetted in the fading light, apparently enjoying the cool breeze and the extensive view.

For hours the girls and I'd sit feeding a cute and cuddly newborn Angora from a baby's bottle by the fire at Drominagh, crying sadly when we lost one. The excitement when female twins arrived in the world was immense, as that's where the money was. The males weren't worth much, so we sold them off as pets, although I'm sure a few ended up on the tables of Greek or Turkish families, despite their assurances this was not going to be the case, particularly as a few families came back time and time again.

We won first prize in the Canberra Show with one particularly stunning female and eventually started to make some money. When we ran out of feed in the paddocks in summer, Rob used to scrounge leaves from around Russell offices, fill the back of our new one-tonne Holden truck and bring a load home. The goats adored the leaves and as Rob said quite reasonably: 'I'm helping the gardeners to clean the grounds up around Russell.'

I found Merrylegs, a small dappled grey Shetland pony, for Charlotte and Georgie – just as strong willed as the Merrylegs of years before in Clonmoylan. Her greatest trick was to bolt down to the dam with one of the children on board. Here she'd hurl herself into the water, saddle and all, refusing to budge no matter how hard we tried. Yet, despite all this, she soon squeezed her way into our hearts, even joining us and a few of the tamer goats, a couple of the ducks and one particularly domesticated goose, (who had decided Poppy was her soul mate and Gatsby her enemy – the only being that I ever saw Gatsby cower from) on the verandah for our sundowners. Here the children would spend hours grooming her mane to perfection. I was also given an ancient horse called Ned to look after. He loved to join us here too, standing with his head on my lap. When we discovered he had cancer, and there was no hope, the vet told me to hold him by the reins and she would shoot him in the head.

'This is the most humane way,' she assured me, as I looked at her in total horror.

Yet, seeing she was smaller and more fragile looking than I was, I didn't want to appear a wimp. So after taking a deep breath, I did what I was told. Whilst I gave the poor unsuspecting Ned a handful of oats I watched her raise her gun to his head and aghast I saw him fall to the ground in a heap, with me still holding the reins of his halter. The next day we sadly buried him in a large hole we dug with a bulldozer up the back paddock over the hill.

Gatsby adored his new home, roaming the paddocks with the goats, swimming in the dams and lazing in the shade on the verandah when the goose wasn't there. Yet he blotted his copy-book more than once, having been seduced by the charms of the Perrymans' two Border collie bitches. Every so often I'd receive a frantic phone call from Pat to say: 'Gatsby's visiting again,' and I'd have to hurriedly get in the car and collect him.

Once we lost him for five days. He'd jumped off the back of the truck when he and Rob were out shopping for supplies for the farm out at the commercial suburb of Fyshwick. Eventually, after many pleas to the radio station he was located and arrived home in grand style to a warm welcome.

Then the rains arrived. For hours we tried to stop the bottom dam's walls bursting by valiantly trying to divert the water. One night I remember being knee deep in mud still trying to do this at midnight. In the end it gave way under pressure. It wasn't long before the low crossing leading into the farm was under flood too, meaning we couldn't get the cars in for days at a time. We ended up using a wheelbarrow to bring shopping up to the house after we'd waded through in gumboots. One day, when Charlotte was sick and needed to go to the doctor, I wheeled her down in the wheelbarrow, a cushion under her head and then carried her across in my arms. It was amazing to see the transformation from the dry to the wet. Almost overnight the grass turned an emerald green and the garden and nut trees burst into life.

Most summer evenings we'd sit on the front verandah surveying our farm with the distant outline of the Brindabellas blazing in a twilight haze. We were so proud of what we'd achieved in such a short time. The house itself had one extensive living area with high raked ceilings, an open copper-beaten fireplace beneath a towering feature brick wall with bookcases each side and a bar dividing the kitchen from the living area. It also had an archway through to the three bedrooms. One evening, when the house was in the throes of being built, I came home from work and the Greek brickie took me in proudly to show me his work. Unfortunately he was a small, stocky fellow and the archway he'd built was only just high enough for him to walk under. Even I couldn't go through without bending my head. He seemed somewhat surprised when I queried the height.

'But yous only gots to dips yours heads the little bits,' he said, standing under the arch and lifting his hand.

'My husband is six foot!'

'Ah. Six foot?'

Suddenly the penny dropped and after much muttering, cursing and throwing around of tools and bricks and mortar, the arch was rebuilt.

Not only did Rob and I paint the outside and inside of the house ourselves, tile the bathrooms and carefully lay every rock in the garden, with Poppy's help we erected all the paddock's fencing. Rob also installed the extensive irrigation system around the nut trees over a few weeks' leave from the army. We worked hard to make our Drominagh our paradise. On returning a few years ago and driving up the avenue between the now-mature walnut and almond trees and seeing the lush haven we'd created it was all worth it. For where the rest of the farms around Drominagh sweltered in yellow grass and dust, Drominagh sat in her separate oasis of greenery.

Our time at Drominagh was a peaceful happy time with many of the Class of '65, making it their country base. Often on a Sunday the phone would ring and someone would ask: 'Okay if we bring some lunch. We'll grab the newspapers too.'

Even the Greek couple that ran our local mini-supermarket at Flynn would come out and cook us up a storm on a stone fire by the creek. Sometimes children would camp down there in tents, staying the night and I'd take them into town the next day when I went to work and dropped Charlotte and Georgie at school.

We had a number of large parties, spilling out onto the verandah, one in particular to welcome me home from six weeks in Ireland with my parents in 1978. Although I was suffering dreadfully from jet lag, having only arrived home the day before, it was great fun, with a band set up on the lawn and a huge barbeque blazing. This was one of the many nights the generator gave up the ghost, only adding to the atmosphere. It was impossible to get electricity connected, so the generator was our only form of power. I often spent hours trying to coax it into life, usually at the end of a long day at the office, before Rob arrived home to take over. It was during this time that my language deteriorated considerably, for it had a knack of stopping right in the middle of dinner preparations or during a great movie or series on the TV, particularly Poppy's favourite, *Fawlty Towers*, almost driving him to drink.

Chapter 28

Ireland Revisited

On the last day of my parents' visit one year, we were sitting on the verandah of our Drominagh, enjoying the late afternoon sun setting behind the Brindabella Ranges, when I said: 'I'd like to go back to Ireland and see where I was born.'

They thought I was joking. I wasn't. For quite a few years I'd had a hankering to go back. I hadn't seen Viv for thirteen years and thought I could incorporate the two. Rob and I'd discussed it at length, and although he wouldn't be able to get time off work and leave the farm, he was more than happy for me to go and take the girls. So nine months later in early December, Charlotte, Georgie, and I were sitting on a Qantas plane bound for London where we changed to an Aer Lingus flight for Dublin.

In hindsight it was a big ask leaving Rob and Poppy to tend the farm on their own, particularly as it ended up being the hottest and driest summer in Canberra for many years. They had a pretty rough time of it, endeavouring to keep the animals and trees alive in the searing heat with little water, while on the other side of the world we enjoyed a white Christmas in Ireland and then Wales.

Returning to the country of your birth is one of the most comforting feelings in the world. The girls wondered why I

Chapter 28   Ireland Revisited

was crying, as I looked out of the Aer Lingus window coming into Dublin, when I found it difficult to contain the tears. After the parched paddocks of our Australian Drominagh, the green chessboard fields of Ireland were a welcome sight.

I've read that Ireland is a story between you and your heart. How true that is. It's difficult to explain how I felt. I loved Australia dearly. And she'd been marvellous to me. But in my heart I'd always held a special place for Ireland, although I never for a moment thought of going back and living there. My life and family were in Australia. I didn't go quite so far as to kiss the ground when I got off the plane as my father did, but I felt like it. Instead I kept my kisses for my parents waiting anxiously for us inside the chaotic Dublin terminal.

After driving over the Liffey River, past St Stephen's Green where ducks frolicked in the lake, and on through the ancient streets of Dublin crammed with scurrying people and bumper to bumper traffic, including the green buses, I could remember from Bray days, we headed up into the Wicklow Hills for Glendalough. It was wintertime so the trees were bare, giving the countryside a haunting beauty. For three wonderful weeks we stayed with my parents at Cloneen, entertaining relations and family friends, walking by the river, the two lakes and along the windswept beach at Britas Bay. The gift shop was closed for the winter, meaning my parents had plenty of time to drive us around in their small VW beetle, including up to Dublin where we had lunch at Drury's Hotel and afternoon tea at the Shelbourne. It was bitterly cold, but even that didn't dampen my enthusiasm for being home. There was just something about it that made my heart skip with joy. It's not as though Ireland looked dapper and sparkling – far from it, with many of the villages drab and unpainted; the people often wearing black beanies and parkers, heads down against the piercing cold. There were far too many young girls pushing prams and young blokes standing on corners smoking and chewing gum. Yet even that didn't take away from the beauty of the land, and the charm of most of the people.

This was before the Celtic Tiger came to Ireland and the whole country suddenly burst into bloom, with the small villages and towns spruced up and painted the bright colours that they are today. The economy was still pretty much in a depression, although in the late seventies not nearly as bad as in the fifties. Yet unemployment was high and morale often low. But the fields were green, the Guinness good and the shopping in Grafton Street out of this world.

This is when we rented the small whitewashed cottage with a thatched roof in Tipperary where we stayed huddled by the peat fire for a week, venturing out to visit both Drominagh and Clonmoylan or listening to Irish music in the pub next door to the cottage. I remembered nothing of Drominagh from when I was a child. Yet walking through Clonmoylan it was as if I'd never left. There was a new central heating system, but not much else had appeared to change. Standing in the kitchen by the old Aga, I could almost feel the presence of Mary and Brownie; smell a loaf of Irish Soda bread straight from the oven. Walking down the front fields to the lake I could see us all there jumping and screaming in delight, Eugene announcing: 'There's not enough room in this lake for me.'

We stopped under the beech tree where we'd enjoyed so many picnics and walked down to the lake. Across on Friar's Island there appeared to be no goats any more, but the walled garden was still there next to the house and the remnants of my father's apple orchard still visible. The many years that I'd spent dreaming of Clonmoylan had to a certain extent kept it clear in my mind. I was happy to discover my dreams and memories were much the same in reality. Everything did seem a little smaller, but that is often the way.

Despite the bitter cold it was so beautiful, with a soft mist rising from the lake settling over the rushes on the shore that I wondered why my parents ever wanted to leave. Yet looking at Charlotte and Georgie I realised that if my family had remained in Ireland I wouldn't have the girls here with me now for I wouldn't have met their father. I wanted to stay for hours breathing in my youth, taking in every last detail, every stone, every last blade of grass. Sadly, the owners, a kindly Dutch couple, had to be up in Dublin that afternoon and the girls were getting tired and hungry. So reluctantly we said our goodbyes and drove down the avenue to the wooden gate, just as we did all those years ago on our way to Australia.

The next day I got my first glimpse of Drominagh. This day the old building appeared to carry age heavily. Centuries of sun and storms had slightly weathered her face devoid of summer vines, but there was no doubt in my mind that my father would have died a sad man had he not had the opportunity to set eyes on her again. And so would I.

For over two hours we roamed through the house, wandered the gardens and sat by the lake where the girls threw stones into the rushes, as my father and his siblings had once done. And so too Dibs, Gill, Eugene and Viv. I was far too little. When it was time to leave, Helen, the caretaker, insisted we have afternoon tea in the front drawing room. And soon we were sitting around a roaring fire with steaming cups of tea in our hands, as my parents told her of how it had been when they were living there before and after the war.

On the way back to Cloneen we visited many relations from Cork to Kerry, ending up at Ballynastragh where Charlotte took a shine to my elderly aunt, Ethne. For years she and Charlotte wrote to each other. This was the first time I'd seen Ballynastragh and was immediately smitten by her gorgeous lake and surroundings.

With great excitement we waited for Viv to arrive. When she walked through the door at Cloneen it was as if we'd never been apart. She was little changed – still as beautiful as ever, and just as much fun and full of life. It didn't take us long to fall back into step, although we both noticed I was no longer 'the little sister', prepared to go along with everything Viv said. Now I had strong opinions of my own. Together we went up to Grafton Street to shop and drove to Rathdrum a couple of times for the girls to buy warm fur boots, as snow was predicted. In the small bedroom to the front of the house we talked until the wee hours of the morning as we used to do. We also threw a wonderful party at Cloneen for many of our relations and friends of my parents, where my elderly, spritely and fun-loving Aunty Eileen, who'd driven up from Cork with her handsome husband, my father's brother, Witham, whipped her cocktail dress out of a silk stocking and donned it in a second.

'If you keep your dress in a silk stocking you'll never need to iron it,' she told me with a girlish giggle, as she patted the immaculate blue fabric and fiddled with her beautifully coiffed hair, at the same time ordering me to do up the back zip. I then watched her twirl and flounce in front of the mirror, much like a ballerina, with a whiff of expensive perfume filling the air.

When Viv took off to catch the ferry back to Wales we were sad to see her go, but as we were to have Christmas with her at Cilwych it was only a week before we'd see her again.

Early one morning, with a thick blanket of snow covering

the ground, my father, mother, Charlotte, Georgie and I drove to Dublin to catch the ferry to Hollyhead in north Wales. It was a tight squeeze in the VW, with the girls and I huddled in the back seat and my parents in the front. The luggage was tied down tightly on the roof rack. I thought of the time Gill had been in the back seat, as my father and mother drove her to the airport in Dublin. My father, being the gentleman he was, had stopped dead still to give way to a car wanting to merge. Suddenly there was a loud bang as a car hit them from the rear, sending my father's tweed hat flying off his head. For a while there was a stunned silence in the car.

'It's okay Gill,' my father eventually stammered, putting his hat back on and turning around to make sure she was okay. 'I don't think it was a bomb.'

At the time the IRA had been threatening to blow up civilians.

'It wasn't a bomb, Daddy,' Gill screeched. 'You just got hit in the back by another car.'

'Ah! Is that all?'

Fortunately there was little damage and they were able to drive on, delivering the car to the garage on their return to Glendalough for repairs.

Driving down through Snowdonia in Wales I felt as though we were in a Christmas post card, with snow sprinkled over the pine trees and covering most of the road. It continued to snow for the next two weeks, meaning we enjoyed a wonderful white Christmas at Cilwych, making snowmen on the front lawns, sitting by the roaring fire in the drawing room or around the huge scrubbed pine table in the kitchen.

Viv and Tim now had two beautiful daughters, Laragh and Dominie, a few years younger than Charlotte and Georgie. It took the cousins a while to get used to each other, but soon they were bosom buddies with the odd tussle now and then. It was interesting to see them together. Viv's two with dark brown hair and luminous brown eyes, my two with blue eyes and fair hair. It was difficult to think they came out of the same brood, more or less.

For hours I rode one of Viv's horses through the thick snow up into the Brecon Beacons looking for stray sheep, having to get off every now and then to remove the snow embedded in my horse's hoofs. The girls and I also helped with marking and drenching of the sheep and cattle down by the sheds near the original farmhouse where Tim's parents still lived.

In the evenings there seemed to be one function after the other where we drove through the snow to various old homes on large estates. On Christmas Eve we went to a large manor home where I was grabbed for a quick kiss under the mistletoe by the notorious Dai Llewellyn, brother of Roddy, Princess Margaret's consort of the time. And at every dinner party we went to I tried with all my might to eat green pheasant, (the Welsh like to hang their pheasants until they're green and gamey) but thankfully Viv and Tim were there to surreptitiously dispose of what I was unable to stomach. Both taste and smell are definitely acquired tastes; not ones I aspire to.

Apart from the wonderful stone cottages Viv and Tim run as tourist accommodation on Cilwych, they also have peasant and clay pigeon shooting. On the numerous occasions I've been back to Cilwych since, I've helped Viv cook huge pans of curry for a hungry group of Londoners at the end of a day of shooting, after I'd sat for hours in a paddock in the freezing cold, shooting the clay pigeons into the air for the shooters to aim at. Other times I'll go with Viv on the tractor to help feed the pheasants in the woods.

Chapter 28 Ireland Revisited

When it was time to say goodbye, I was devastated to leave. I knew my parents would be coming to Canberra the following year; however, I wasn't sure how long it would be before I'd be able to make the long trip back to Cilwych. It turned out to be quite a while, although over the years I've been back many times. I love to stroll down with the dogs through the marzipan fields to the River Usk for a swim or just to skim stones for the dogs to fetch. Or sit on the banks watching the ducks gambol and the trout jumping. In springtime I often ride with Viv through the laneways lined with thick hedgerows where glorious tulips and yellow daffodils have popped up from their winter hiding places, whilst all around us is the merry song of the newly awakened birds as they burst into life after the long cold months. Or we might sit around the wooden tables on the front terraced lawn (beautifully manicured by Tim) watching the sun set above the hills sloping down from the towering Brecon Beacons, where splashes of purple heather, yellow gorse and black and white sheep are etched into the vivid landscape.

When we finally flew into Canberra it was still incredibly hot. Our Drominagh was even drier than when I left, with both dams empty, and the garden parched. But somehow Rob and Poppy had managed to keep everything alive. During the rest of that long hot summer Rob and I canoed down the Murrumbidgee from Jugiong to Gundagai where we camped on the banks of the river, often waking up in the early morning to find a herd of cattle surrounding us as we were camped in their watering spot. We towed the boat down to the ocean at Bateman's Bay on some weekends and sailed each Wednesday evening in the twilight races on Lake Burley Griffin. In the winter we went up to the mountains at Thredbo where a group of us stayed in the army lodge. For hours the children romped in the snow on homemade toboggans and a few of the adults skied. In the spring we went up there again to walk through the hills covered in a blanket of wildflowers of every imaginable variety and hue.

Rob did a sailing trip with Josko Grubic on his 80ft yacht, *Anaconda*, (a contender many times in the Sydney to Hobart race) from Perth to Sydney. Although it was tough he enjoyed it enormously, only increasing his desire to sail further afield than Lake Burley Griffin and down the south coast. And all the time our flock of Angoras flourished, the garden took shape and the groves of almonds and walnuts started to burst into bloom. But even so we were restless. Rob had long since decided the army was not what he wanted in the long term. As his twenty years of service were coming up (when he could retire) we decided to look around for another path for our lives to take.

A friend suggested that we take a trip to his home state of Tasmania. As we still wanted to farm, but be close to the sea so we could sail, we'd thought of moving to the north coast of New South Wales to Coffs Harbour or Byron Bay. However, we decided to take the friend's advice and go for a trip to Tassie. Rob's old school mate, Max Doerner, and his wife, Viv (whom we see often, meeting most weeks that we are in Hobart for a Guinness at the Irish Pub in Salamanca), had also just moved there, where Max had purchased an abalone licence.

They told us they loved it and coaxed us into taking a look.

CHAPTER 29

A New Life in Tassie

It didn't take us long to decide that Tassie was where we wanted to live. After flying in over the magnificent Western Tiers the following July, we picked up our campervan from the small airport near the historic town of Evandale, not far out of Launceston. From there we drove through the Fingal Valley (where many Irish have settled over the years) to the glorious east coast. We camped the night in a flourishing green field speckled with yellow gorse, newly shorn sheep, and an outcrop of grey rocks overlooking the stunning blue waters of Great Oyster Bay. We couldn't get over how green Tassie was. It reminded me of Ireland. Sadly the east coast has suffered so many droughts over the past few years that the green grass has faded somewhat and the sheep often struggle to survive.

Even though it was mid-July the sun was shining brightly, enticing Rob to grab his swimmers and jump into the water. When he got out he declared with the understatement of the year: 'It's a bit chilly.'

In 1924, Thomas Grattan Esmonde, my great uncle, had published his book *Hunting Memories* – an account of his hunting days around the world.

Of Tasmania he wrote: Southward of the Australian Continent lies Tasmania: lovely land of pathetic tragic and historic memories, nowadays happily transformed into an Eden of placid content. A specially favoured and attractive land with its salubrious climate, its wildly picturesque scenery, its heaped up mountains, its level lakes set in stately forests and its flashing rivers, rushing to the Southern Ocean through the endless bays and estuaries of its rock bound coast.

I had read this extract many times and now here I was to see for myself what my uncle had discovered nearly sixty years before. He goes on to say: *A fisherman could do much worse than explore its tempting waters which a wise and practical Tasmanian Government has stocked abundantly with Salmonidae. I have spent happy days amid its peaceful hills and woods, on the banks of its streams, or wading in their shallows, my ear tuned to the music of their waters as they speed past, mirroring the rocks and trees and giant ferns with their every varying background of hill and cliff, while the speckled trout leaped in the pools like glistening ingots of silver.*

He also wrote: *With luck on these occasions one may sometimes bag a specimen of that very rare animal The Tasmanian Tiger, a striped and brindled leopard with a very handsome well marked coat, but much smaller than his famous Asiatic namesake.*

It was unlikely that we'd spy such an animal, as sadly the Tasmanian tiger has long been extinct, but that didn't stop the girls from keeping an eagle eye out.

The next day we drove south to Eaglehawk Neck, the gateway to the Tasman Peninsula, where we stopped for a blustery walk on the wide stretch of white sand with thundering waves rolling in from the Tasman Sea. In convict days a long line of savage dogs were stationed either end of the

Neck to stop prisoners escaping from the penal settlement of Port Arthur, where convicts were incarcerated in the most awful conditions.

Our next stop was at Dell's small bakery in Taranna where we bought scrumptious homemade Tasmanian scallop pies before heading down to Port Arthur to have a look around the old sandstone ruins in the historic site, and for Rob to watch a rugby match in the pub on the hill.

Port Arthur was one of the British Empire's major penal settlements of the 19th Century and a vital link in the development and colonisation of Australia. It was named after the Governor of the day, George Arthur, and apart from being a penal settlement had flourishing industries, including timber, ship building, brick manufacturing, coal mines, flour production and nail making. It was the site of Australia's first railway, consisting of small carriages on wooden rails propelled by convicts between Port Arthur and Taranna. It was also an utter hellhole, with many of the convicts that were incarcerated there being from Ireland, including the famed Smith O'Brien.

Unfortunately Port Arthur has become notorious once again for the horrendous massacre that took place there in April, 1996, when a lunatic gunned down over thirty people, some of them locals, including the chemist's wife and his two beautiful daughters. Yet there's no taking away from the port's haunting beauty, with the eerie sandstone ruins sitting in the midst of manicured jade lawns, (often with a cricket match being played, or a concert filling the air with music), sandstone walks, water lily ponds, colourful garden beds, stone bridges spanning small rivulets and stands of old English trees; with the added beauty of the sea lapping against the shore. Now, where the massacre took place in the small Broad Arrow café, there's a tranquil remembrance pool, and an impressive new visitors' centre stands next door where thankfully hordes of tourists flock in once again, providing much needed employment to the small community.

Back in 1980 when we told one of the local farmers, watching the rugby in the pub, that we were driving around Tassie looking for a possible place to farm and be close to where we could keep a yacht, he gave a broad grin.

'I know just the spot,' he told us, taking a large gulp from a Cascade stubby. After a moment he plonked the bottle down, splashing beer onto the counter. 'Could well be what you're after. At Koonya. Bruce Heyward up at Windermere's selling. It's an apple orchard with a good piece of farming land. It's been on the market a while, but it may be worth taking a gander. You can keep a boat at Taranna, not far down the road.'

'How do we have a look?' I asked, thinking this sounded promising.

'Not a problem,' he said. 'I'll give Bruce a holler.'

The next morning we were sitting around the Huon Pine kitchen table at Windermere, talking to the affable Bruce Heyward, a tall, fit heavy-set man with kind eyes and a thatch of grey hair. We'd fallen in love with the green valley that Windermere was nestled in the moment we rounded the top of the wooded headland at Sympathy Point on the Taranna Nubeena Road. On one side of the road were the sparkling blue waters of Norfolk Bay; on the other side there was an apple orchard, and a paddock of hop vines where we had turned left and driven up the long driveway lined with tall poplars, past a huge dam with ducks weaving between the thick reeds on the edge. Further on was a small convict cottage, sitting on a hill overlooking a beautiful flat paddock fronting the river. To the left of the dam was a long timber hut with a shingled roof. Next to that stood two enormous iron sheds for apple storage and packing. We later discovered Bruce had erected them both entirely himself, using a tractor and pulleys.

For over two hours we wandered around Windermere with Bruce, inspecting the numerous paddocks, wooded groves, the extensive orchard with many varieties of apples (from Granny Smith, Cox's Orange Pippins, Red and Golden Delicious to early Gravensteins), the pickers' quarters, the derelict convict cottage, another small cottage by the woods on a separate title and the apple sheds. Bruce seemed amused that I wasn't all that interested in the house, once I'd seen there'd be enough room for us all, if Rob and I slept on the open verandah and Poppy had the main bedroom. I was much more interested in the stunning garden of camellias, fuscias, roses, rhododendrons and silver birches and whether it would be possible to make a living out of the orchard and the remainder of one hundred and forty odd acres of pasture. The somewhat dated brick house we could deal with in our own time.

Bruce is one of the most genuine people I've ever met. Immediately we felt comfortable with what he was telling us. He didn't make a fortune, but he'd made a good living over the years, enough to educate the children and give him and his wife, Marjorie, a comfortable existence.

'Mind you,' he said, looking out across the orchard, 'it can be challenging work.' This was to prove an understatement.

Yet Rob and I immediately felt we'd found what we were looking for. However, this was the first place we'd seen. There were many questions still to be answered. Would we be happy living in the area? Would the girls have any friends nearby? What were the schools like? Was it a reasonable buy? Would it increase in value, or was it a depressed area? What about hospital care, as Poppy got older? Most importantly, could we make a living here once Rob got out of the army?

We decided to tell Bruce we were interested, but needed time to have a look around the rest of Tassie. He fully understood. So we agreed that we'd get back in touch early the next week, when we'd had a chance to explore the island and see what else was for sale. He gave us the name of his real estate agent at Henry Jones in Hobart and we agreed to keep in touch.

However, no matter where else we travelled, we couldn't get Windermere out of our minds. And we didn't leave many stones unturned in our search, from the apple orchards of the Huon Valley in the south to the picturesque Tamar Valley in the north. We even looked on Bruny Island, but disregarded that as we'd have to go to and fro by ferry. There was just something about Windermere that had grabbed us both. The girls had fallen in love with the Peninsula too, dreaming of swimming and sailing in Norfolk Bay and riding horses amidst the rolling hills.

So in the end we made an appointment with the real estate agent at Henry Jones, an elegant sort of fellow, who arrived wearing a tweed Saville Row suit, not exactly suited to pacing Windermere's unruly boundaries. As you can imagine he was somewhat flustered by the time we'd walked every nook and cranny. Once again we sat at the kitchen table with a roaring fire in the grate, this time with Bruce's wife, Marjorie, serving piping hot scones and scalding tea. Soon an agreement was reached.

We were now the proud new owners of an apple orchard (of which neither of us had the faintest clue how to run) and one hundred and forty acres of prime farming land. It was agreed that Bruce would stay on for six months and would take the profits from the first season. This seemed more than fair, as he was giving us six months before we had to come up with the money, hence it would be Bruce who produced and packed the crop. It all sounded a good arrangement, particularly as Rob would still be in the army when we came down.

After final farewells we drove back up north where we stayed a night in Launceston, before jumping on a plane for Canberra. Within a week we'd put both our properties on the market. At times I lay awake at night wondering if we'd done the right thing. Yet seeing how happy Rob was I soon lost any thoughts of regrets. But I knew I'd be sad to leave my job at Perrymans and the many friends we had in Canberra, not to mention our Drominagh, although I was realistic enough to know there was no way we could make a worthwhile income from forty acres. Were we mad to throw all we had in Canberra away to go and live in a remote country community on the small island of Tasmania? Perhaps not quite as mad as my parents had been when moving us all to Australia. At least we would be in the same country.

Not long after we got back to Canberra we flew down to Melbourne to Dib's wedding. Years before she and Peter had decided they weren't suited to each other and had divorced. A few years later Dibs met Kevin Scott, a past editor and production manager with News Corp, who now ran his own business. Eugene was to give Dibs away and I was to be her maid of honour. She looked so happy and gorgeous, standing in the front garden of her home in Royal Avenue next to the dashing and athletic Kevin. We were all thrilled that she'd found the great happiness she deserved very much.

That summer my parents were once again back in Australia. It was agreed we'd have a family Christmas at Gill and Colin's property at Wallabadah south of Tamworth. Packing up the car, we dropped Poppy off in Goulburn for Christmas with

Dick and Fran and headed north. It was blistering hot, so we were more than glad when we finally arrived at Hardigreen Park on Christmas Eve. What followed was a wonderful week with all the family, except for Viv, spending long hot days lolling by the river or under the huge weeping willows in Gill and Colin's garden, with the odd heated argument on politics and religion thrown in for good measure.

The children, Gill's Andrew, Allison, Mia and Liam and our two girls got on famously, riding the horses, yabbying in the river and playing endless games of cricket in the paddock next to the garden. All too soon our time at Hardigreen came to an end. Early one morning we said a sad goodbye before heading back to Canberra to get ready for the move to Tasmania. My parents had agreed to come and visit us on their way to Ireland, so we knew we'd be seeing them before too long, but I'd no idea how long it would be until I saw the rest of my family, particularly my precious Gill.

We found a buyer for Drominagh easily (the nephew of Damien Parer, the famous war photographer, who'd taken so many harrowing images of the Kokoda Track). The house in Flynn took much longer. John and Pat Perryman had decided to go into goat breeding, so they took our flock of angoras, including the lordly buck Simon. We'd thought of taking the goats to Tassie, but were advised it would be too wet and cold for them on the Peninsula.

If it was too wet and cold for Angoras I did wonder for a moment how on earth we would cope.

Rob had managed to get a posting with the army to the barracks at Brighton just north of Hobart, which he was to take up early in the New Year. So on a blistering hot January day, after a horde of farewell parties (including a special dinner at the luxurious Lakeside Hotel put on by the Perrymans for me) Rob and Poppy headed off first, in the Holden one tonne truck packed to the hilt and trailing the Boomeroo.

Behind them the girls, Gatsby and I followed in the Lancia – down the long driveway between the walnut and almond trees, past the cracked and dry dam and over the stone crossing, now surrounded by a mass of weeping willows, which had grown in the blink of an eyelid from when we'd planted the cuttings. As I got out to shut the gates for the very last time I glanced up at the homestead and felt a tear threaten.

Slowly turning my back, I wiped the sweat from my forehead, pulled the gate shut and got back in the car. With a sad smile to Charlotte and Georgie, who were both in tears as they'd had to leave their pet goats and Merrylegs behind, I placed my foot hard on the accelerator and commenced the long drive to our new life in what I thought would be the cooler climate of Tasmania.

Chapter 30

She'll Be Apples at Koonya

Yet when we arrived in Tasmania, after stopping for two nights with Dibs and Kevin in Melbourne, it was the hottest day the state had experienced in years. From memory it was 37 degrees. As we pulled into the garage at the historic village of Campbelltown to fill up with petrol and get a cool drink, I had no doubt at all that we were going to expire.

In fact poor Poppy almost did. I often wonder what he really thought of this move. He never complained, as we dragged him from one adventure to the next. Yet surely he must have wished for a less gypsy style existence. As a bank manager, he'd constantly been on the go from one town to the next. And later, after he retired, Hazel seemed to have him on the move often too. But he was a lot older now. However, as Rob assures me, to remain living on his own would have been much worse. At least with us he had someone to share a meal and a glass of wine with each evening and the girls to constantly keep him young. He was certainly never lonely or bored. Surely though, at seventy-seven, this move to Tassie must have been somewhat traumatic for him.

After a few days in a motel in Hobart, awaiting the removal van to arrive, we headed south past the sprawling paddocks with cows grazing languidly in front of Government House. We drove over the Tasman Bridge spanning the magnificent

Chapter 30 She'll Be Apples at Koonya

Derwent River dotted with yachts competing in the mid-week race. A little further along the river was the unmistakable tall sphere of Australia's first casino perched on the shore and I could see the towering and majestic Mount Wellington gazing down as though she was a mother hen keeping an eagle eye on the city. At the small coastal town of Dunalley, where much to my astonishment we had to stop to let a crayfish struggle across the sea-splashed road, we collected the key to our new home from Bruce, who was building a fifty-five foot steel trawler, *The Norfolk Bay*, out of disused oil tanks. This was to be Bruce's new life, running tuna fishing charters out of Eaglehawk Neck.

As we drove up the long avenue beside the orchard at Windermere (with the trees now laden with tiny apples) and pulled up outside the vine-covered fence surrounding our new house, I was once again overcome with the beauty of the place. Even in this searing summer heat it didn't seem to have wilted. The dam wasn't as full as in the winter, but the ducks were still playing in the reeds and Bruce's cattle sat chewing the cud lazily in the river paddock. Further on, flocks of sheep huddled under the shade of the Blackwood trees, escaping the heat, with others traipsing down to the dam for a drink. All in all it looked much like a Tom Roberts' painting.

When the removalist truck failed to turn up, it was obvious we'd have to spend the first night camped on the floor. At five 'clock it was still so hot that I showered, put a long red towelling dress on (all that I could find that was clean) and sat under the silver birch in the front garden, where Rob brought Poppy and me a glass of wine. The girls were happily playing on the swing and Gatsby was busy exploring. A truck pulled up out the front and in it was Don Clark, an eye-catching guy with a mass of greying hair and huge expressive eyes. Don had heard he had new neighbours. He'd also heard we were sailors. As he'd just built himself a 36-foot fibre glass Roberts Mauritius, he was keen to see what sort of boat we had.

'G'day,' he said, holding out a farmer's hand, 'welcome to Koonya. Sue and I live down the road at Cascades. Reckoned I'd just drop in and see if you need anything.'

Joining us for a glass of wine, he told us how his family had lived on Cascades, a property spanning both sides of the road going down and into the small village of Koonya, for a number of generations. He also had an apple and pear orchard and large packing sheds, although much older and more basic than the ones Bruce had built at Windermere, so Bruce had been storing and packing Don's apples for the last few seasons. Cascades had been the outstation for Port Arthur and had many old historic buildings, which he and Sue were about to do up and turn into colonial accommodation.

Sue told me later that when Don got back to Cascades he scratched his head in consternation and exclaimed: 'Gawd, Sue, don't reckon they'll last long. She was sitting out under the tree in a long dress, having a glass of wine at 5 o'clock. Don't look much like farmers to me.'

Sue with her Nordic blonde hair, eyes the colour of the sea on a sunny day and forthright attitude and Don became our great friends and still are to this day. Their son, Marcus, and daughter, Karina, and our girls soon formed a strong friendship, although Marcus was somewhat overcome with having three giggling girls to contend with.

Over the years we were at Windermere, Don, like Bruce, used to shake his head in wonderment as we came up with what we thought were good ideas on how to farm this Peninsula land. Yet he gave us the greatest help and encouragement with whatever brainwave we had, no matter what he thought. He only balked once, when Rob asked him to help chase our wayward boar, Hitler, around the orchard in order to put a ring through his nose to stop him ploughing up the paddocks. After two hours of chasing and then trying to hold the screeching Hitler down on the ground, he shook his head and exclaimed to Rob exasperatedly. 'Bloody Hell, Rob, there must be an easier way than this.'

Not having had much to do with pigs before (Cascades is a cattle and sheep farm), he wasn't sure what that was.

Hitler got his own revenge. A year or so after the orchard episode we eventually caught him again and off to town he went in the trailer attached to our small Mini Moke. His day had come. I was somewhat sad, but realised this was part of farming. He came back all dressed up and ready for the spit. We decided to make a day of it and set the spit up over a log fire under the walnut tree within the old convict ruins at Cascades. We left the spit in the charge of Marcus, as we helped Don and Sue move a flock of sheep from one paddock to another by the convict Mess Hall on the shore.

It wasn't long before Marcus came bolting down to find us. 'Hitler's on fire. Hitler's on fire,' he screamed at the top of his voice, pointing to the huge flames visible over the sandstone wall around the ruins. By the time we rushed up to see what we could retrieve there was just a charred mess with only a few morsels of very tough flesh left. He'd certainly got his revenge!

Soon we settled into our new life at Windermere, with Rob commuting to the army barracks in Brighton, where he was in charge of school cadets throughout Tasmania, coming home at weekends and Wednesday nights.

In the meantime I learned the ropes in the apple sheds from Bruce. Each day I was on the assembly line, packing some dozens of boxes of apples every hour, which had to be wiped, wrapped in tissue paper and gently laid in the boxes. I then had to pick the box up and carry it to a conveyor belt opposite. The other women on the assembly line, including the wonderful Blossom with her mass of fairy floss ashen hair, floral aprons, coloured socks and lace up shoes, being the oldest and most experienced, had been doing this job for years. She told me later that she and the other women doubted my stamina to stick it out. Mind you, I don't think I've ever looked forward to a morning tea and lunch break so much in my life, when we'd sit on the dilapidated vinyl chairs under the window often listening to the broadcasters, Sue Becker or John Laws, conducting their talk-back shows on the radio.

I also learned how to make the apple boxes, how to grade and sort the apples at the beginning of the assembly line and how to drive the fork-lift truck to move the pallets around. Rob learned all of this on his odd day off from the army and at weekends. It was more than satisfying to see the apples head off in large container trucks, which would arrive to the front doors of the shed to be loaded up for the markets around the world. Apple orcharding in the 1980s wasn't what it had been just after the war, when five acres was enough to make a good living and huge container ships would leave the docks of Hobart laden down with apples bound for the United Kingdom. The Common Market ruined this for many orchardists, for suddenly Australian apples were not as competitive as they once were in Britain. Fortunately we now had cool storage in Tassie, allowing orchardists to keep their apples until a market was found. Even so the golden days of Tasmanian apple export had long since gone. So despite the long hours in the orchard and sheds we certainly weren't going to make our fortune in the short run.

The earliest variety of apples to be harvested is Gravenstein.

Chapter 30   She'll Be Apples at Koonya

The first year we had a glut. It was my job to find a market. I rang around all the fruit and vegie merchants in Hobart and found a sympathetic ear at one outlet fairly quickly. I must admit at this stage, although I could sell a house fairly easily, I had little idea of how to market apples.

'How many in a box?' the man on the other end of the line asked warily.

I hesitated, not having any idea at this stage. 'Are there eighty?' he probed.

I was pretty sure there were far more than eighty. 'Oh yes… there certainly are.'

'Well, bring them in then.'

That afternoon I packed at least twenty boxes of apples onto the back tray of the Holden and drove up to town. At the fruit and vegie outlet the man came out to inspect my offerings, as I stood back proudly.

'There aren't eighty in here,' he sighed in disgust. 'There must be at least a hundred and fifty…these are nothing but bloody marbles.'

Needless to say he refused to take any boxes and I realised I'd made a huge tactical error, for he was obviously after 'big' apples, not 'tasty small' apples. I wasn't sure what to do next. Refusing to give up, I continued around the outlets until I got rid of the lot, including to the delightful Mrs Chung and her sons at Chung Sings in North Hobart. Mrs Chung, with her wispy grey hair tied up in a scarf and wearing a colourful apron, ran the floor of Chung Sings until what would appear to be well into her eighties. I used to love to stop and have a chat with her or Michael, as we dropped off boxes of apples and apple juice for the next six years or so.

On their way back to Ireland my parents came to stay in the little cottage by the woods and my father, being an old orchardist, gave us constant advice. Rob continued with the army at Brighton and sent a truck-load of sheep home every second week from the Bridgewater market nearby, until we were so saturated in sheep that even Bruce and Don panicked.

In order to cope we got Shep the sheepdog. Unfortunately herding sheep was not her forté. Sitting on the back tray of the truck, with us herding the sheep was much more her style. When she came on heat, Rob put her kennel onto the roof of the carport. (He'd read this in *Footrot Flats*, a New Zealand comic strip.) Even that didn't stop the neighbour's dogs and Gatsby collecting underneath in lustful hope.

It was no sooner than we installed all of our new sheep in the paddocks that Bruce announced to me apologetically one sunny afternoon that we were in quarantine as his sheep had lice. Now his sheep and ours were unsaleable, including the fat lambs we thought we could sell at a hefty profit. As you can imagine we were slightly overstocked for a while, with every single sheep and all the cattle having to be deloused, checked and checked again before the quarantine was finally lifted three months later, meaning the income we thought we'd be getting from the fat lambs went down the gurgler.

Gatsby took an instant dislike to Bruce's dogs, Bill and Ben, and they to him. This didn't surprise me, for they were a terrifying pair of blue heelers, baling me up time and time again, unless Bruce was there to tame them with a glare. One day, after much niggling from the two, Gatsby decided to take to them with a vengeance. With blood and fur flying everywhere, I screamed hysterically. They took little notice. Eventually Bruce came running from the apple sheds. Grabbing an oar by the side of the dam, he managed to chase the three dogs into the water. They continued to fight until they were in imminent danger of drowning, then let off long enough for

Bruce, who'd now bravely waded into the water (still with the oar) to whack them apart. Gatsby ended up with teeth holes all over him and having to be rushed to the vet at Sorell. Bill and Ben looked reasonably unscathed as they swaggered off to the back of Bruce's truck. Another time Rob put his leg between the three to try and kick them apart, ending up with six stitches in his calf.

Running the farm with Rob still in the army had the odd perk. One day there was a knock on the door. There stood the local agricultural officer. He'd just been down to Cascades and Sue had told him we'd moved in, and with Rob still in the army, I was running the place on my own with Rob's father. Now this fellow was somewhat easy on the eye and charming to boot. Poppy and I were having lunch at the time, so I invited him in for a coffee to join us. In the excitement of finding such a specimen on my front door I'd forgotten I'd just turned the tap on in the sink in the laundry. After about half an hour he looked down at his feet and lifted them in the air.

'Is it always under water in the kitchen like this?' he asked with a lopsided grin, at the same time running a hand through his mop of dark hair.

It was only then that I realised I'd clean forgotten to turn the tap off. For over an hour he helped us mop up – and from that day on often popped in to see how Poppy and I were getting on, staying to give us a hand with the sheep, followed by a cool beer or a glass of red.

When the worst hailstorm in twenty years annihilated our crop of apples, just ready for harvesting the next year, we had to do some quick thinking. After much swearing and cursing about the injustice of the gods up above, we decided to go into juice production. We'd no idea how to make apple juice; however, that didn't daunt us. Don arrived one day when I, with the help of a friend from Ireland, was trying to coax the juice from a batch of apples going through the new press Rob had brought home from town to experiment with.

In my column, *She'll Be Apples*, that I later wrote for the *Sunday Tasmanian Newspaper*, I described Don as being 'The Know it All Bystander'. In this instance he certainly was. He suggested that we cut the apples up into small pieces first before putting them into the press. This needless to say was a great step forward and before too long we were producing more apple juice in Tasmania under the Apple Maid label than anyone else, outselling orange juice in the large supermarkets.

With Bruce's help, Rob, now retired from the army, became an expert in all angles of juice production. He managed to find a great recipe, mixing a variety of apples to produce what some described as the best juice they ever tasted. I took my hat off to him, for it wasn't an easy ask for an army officer to change into a successful orchardist and juice and cider producer within the blink of an eye. He spent hours testing and tasting until he came up with a recipe we were all happy with. The uniqueness was that each batch tasted slightly different depending on what apples we had available. Gravensteins and Golden Delicious were sweeter, Red Delicious fruitier, Granny Smith's tarter. Sometimes we mixed them all together. Our customers loved the variety and we often got phone calls telling us which was their favourite. Rob employed industrial chemists to show him the best way to preserve the juice without using preservatives and how to retain the best colour. We designed labels and advertisements. We chased Australia to get the correct bottles to put the juice in. We'd found Don Calvert (one of Tasmania's foremost yachtsmen who represented Australia in the Admiral's cup), a plastic bottle producer in the Huon, but the glass ones needed to come from further afield.

Chapter 30   She'll Be Apples at Koonya

Bruce was invaluable. He helped us set up the equipment we needed, including a fancy apple washer he managed to put together with bits and pieces lying around the shed. Even after five years Bruce still had bits and pieces around the shed.

'I know there's a twelve-inch screw in that box up the back,' he'd say scratching his head in deep thought. 'And whilst I'm here I'll have a look for that gasket I left in the hayshed.'

Needless to say when we needed a part for anything, Bruce could usually lay his hands on it fairly quickly. We also travelled to the Huon Valley to purchase another larger press and some steel vats from a defunct wine producer, ending up with boxes and boxes of the worst wine ever produced (Chateau Lorraine) as Rob was so overcome with the great packaging. For years we used to take a batch to give away at the Tasman District School fair, where others were also seduced by its appearance. Then no doubt they'd cook up a feast to do justice to this great-looking wine, just as we had done. After tasting it they'd soon realise there was no way you could finish the bottle. The next year you'd see it back again at the fete. And once more it would go off to unsuspecting connoisseurs of fine wines, only to reappear the next year. It may still be doing so for all I know.

The girls started at the Tasman District School over at the seaside town of Nubeena, catching the school bus at the end of our driveway, which would take them over the dirt road lolloping up the steep hill behind Koonya to Nubeena. I often did tuckshop duty in the canteen, run for many, many years by the renowned larger than life, Lola, with a heart of gold and a no-nonsense manner. Charlotte and Georgie made many good friends at Tasman, some of whom they keep in touch with today, although tragically Charlotte's special friend, Elizabeth Campbell, was killed, together with her cousin, in the Port Arthur massacre, as they crouched in terror behind the counter trying to hide from the lunatic gunman. (I refuse to mention his name.) Their funeral and many others were held at the small Koonya chapel on the shores of Norfolk Bay, followed by a sad wake at the Mess Hall on Cascades.

After school the girls would help in the apple sheds, washing out the vats and cleaning up the apple press. As Georgie was still tiny, the best way to clean a vat was to put her inside with a hose; not a good job on a freezing cold winter's day, when the only way we could keep our feet warm was to cut up old sheepskins, putting them inside our boots. To give them their due, young as the girls were, they never complained, seeming anxious to help, with the odd bit of pocket money an incentive.

Not long after we arrived at Windermere I found Devil – Devil by name and Devil by nature. Once again I was overcome by good looks. He was about fifteen hands, with a white star running down his aristocratic Arab face. I probably would have been better off getting something older and quieter, but once I spied Devil in a paddock the other side of Port Arthur, I was smitten. For the years we lived at Windermere we had a love-hate relationship. In reality he was far too much for me to handle, often bolting through the orchard (once I caught my neck on a Red Delicious tree and was ripped out of the saddle), or dumping me (Rob too) in a heap of blackberry bushes. Yet I persevered and eventually Charlotte was old enough to ride him also, both of us winning a few ribbons at the local gymkhanas. For hours I'd ride through the countryside, sometimes ending up down at Cascades or a little further along at the small Koonya shop (stocking everything from garden spades and chicken feed to bread and milk), where I could grab a few things and ride on back home.

Cascades is a lush green farm of some 700 acres of prime

grazing land spreading inland from the shores of Norfolk Bay to the far reaches of the hills behind Koonya, with spectacular views across the sparkling waters of the bay. At its peak in the 1850s there were between 300 and 400 convicts at Cascades, gainfully employed in the timber industry. When we arrived at Koonya Sue and Don were living in the weatherboard house, which Don's father had built after the war overlooking the Cascade River (where the cascading water provided one of the first hydro schemes in Australia). The house where they now live was the convict hospital. Across the road is the original convict Officers' Mess and Officers' Quarters, which they've now completed the restoration of (winning a nationwide heritage award for restoration). During the Second World War a group of Italian prisoners lived in Rotten Row (another heritage building they've restored) while working on Cascades' orchard. Photos of the prisoners, appearing more than happy with their lot, are displayed on the thick stone walls.

Our life at Windermere wasn't all work, however. At the time there was a great group of people living on the Peninsula and we constantly seemed to be at parties or giving parties, leading Rob to mutter one day, as we were shearing the sheep in the old wooden hut off the apple sheds, 'Not sure if I can keep up with this social life.'

For not only did we have the local people to socialise with, including, to name a few, Sue and Don at Cascades and Marg and Paul Hansen at Highcroft, where apart from the magnificent job Marg has done in restoring a significant Hobart property, Summerhome, in Moonah, which has been in her family for generations and where we still often party, they have one of the best peony farms in Tasmania. There were also Kate and John Hamilton who ran the popular Tassie Devil Park, John's wonderful parents, Bill and Meg, Tom and

Brenda Newton who started the *Tasman Gazette*, Alistair and Caroline Mathieson, a former Miss Tasmania, at the renowned Bush Mill where Alastair had installed a steam train he'd imported from the UK, which ran from the Fox and Hounds to the Bush Mill and where I'd help out when they had huge busloads in for cray bakes, and Phillip Thomson, the local doctor (who still looks after Rob) and his wife, Carmel, (with whom Rob's Uncle Keith fell madly in love). Then there were quite a few of the class of '65 and their families visiting, plus many other friends from the mainland. In fact in our first two years at Windermere we had no less than thirty visitors from the mainland (more that they were curious to see what we had let ourselves in for), some of whom stayed for weeks on end, giving us a welcome hand. The summer of 1982 was one of the hottest on record, so there was a lot of carting irrigation pipes around the orchard. Eugene arrived and was there to help with putting rings in the pigs' noses to stop them harrowing the orchard. I've a wonderful photo of him attempting this job with a long pair of white gloves on. I can only imagine this was to stop him being bitten by a furious pig. Dibs and Kevin came for Christmas with Kevin's two children, Cameron and Minnie. For hours we played tennis on the courts at Taranna and golf on the Port Arthur Golf Course, surely one of the prettiest courses in Australia, straddling the high cliffs looking towards Tasman Isle.

Rob's Uncle Keith (the Rat of Tobruk and the one who fell for Carmel) also used to come for months at a time as he had now been widowed. He loved to stride through the orchard like a sergeant major pointing out how things could be regimented. And he was forever giving Poppy (his brother) advice on how to grow vegetables, which used to drive poor Poppy to despair. As an ex-sheep farmer he also had plenty of advice with regards to the stock. As he was now living in Sydney on his own, he found Windermere a haven to escape to. Although he was a great character, I must admit there was a collective sigh of relief when he would announce it was time to return to the 'big smoke.'

The Badger Creek Regattas were a highlight of our summers. Together with Cascades we'd sail around from Taranna and anchor in Badger Creek not far from Nubeena. Here we'd take part in riotous activities, including dog races and rowing competitions, ending up at the shearing shed belonging to the Shoobridge family for a cookout and more games, followed by a concert put on by the talented Shoobridge clan.

As we didn't have many restaurants to go to, a bit like New Guinea, we mostly entertained in our own homes or met on the beach for a barbeque. The Fox and Hounds at Port Arthur was a favourite haunt if we wanted to dine out, or otherwise it might be the RSL Club at Nubeena or the Fairway Lodge.

Poppy was very much part of life on the farm. He was now in his eighties and going blind from glaucoma, but still managed to hike down to the apple sheds each day to help make boxes, when he wasn't working in his extensive vegetable garden. For even then he was as fit as a fiddle. Having been a good swimmer in his early days he never lost the build. He was more than proud when they produced a television show about us called *Making it in Tasmania*, and he was a star, striding down from his cottage on the hill, swinging his walking stick (we built him a small cedar cottage overlooking the dam), past the pickers' quarters and into the sheds to make boxes. He loved to socialise at our parties, on many occasions outlasting us all, having another wine, followed by a port, which we eventually had to ban as he became far too argumentative, particularly if Uncle Keith was there.

Our apple sheds became the venue for many Peninsula occasions; from political and school fund-raisers to just a good old apple shed party. We'd light discarded steel barrels as barbeques, place lanterns around the rafters, and hire a bush band. With the tantalising smell of cooked sausages and onions filling the air we'd all sit on hay bales or take to the floor dancing to the old cassette player on the windowsill. This is also where we'd hold our end-of-apple-picking season bashes. Here I'd award the pickers with a certificate of accomplishment for their weeks of hard work in the orchard. These were usually hilarious nights, as most of the pickers were from all ends of the earth and there was no common language, apart from the appreciation of a cool drink and a bit of fun. I gave certificates for the 'best drinker', 'best pool player', 'best singer in the orchard', 'laziest picker' (Jean Paul, a tiny Frenchman sporting a wispy goatee beard, who spent more time lying dreaming within the rushes by the dam than apple picking, won this hands down), 'quickest picker', and 'sexiest picker' (Rob employed her without me seeing, mainly due to her never-ending brown legs.)

When I asked him what she looked like he lied through his teeth. 'I didn't really notice,' he said. 'But she seemed keen.'

Much to my chagrin she turned out to be very good. She was also great fun and with her long flowing blonde hair she kept her male colleagues as keen as mustard too, which Rob assured me was a bonus in itself.

For months on end the pickers would live in the long row of white painted fibro pickers' quarters by the apple sheds. Some also came for the pruning and thinning, although Rob and I mostly carried out this laborious and boring task ourselves, with the help of the highly efficient Murray Boon, who had worked the orchard for years. We also had Michael, an ample fellow, who always wore a short-sleeved T-shirt, no matter how cold it was and whose trousers never seemed to quite adequately cover his extensive rear end, revealing a huge plumber's crack. Then we had Nick with a mop of long blond hair. At one stage we had thirty people working shifts.

On a blistering hot summer's afternoon I opened the door to find Michael, whom I'd last seen lugging the heavy irrigation system around the orchard. I had been perched on a log keeping an eye out for blackbirds with my shotgun posed to shoot. Blackbirds are the orchardist's enemy. Much as we tried putting scarecrows and many other deterrents in the orchard, nothing seemed to work. So it was my job to try and shoot them, or at least scare them away. With my gun aimed, I diligently followed one bird down and pulled the trigger. But by that stage it was close to the ground and an unsuspecting, happily grazing prized ewe got in the way. Needless to say I was not popular when I had to admit I'd killed the poor thing.

'I've been bitten by a bloody snake and reckon I'm for it,' Michael told me with a painful grimace, holding his behind and looking ashen, as he grabbed hold of the door handle to steady himself.

I gasped in horror. First I'd killed a sheep and now this. Not a good afternoon. 'My God! Did you see what sort it was?' I asked him.

He shook his head. 'I reckon the bugger was in the blackberry bushes. I probably disturbed it and he got me when I was leaning down to join one of the irrigation pipes.'

I had a vision of Michael's ample bare behind right in the firing range of an enraged Tiger snake on the rampage. There was obviously no time to waste. The poor bloke was in dire straits.

I asked to look at the bite, but knowing it was in a delicate spot, I wasn't sure if he'd be embarrassed to show me. Not to be deterred, Michael swivelled around and gave me a full view of his shiny derriere. I looked hard at the small red mark, but couldn't see any puncture holes. However, not ever having been bitten by a snake, nor in fact ever having seen a bite on anyone else, I wasn't too sure what I was looking for, even though I'd studied my first aid book at length. I knew you were supposed to put a tourniquet on. How on earth I could tie a bandage around Michael's rear end I had no idea. A leg or an arm would have been a far more convenient spot to have been bitten. A large fat behind was beyond my knowledge of first aid. The doctor's surgery was the only answer. And obviously there was no time to waste.

Before Michael had arrived at my door, I'd just put a dark hair rinse through my long hair in order to cover the rapidly appearing grey hairs I'd been getting of late, due I felt to the stress of being a farmer, orchardist, juice producer, wife, mother and real estate agent, for I'd just started with Henry Jones selling property on the Peninsula. Plus I was now a sheep murderer.

But seeing the emergency before me, I knew there was no way I'd have time to wash it out. Instead, I grabbed a scarf from the cupboard and rushed out the door. After manoeuvring Michael into the passenger seat of the Holden, I jumped behind the wheel and backed out from the fence, whereupon there was a bellowing BAA, BAA!

'Bloody hell...it's Milly,' Michael exclaimed in alarm, as he looked out of the window.

My God! I'd forgotten I'd tied Milly the goat to the back-tray so she could use it as shelter from the sun. I leaped out, saw that she was okay, with only her pride in tatters, undid her chain, and tied her hurriedly to the fence. (If you left her free for a moment she was into everything including Poppy's prize garden.) Hearing all the commotion going on, Gatsby came flying out from under the oleander bush and leaped into the back-tray. Soon all three of us were sitting outside the waiting room (Gatsby giving a ferocious growl at anyone who dared to look at him), at the Nubeena surgery waiting for the affable Dr Phillip Thomson. He took a quick look at the bite, got out a magnifying glass and then proceeded to laugh, which I thought was a bit off in the dire circumstances.

'Did you actually see the snake?' he asked Michael, whose face was still the colour of a large bucket of creamy milk. He appeared even more put out than I was with the doctor's seemingly uncaring and unprofessional mirth.

'No. But I bloody well felt it.'

Phillip picked up his stethoscope and after listening to Michael's heart, he took a deep breath and winked at me. 'I think it might have been a bull ant,' he said to Michael, giving him a pat on the bum. 'They can give a nasty bite.'

Immediately I saw the colour come back into Michael's ashen cheeks. Maybe he wasn't going to die after all. 'Are you sure about that, mate?'

'Well, it certainly wasn't a snake and you seem fairly healthy… nothing that a good diet wouldn't fix.'

Back outside the waiting room, I grabbed hold of Gatsby (I'd tied him to a downpipe), and soon we were all in the truck heading home over the dirt road to Koonya.

'You reckon he was right. A bull ant, eh?' Michael said, winding down the window and shouting for Gatsby to stop barking. 'Well, I'll be damned.'

It goes without saying that I had very dark hair by the time we got home.

Yet to say I was relieved was an understatement, for I knew we'd lots of snakes at Windermere, mainly in the blackberry bushes – a bit of a hazard when trying to harvest the huge crop of berries surrounding the apple orchard. For hours Charlotte and Georgie would sit on the side of the road at Taranna selling punnets to tourists going past, or otherwise we'd supply some of the local shops.

When we'd finished pruning our orchard, Rob, Murray and I headed down to Cascades, as we'd now taken over their orchard for a year. Often Sue would join us, more so that she and I could have a good gossip. The steel ladders were heavy and not easy to manoeuvre and many a day I ended up with large blisters on my hands from the pruners and a bruised leg where I'd either fallen off my ladder, or given myself a nasty knock. We really had to push ourselves on wet winter days when the rain would run down our arms or get in our eyes.

'We're stark raving mad. Totally insane,' I shouted to Rob across a Golden Delicious tree one freezing cold morning, getting off my ladder and throwing my pruners down on the grass in a wild rage, before heading inside for a warm drink to defrost my limbs.

But, of course, before too long I got the guilts, going back out again to continue the job.

There was a definite knack to pruning; one I didn't always get. I lived in terror that Murray would discover I wasn't doing it correctly. If I wasn't, as was often the case, all hell would break loose (well in a nice sort of way). I was always glad when the school bus came and I could down tools to go and pick up the girls. Rob, being of hardier stock, stuck at it out through thick and thin, often not coming in till late at night. One day, whilst waiting for the school bus to arrive, I thumbed through a copy of *TV Week* magazine and was fascinated to see a photo of my friend Vera Toll and Tony Barber, famous for his TV show, *Sale of the Century*, staring out at me. I remember thinking crossly how much I'd rather be Vera, who was running a ski resort in Mount Bulla with her husband and doing ski weather forecasts with Tony Barber, instead of spending hours in a freezing cold orchard scaling thousands of apple trees.

Our juice business continued to thrive and we formed The Port Arthur Cider Company. We also registered the names Apple Maid and Orchard Fresh, still going to this day. To begin with we did our own deliveries around the Peninsula from a trailer towed on the back of the small Mini Moke we'd bought when we'd first arrived. Yet before too long we couldn't keep up with production using our antiquated equipment. Hence Rob flew to Adelaide to try and find a more efficient press. There he found Bernard, a large rotund German (with half a dozen strands of died yellow hair lashed across his pasty head and who wore his shiny black trousers, kept up with black braces, high over his humpty dumpty stomach) to install the most modern of German presses available. It worked in a rack and cloth kind of way. We crushed the apples, placing the pomace into cheese cloths. Then we laid them between the racks until we formed a large stack, which hopefully wouldn't fall over. The hydraulics would push them all together with the juice flowing out the bottom. From here it went into stainless steel vats and through a pasteurising machine before being piped into bottles. A cold and wet job. For two weeks Bernard lived with us, going up to Hobart with a small brown leather suitcase packed with his Freemason gear to attend meetings. He became enamoured with our friend, Marg Murray, who was down from Hobart helping us during the lambing season. Unfortunately for him, Marg found him about as attractive as one of our large cider barrels. Besides, we were pretty sure there was a Mrs Bernard back in Adelaide somewhere.

All the machinery in the apple sheds never seemed to work at the one time. Either the press was broken or the pasteuriser was out of steam, or the bottling machine was not bottling. On one occasion we waited for a new shipment of bottles to arrive that were supposed to take the boiling hot pasteurised juice. Just when we were panicking to get an order out on time, they all collapsed into a sticky mess when the first lot of juice was poured in. Another time I looked at the bottom of one bottle and found black floaty objects there. I looked at all the others. They too had black floaty objects. The pasteuriser had burned the apple and all of that batch had to be thrown out. At moments like this I'd sit on the floor crying at the injustice of it all, wondering why the hell we were doing this.

Rob would try valiantly to cheer me up, at the same time trying to keep cheerful himself. One day all the lids on the bottles leaked and the juice got mouldy. That batch also had to be ditched. Another time, as I was doing the rounds of the supermarkets promoting the juice, I noticed that the pear had coagulated in the bottles on the shelves of Coles in Burnie. (At that stage we were producing mixtures of apple and pear and apple and berries). All that had to be withdrawn. But, despite all this, the orders kept rolling in and we were flat out trying to keep up.

My job, apart from helping to make the juice, was to promote it. I did this in every supermarket throughout Tasmania, sometimes with the help of Don Calvert, who'd not long before returned from sailing in the Admiral's Cup. David Boon, the solidly built, moustached, and brilliant Tasmanian cricketer, made a commercial for us. It was so bad it was good.

He had to say. "The thing I like doing best is opening for Australia and the thing I like doing second best is opening a bottle of Tasmania's Pure Fresh Apple Maid Apple Juice…it's a real BOON for your health."

How corny is that!

When I asked David to put a bit more oomph into his voice, he said, fairly, 'I'm a cricketer, Rosemary. Not a salesman.'

Mind you these days he makes many commercials and has improved somewhat, although he still sounds more like a cricketer than an actor. We did have a fun day making that commercial and another one, where we used a Hobart model, dressed in a blowsy Apple Maid costume, frolicking down the orchard carrying a pail of apple juice. The girls were so embarrassed that she was so obviously wearing a blonde wig and the ad was so twee that they refused to watch it. However it sold lots of juice.

Apart from appearing on television in the series, *Making it in Tasmania*, and *You've got it made in Tasmania*, we also appeared on the front page of the *Mercury* and *The Age* newspapers in Victoria when we sold our juice to the Jewish Community in Melbourne. The day the Rabbi and his followers (including Enzra, a huge boulder of a fellow who seemed to be the Rabbi's bodyguard), arrived to make sure all was 'kosher' it was pouring rain, with huge rivers pouring off the gutters onto the ground. The whole entourage were all in black suits with large brimmed black hats and sporting long flowing black beards, which they spent a lot of time patting. The Rabbi, an elderly gentleman with a stooped back and wearing thick black spectacles and sporting a longer beard than the others, sat in a dilapidated armchair in the sheds reading his verses until he nodded off to sleep, producing a loud snore.

Much to my horror I saw that a dozen of our nosey piglets (we were breeding them to eat the apple pomace) had escaped from their pens and were trotting in, squealing in delight.

Before I could get to them they rushed up to where the Rabbi was sitting and started sniffing around his feet. As you can imagine, for a Jewish Rabbi, pigs in the apple shed would have somewhat tainted the idea of the juice being produced in kosher fashion. Thank God the good man didn't wake up before I managed to shoo the piglets out. Till two o'clock the next morning we produced bottles and bottles of kosher juice for the tables of the Victorian Jewish community. The next morning a truck came to collect it all and take it to Devonport for the ferry crossing to Melbourne.

They took forever to pay. In fact they didn't. Not until I threatened to get them the same sort of publicity we'd got in the first place for being the only juice producer in Australia able to provide them with kosher juice.

The pigs were a necessary sideline. The apple pomace had to be disposed of somehow, so mixed with dry feed this provided an ideal way to fatten pigs. In the end we had a herd of eleven, producing a heap of little piglets. And although I got the top price at the Bridgewater sales one week (where I'd taken a load up myself with the local stock carrier), they still caused a bit of friction between Rob and me. It was always 'your damn pigs' who'd broken through a fence or dug up another paddock.

One year we swapped a dressed pig for three dozen crayfish and fifty dozen oysters (not all coming in at once) with a local fisherman and continued to barter in this way with a few others. Rob tried to convince Phillip Thomson to go into 'Piggy Bank' rather than 'Medi Bank' seeing as we seemed to spend so much time sitting in his surgery with one injury after another. He politely refused.

Another day I had to hurriedly fly to Brisbane to dispose of five pallets of apple juice that had gone up the week before. There had been a stuff-up with our agent and the supermarket had over ordered, refusing point blank to take delivery. From five o'clock five mornings in a row I sat at the Brisbane markets selling apple juice to local businesses, eventually getting rid of the lot and arriving home with a most unbecoming permed hairdo, (the girls christened it 'the busby') which had seemed a good idea at the time when I'd a few hours to fill in before catching the plane home.

It was during this time that we bought a new yacht. Although our sailor trailer, *Prauwin*, was great for sailing around Norfolk Bay we were keen to go further afield. We'd done a few trips away with Sue and Don and all the children on their boat, *Cascades*, down the D'Entrecasteaux Channel and up the East Coast. Now we were keen to have our own boat to go exploring in. After much searching we found a 38-foot Huon and King Billy pine sloop in an old shed at the bottom of the noted boat builder Tom Pilkington's house in Marine Terrace in Battery Point. She wasn't quite finished, but Tom was getting on in years and was keen to off-load her. For weeks we worked on her at Purdon's slipway in Battery Point, finishing her off, installing a new engine, decorating her with plush cushions and curtains and varnishing her woodwork. Soon she had a name: *Charlotte Rose*, and was bobbing up and down on a mooring in the picturesque tree-lined bay at Taranna beside Don and Sue's *Cascades*.

Often we sailed extensively around Tasmania, from Recherche Bay in the far south to Maria and Shouten Islands on the east coast, at times in the company of *Cascades* or Bruce's *Norfolk Bay*. These were the days when you could throw a cray-pot over the side and know you'd end up with four or five good crays for dinner, or catch up to thirty flathead in a few hours of dangling a line over the side.

'Not crays again for breakfast,' was the cry one morning as the icebox was overflowing with succulent crayfish.

Nowadays in Tassie one has to pay over sixty dollars a kilo for crays, and even then they're often not available, unless there's been an upset in the lucrative Chinese market and fishermen are selling them directly off their boats.

We'd only been at Windermere for a few months when I decided to take up selling real estate again. The Peninsula was situated some one and a half hours from Hobart (it's a bit closer now with the new road at Eaglehawk Neck). There was no real estate agent on the Peninsula, although Robert Stewarts had an agent working the area from Hobart. I decided to start where I knew someone. I called in to Henry Jones IXL, the office of the dapper fellow who'd sold us Windermere, assuring them they needed an agent on the Peninsula. I was pleased, if not slightly nervous as to how I was going to fit everything in, when they offered me a job to start straightaway. Within a short time, much to my amazement, I had a load of listings, mainly by going around and introducing myself and advertising in the local gazette.

I must have been doing well for I was asked to judge and present the prize to Miss Nubeena at the Nubeena Regatta – a great honour. Then Robert Stewarts (now Roberts) the well-known rural Tasmanian company approached me to join them. After a bit of persuasion I agreed. Shortly afterwards Henry Jones closed their real estate section anyway.

At this stage on the Peninsula the average block of land was selling for about five thousand dollars, so as you can imagine my commissions weren't going to set the world on fire. Yet it soon started adding up and we had a good extra income coming in to supplement the orchard, farm, and Rob's army pension.

My sales varied from a pig farm in Nubeena to the most expensive residential property sold on the Peninsula at Eaglehawk Neck (from memory it was fifty thousand dollars).

I managed to fulfil my real estate obligations between working on the production line in the apple sheds and in the orchard. I either had an answering machine when I was in the orchard, checking it regularly, or if in the sheds I'd hightail it up the stairs in my overalls and gumboots to answer the phone. People on the other end of the line would imagine I was sitting in a plush office somewhere, not in a grotty cubby-hole covered from head to toe in apple pomace. If they wanted to look at a property I'd have a quick shower and change into something more becoming, before heading off to show them around. My main real estate outfit consisted of jeans, leather boots, and a tweed jacket, even if I was going in to have my fortnightly rostered day in the office in Hobart. One day, when some of the board were coming in for a meeting, the manager of Robert Stewarts asked me cautiously, 'Rosemary…do you think you could possibly rustle up a dress to wear?'

How I wasn't murdered in this job I'll never know, for I ventured from one end of the Peninsula to the other – to the remotest farms and isolated wilderness areas to show prospective purchasers their dream. Anyone of them could have been a nutter. When I was really nervous I'd put Poppy and Gatsby in the car with me (Poppy more for the ride, rather than any great deterrent to a would be attacker, as he couldn't see much anyway, but he did bring his walking stick just in case). Yet fortunately no-one seemed in the slightest bit interested in doing me any harm. I became bogged in a few places and had to walk to the nearest farm to get a tow, once having to wade through a river fully dressed in order to get help. Other than that I wasn't worried at all.

Tragically a neighbour shot Gatsby. I can't say I blame the man, as he'd been caught chasing their sheep. Gatsby was always a wanderer, no matter how hard we tried to curtail his outings. He grew far worse after he and the rest of the dog population on the Peninsula were compulsorily drenched for hydatids. Somehow he never seemed quite the same thereafter. Not long before he was shot he'd disappeared for a few weeks and we'd searched high and low. Eventually he wandered back up the driveway with his hair all matted and with the pads on his paws worn to a frazzle. For a while he stayed near home.

We hadn't realised he'd disappeared until one of the girls in Georgie's class at school was telling the children how her parents had shot a dog that morning who was chasing sheep. When Georgie asked what the dog looked like it sounded just like Gatsby. Poor little thing had to get through the rest of the day at school before she could tell us. That night we went up to the neighbours' farm and found him. We brought him home to Windermere and buried him in the back garden under a pine tree near Poppy's vegetable garden, all of us with tears rolling down our cheeks.

From apple juice we diversified into scrumpy cider and coolers. The scrumpy cider was so potent that it produced some unexpected results. One night, when we were having dinner at the Lufra Hotel at Eaglehawk Neck (which used to be owned by Reg Ansett), with some friends from Canberra and the Peninsula, we were treated to an impromptu floorshow. Next to our table was a group of attractive young women from overseas doing a tour with The Camping Connection. Rob offered them a bottle of our scrumpy cider, which they readily accepted. Within half an hour two of them were dancing naked on the staircase. We were all entranced, apart from Poppy who couldn't see a thing and was furious he was missing out. The next week written up in the *Peninsula Gazette* was 'The Great Scrumpy Cider Episode', doing wonders for the publicity of our new product.

Chapter 30 She'll Be Apples at Koonya

During this time we became quite well-known in Tassie through the many radio, TV, newspaper and magazine interviews we did about our apple juice and cider business. We basked in the glory when we weren't in a screaming heap on the floor of the sheds with one machinery breakdown after another and a deadline to meet. At one stage we were pressing more apples for fresh juice (from as far away as the Huon down south and Tamar Valley up north) than any other apple processor in Tasmania, including Cascades and Clements and Marshall. In the end we decided we needed a distributor. It was becoming impossible to keep up with the distribution as well as production.

We employed a fellow who owned one of the biggest orange juice and mineral water businesses in Hobart. Unfortunately a few years later this ended up in a long protracted court case when he appeared to pocket some of the profits without declaring them to us. We were only made aware when we got a phone call from Coles and Purity asking why we'd put up the prices of our juices. When we informed them we hadn't, it all came out.

Fortunately, we won the law case but it had taken its toll, both financially and emotionally, particularly as the fellow told me he'd run us out of town when he thought he was being shown up and about to lose the case. Also, in the confusion both Coles and Purity suspended any future orders until the court case was resolved, meaning our income was devastated. The day the verdict came out in our favour we went to the Sheraton Hotel with the girls to celebrate. I must admit the whole episode, not surprisingly, had taken the shine off the apple juice business and put a strain on the whole family.

Although at the time we thought it was the end of the world, a number of years down the track it was hard to even remember the finer details, apart from the fact we lost nearly all our money and had to completely start all over again. We also learned a valuable lesson that most manufacturers learn. No matter what product you produce you are at the mercy of the retail chains and distributors.

CHAPTER 31

Overcoming Adversity...Hobart

Well before the court case took place we decided to move to Hobart in late 1985, as both girls were boarding at Fahan School in Sandy Bay. Tasman District School only went to year ten and Charlotte was ready to go into year eleven. She'd boarded with a family in Sandy Bay for a term the year before when she went to Mount Carmel Convent, but she didn't particularly like living with a strange family, so we thought boarding school for both of them was the best option.

This left Rob, Poppy and me on our own on the Peninsula. We felt that this was not the reason we'd come to Tasmania. It was also a long trip up and back each Monday morning to make the deadline for school at 8.30. And then there was the long trip up to bring them home for the weekend on Friday evenings. They were feeling unsettled and so were we.

I spent hours driving real estate agents in Hobart batty, trying to describe what we were looking for and not having a clue myself. Every time I'd find anything slightly suitable, I'd then drive down to the Peninsula and think we were crazy to be moving. Our apple sheds were so enormous that anything else looked tiny, until we found Hampton, a two-story Federation weatherboard divided into three flats on the bluff at Bellerive with spectacular views across the Derwent River to Mount Wellington. After we turned it back into one house, with Poppy having part of the downstairs as his living quarters, it was featured in the local press as *Home of the Month*, yet not before we'd ripped up acres of lino, pulled out thousands of old nails, knocked down numerous mock walls put in during the fifties, and installed a brand new Bosky stove, which ran the central heating, and nearly burned the house down at Charlotte's 18th birthday when we tried to crank the heat up. The chimney caught fire, resulting in the fire brigade arriving (to the joy of the revellers). We also sanded the floors, painted it throughout, re-established the gardens and built a huge fence along the front to protect us from the prevailing winds howling across the water from Mount Wellington. We let out the house at Windermere to our production manager, who was continuing to run the sheds and produce the fruit juice, with Rob commuting a few times a week.

The girls and I would go down with him on weekends (staying in Poppy's old cedar cottage) where we all worked frantically trying to keep the farm going and getting the next week's production in the sheds organised. As I had now started in real estate again in Hobart, this soon began to take its toll. After much discussion we decided to sell up and move to Hobart permanently. We were sad to leave the Peninsula and the many friends we made there. Yet we go back often, staying with Sue and Don at Cascades. We have a wonderful room overlooking the luxuriant green valley fronting the Cascade River – where years ago we used to sit on fallen logs with a huge bonfire burning in our midst, and where sheep and cattle now graze languidly under the tall stands of blackwoods and bluegums.

After the first couple of weeks in Hobart I was offered a job selling real estate at an office in Sandy Bay and accepted. The next day I was offered the job I'd wanted in the first place and had to go down with a bottle of whisky to appease the manager at the Sandy Bay office. I started the next week at the office of Edwards and Windsor in the centre of town, moving into a tiny cubicle at the end of a passageway. It was from this cubicle that I managed to sell some of the most expensive houses in Hobart (including the record price ever achieved), but not without the guidance of Rob Windsor and Andrew Edwards, who'd started the firm a few years before. I went on to get my Auctioneer's Licence and as far as I know I was the only woman conducting auctions in Tasmania at the time and one of very few in Australia. Some days I'd conduct up to five auctions. I adored doing them, particularly chattel estate auctions, often going on for a whole day and leaving me with a voice like a croaky frog. I also studied to renew my Manager's Licence. The law in Tassie was different to Canberra so there were other subjects I needed to do. There were only a few of us selling at Edwards Windsor when I started. Then we expanded, eventually moving across to the other side of Collins Street to larger premises where I became the Sales Manager with twelve sales staff. Over the six years I was there I made many great friends with other staff members and the people I dealt with. It was a fun office. We worked hard, but we also had plenty of time for partying. Recently the talented writer, Rosie Dub launched my novel *Bird of Paradise* at Fullers Book Shop and I stood up and gave a speech to a large gathering in the very same spot my office used to be, for Fullers have now taken over the premises.

I became a National Real Estate Trainer, conducting training seminars all around Australia. On one trip I was sent to Echuca on the Murray River to train a group of Victorian country agents. It was during the airline strike. I had to fly out of Hobart on a Caribou Army plane to Melbourne, followed by a light plane to Albury and then a four-hour drive up the longest, flattest, and hottest road to Echuca, an old-fashioned paddle steamer town in Victoria on the Murray River, opposite its twin town of Moama, New South Wales. I arrived back in Melbourne the next day to conduct another seminar with a huge dead bird attached to my front bumper bar, wondering why people were calling out and pointing as I drove past. The next day I hopped back on the Caribou for Tasmania.

I enjoyed the training side and the travelling it involved plus all the people I met. I also loved writing columns for the *Australian First National Training Magazine*, doing so for many years. My numerous trips to Victoria allowed me to visit Dibs on her new farm, Glendalough Park, in the rich rolling countryside of the Gippsland area, where she and Kevin have set up their kennels and cattery at the bottom of the manicured lawns surrounding the homestead. Here they'd made a new life for themselves, both becoming absorbed into the local community as if they'd been there all their lives.

I was also able to visit Gill and Eugene. He and Jenny now had three children: Godfrey, Eugene and Grania. I hadn't seen Gill since I flew up in 1985 for a grand celebration for my father's eightieth birthday at Hardigreen Park where all the family gathered for a double celebration, as it was also Gill and Colin's son Andrew's 21st.

Sadly this was to be the last time we were all gathered together as a family, apart from Viv, who hasn't been together with the rest of us as a group for close to fifty years, although we all visit her at separate times. When I look at the photos I feel a dreadful stab of sadness, for shortly after this photo was taken my parents decided that the long trip from Ireland was becoming too much for them to cope with. Neither ever came back to Australia again, relying on us to visit them in Ireland whenever possible. I look at the happy faces of the children. The rugby-mad Andrew, who has set up an enormously successful world-wide business in North Wales where he lives with his family, wife Jane and daughters Sian and Catrin; Allison, who has bravely overcome many health set-backs and Mia, a talented teacher to children with special problems; our precious Liam, who loved animals so much and is sadly no longer with us; and our two blonde blue-eyed girls, such a contrast to Gill and Colin's brown-eyed lot. In a way it all seems so long ago. In other ways it seems like yesterday.

A house with children but without a dog is not the same. So it wasn't long before Rob and Georgie set off to buy Georgie a birthday present. Hence, Polly, a wriggling shiny black Labrador, came into the family. For the next thirteen years she gave us incredible joy. Sadly she became so ill when she got old that we had to have her put down, leaving an enormous hole in the family. Not only was she a wonderful watchdog (taking to a burglar when Georgie and Charlotte were flatting together later and baling up a couple of blokes stealing from under our house), she was also great company, particularly for Poppy who adored having her around.

During our legal battle with our juice distributor, finances had become scarce, so we decided to sell Hampton and move to a smaller house in Albuera Street across the river in Battery Point. It adjoined the Anglesea Barracks, where we were often invited by our army friends.

Our new house needed a lot of work, but we weren't daunted, as Rob had decided that with the help of a tradesman he could do most of the renovations himself. There was a large crowd at the auction, but few bidders. Not realising we were the successful bidders, Sue Becker, the radio personality and a client of mine, walked up to me afterwards, exclaiming in a loud Cockney accent, 'My God Ro! Who in their right senses would buy a place like that? Have you seen the state of the roof?'

CHAPTER 32

Finding Our Feet and Sea Legs

The house at Albuera Street was on a long narrow block with an overgrown vegetable garden and chicken sheds up the back. I wasn't all that sad to leave Hampton, for the wind howled relentlessly and in a way the house was far too big for us. Albuera Street was cosier; the rear garden a delight, with a wonderful walnut tree and a mass of spring bulbs and a huge jasmine vine covering the trellis off the back room.

Sue Becker was right – the house certainly needed work. The roof was in a dreadful mess with the outside eaves channelling water straight into the rickety sink in the small lean-to kitchen. There was only one tiny bathroom and the girls' bedrooms upstairs had no power points whatsoever, a slight problem we'd somehow overlooked. Poppy was given the room running the whole length of the eastern side, with his bedroom being the enclosed verandah to the front. He was soon supplying us with lettuces, tomatoes, zucchinis and cucumbers from the garden.

From Albuera Street, after many renovations and a few additions, we had Charlotte's 21st at Salamanca Inn (with what seemed to be the entire Hutchins Rugby Union team downing what we thought would be enough beer for the whole night in half an hour, sending us flying for more) and Georgie's eighteenth.

After a month of living here we put in a chicken run up the back and then Rob decided that what we really needed to add a bit of class and colour were a couple of peacocks. He and Georgie ventured forth, returning with Andrew and Susan, so called after Andrew Peacock, the past Minister of Defence and his gregarious wife Susan.

It wasn't long before both peacocks got their wings, so to speak, and ventured out and about to socialise: Andrew was the epitome of a well-behaved peacock but Susan was a different kettle of fish. One day at work I received a distressed phone call from an elderly neighbour. 'Do you happen to own the monstrous bird in my kitchen?' she shrieked with terror. 'The damn thing is screaming and trumpeting ferociously? It sounds like a braying donkey and I can't get in the door.'

After rescuing the unfortunate lady from the claws of death, we eventually succumbed to pressure, returning both peacocks to the large farm they'd come from. There they were more at home with lakes and fields to roam around.

Next to the house was a small shop (originally the tuck-shop for the Albuera Street School). Although we'd sold Windermere we were still producing apple juice, now down at Castle Forbes Bay about forty minutes south of Hobart. Rob was distributing it around Hobart in an Apple Maid van, but in addition, Charlotte and Georgie decided to sell the juice from the shop to make some extra pocket money. Charlotte also took a stall amongst the ancient sandstone buildings at Salamanca Market during the time she attended Drysdale Hospitality School, after graduating from Fahan. Together with jobs she had at the Theatre Royal Pub, the renowned Dear Friends Restaurant, run by the well-known restauranteur, Geoff Copping, and Kopwoods Tavern (Knoppys) owned for many years by my friend, Peggy James, she made enough money in a year to finance a trip overseas, after which she took up a prized position with the Regent Hotel in Sydney, where she managed the Lobby restaurant.

In the meantime, Georgie continued at Fahan, becoming amongst other things the cox for the men's University Rowing Team, which she loved. After Fahan she took herself overseas for a few months, like Charlotte, visiting her grandparents in Ireland and Viv in Wales. She even had New Year's Eve in Edinburgh with a friend from school. When she came home she went to the University of Tasmania, graduating in Arts Economics. Whilst there, she too worked at many jobs, including the Theatre Royal and Dear Friends. After a brief spell with Trust Bank, she went to Hong Kong where she met up with Charlotte who'd been in England on a working holiday, looking after an elderly couple, followed by a stint in Harrods. Together they did a trip around China, terrifying the life out of Rob and me as they were totally on their own – two young blondes amidst a sea of dark haired Chinese. They walked the Great Wall of China and sailed along the coast back to Hong Kong by steamer from Shanghai. After that they worked in Japan teaching English to the Japanese. Looking back, and only now hearing some of the tricky situations they found themselves in whilst in China, I feel they were pretty adventuresome.

We continued to sail on the *Charlotte Rose*, the highlight being the Bi Centennial Tall Ships Regatta, which brought the whole of Hobart to a stand-still as tall ships from all around the globe collected on the docks in Salamanca.

We followed the boats down the Derwent, including the Irish entrant the *Asgard*.

What a wonderful spectacle it was with huge bowsprits heaving and lifting, sails flapping to and fro in the stiff breeze, and the happy sound of accents from all around the world calling across the wind to each other. After rounding Tasman Island we were left behind in their wake, pulling into Fortescue Bay, where we anchored behind the old shipwreck, as we've done so many times before and since. Here in the bracken waters Marcus Clark sometimes catches a few crayfish or abalone, which he brings home for us all to devour.

Later in the year my parents had a bad car accident in Ireland. After a few hasty arrangements, I took off to be with them. Fortunately by the time I got there my father had recovered enough to collect me from the train station at Bray, but my mother was still somewhat shaken up and bruised. For two weeks I stayed with them, going up to Dublin a couple of times to help my father with research at Trinity University. (He was writing his memoir and compiling the family trees for both the Esmonde and Peterswald families.) At Trinity he showed me the wonderful Book of Kells and we sat in the ancient library, which was brimming with history within leather-bound books, and wandered the magnificent hallways resounding with the clatter and chatter of smart young students rugged up in their Trinity scarves and warm Aran pullovers.

When I wanted to shop in Grafton Street, my father sat patiently in a small church waiting for me. Later we ambled through St Stephen's Green, one of his arms tucked through mine, the other firmly gripping his walking stick, where we fed the ducks swimming amongst the water lilies on the pond and watched the squirrels forage for nuts – just as I've done so many times with my mother after lunch or afternoon tea at the Shelbourne Hotel.

Another time he took me to the Art Gallery and Museum, all the while telling me in his melodious voice about Irish history and what part the Esmondes played in it all. He even

Chapter 32   Finding Our Feet and Sea Legs

showed me the spot where the British hanged my ancestor, John Esmonde, in 1798. After a cup of coffee at Bewleys we caught the train back to Rathdrum where he bought my mother a bunch of yellow daffodils as a peace offering after the slight altercation they'd had before we left that morning.

'You should let Teeny go on her own to Dublin,' my mother had told my father sternly. 'You'll slow her down.'

'I won't slow her down one bit,' my father answered stubbornly, hauling his walking stick out of the brass holder near the front door and plonking his Donegal tweed hat on his head. And with only the slightest hint of a goodbye he crankily shuffled from the door to the car where we drove to the train station at Rathdrum to catch the DART to Dublin.

I was glad he'd put his foot down so to speak, for I wouldn't have missed that day with him for quids. Fortunately when we got home the daffodils worked a treat and my mother was in fine form, serving us a piping hot Irish stew from the pot on the old fuel stove.

Again we went to Ballynastragh for Sunday lunch, and had regular meals at the Wicklow Heather or Lynhams Pub straddling the Avonmore River in the nearby village of Laragh, or at The Meeting of the Waters near the small town of Avoca – where they made the popular television series *Ballykiss Angel*. When I was happy they were okay, they drove me through the narrow winding country roads (where we were held up for ages behind an army convoy, as there'd recently been an IRA scare) to the train station at Carlow where I once again sadly said goodbye. Each time I left them in Ireland my father seemed to be getting frailer. What I didn't realise then was that this would be the last time I'd see him before he was admitted to hospital with terminal cancer and I would rush to his bedside. From the train window I watched them standing there, my mother dabbing the tears in her eyes, my father lifting his tweed hat in a salute and with his other arm around my mother's shoulders. I too wiped my eyes, before the train let out a bellowing whistle and pulled out of the station. Now they were just two tiny dots in the far-off distance.

Soon I was whizzing through meadows of wild flowers and green fields full of contented bleary eyed cows and black and white sheep, to meet Viv in Cork where she was looking after a friend's five children in a rambling two-hundred-year-old house on the banks of the River Lee. It had been nine years since I'd seen her and as ever she looked divine, as slim as a pencil and her hair a bit longer. We had a fun time together, picnicking at Kinsale, driving around the countryside and visiting our eccentric and lovable Aunt Eileen (the one who placed her dress in a silk stocking) on her family estate, Ballyellis, not far out of Cork. Sadly my Uncle Witham had died a few years before and Eileen was now living there with her two sisters. We even took all of the five children we were looking after to kiss the Blarney Stone. And, as an Aussie guide held our legs, we did what nearly every tourist visiting Ireland wishes to do: leaned over backwards and kissed the stone that is supposed to bring you good luck. The only problem being that we were laughing so much the poor bloke could hardly hold on to us.

After the children were safely tucked into bed, we'd spend hours sitting around the huge pine table in the kitchen with a fire roaring in the stone hearth, dreaming of the possibility of buying a farm in Ireland. We even looked at a few, once being chased off the grounds by an angry tenant with a gun pointed in our direction, who didn't want the farm sold up from under him.

'Jesus, Mary and Joseph,' he shouted across the front lawn.

Chapter 32 Finding Our Feet and Sea Legs

'You two be getting off this place now before I take the gun to you.'

In the end we decided, not only was it a risky business looking at farms in Ireland, it was highly impractical to own one, with all of us in Australia and Viv and Tim already having a farm in Wales. Yet it didn't stop us dreaming.

From Shannon Airport we flew to London. I'd never been before and adored it all, from the gleaming London cabs, the window boxes brimming with spring bulbs, to the Tower of London and shopping in Harrods. The only disappointment was when Viv hurried me to bed the first night we were staying at an inner city hotel before I'd hardly finished my dinner, warning me in no uncertain terms that we were being given the once over by a group of Arab gentlemen at the next table. Personally I've nothing against gentlemen from Arabia giving me the eye, but Viv assured me they didn't have good intentions, so reluctantly I meekly followed her upstairs to our room.

When I arrived back in Hobart we decided to do away with the apple juice business altogether and Rob started working with a firm selling commercial real estate, which he enjoyed and was very good at, holding us in good stead for when we opened our own business a few years later.

CHAPTER 33

Heading North on Reveille

At this stage we were keeping *Charlotte Rose* at the marina in the picturesque seaside village of Kettering about half an hour's drive south of Hobart.

One day Rob came home from working on her. 'I think I've found us a new boat,' he exclaimed, giving me a kiss and a hug to ensure I was going to be as enamoured as he. 'One we can sail the coast of Australia safely in.'

Although *Charlotte Rose* was a comfortable cruiser, we felt that if we were going to go sailing further afield we'd feel far happier in something a bit more suited to ocean sailing. For although we'd made her special, it was difficult to ensure the aft cabin was totally waterproof, as it opened into the cockpit and no matter how much we tried we couldn't keep a rough sea out. Also, she was still lacking a proper shower and the head formed part of the foreword cabin. Hence *Reveille* came into our lives and sadly *Charlotte Rose* went to a new owner.

Reveille, known as the *Elsie J* when we bought her, was a Roberts Mauritius 43 built by a Scottish Engineer out of fibreglass. She was more than comfortable, with three separate cabins. After a bit of titivating she became warm and cosy below and gleaming on topsides. To begin with we undertook a number of trips around Tasmania to familiarise ourselves, but finally the wanderlust got to us both and we

Chapter 33   Heading North on Reveille

decided to take absence of leave from our jobs and sail north to Queensland.

Georgie in particular spent many hours working on *Reveille*, painting the hull on her own in freezing conditions, as she too had decided to come sailing north. Georgie had not long before met Simon Merchant to whom she's now married. At that time Simon was only nineteen (and studying in the first intake of Real Estate Scholarship holders in Tasmania) and Georgie seventeen. Coincidently Simon is the son of Geoff Merchant, who used to manage Chilton Thompson, our agent for selling apples at Windermere. We'd met him a number of times and thought he was a great guy. Now here was Georgie stepping out with his son. Simon had also decided to come on the trip north so it was all go, getting *Reveille* ship shape. Luckily for Rob, Simon, a delightful handsome young fellow, was an avid rugby enthusiast, and still is, having represented Tassie in his age group.

On November 30th, 1989, we set sail after a champagne farewell at the Cruising Yacht Club, where we'd bought *Reveille* up for final preparations. We were a crew of six: Rob and I, Georgie and Simon, Honey Hogan (who later married Jim Bacon, the Premier of Tasmania, who sadly died), and Dan, an experienced Sydney to Hobart yacht racer and friend of ours. Although I was excited to be heading off, I was also nervous about crossing the notorious Bass Strait for the first time.

Our first stop was at Connellys Marsh before we headed across Norfolk Bay, where we threw our money in the bucket on a pole going through the Dunalley Canal as we'd done so many times before. From there we stopped at Maria Island and then Wineglass Bay, where we swam in the clear blue water off the magical stretch of white sand that's so famous around the world (the Queen stopped here for a barbeque whilst on the *Britannia*), and ate magnificent crayfish supplied to us by friendly local fisherman. Our initial night in Bass Strait was so calm we fired up the barbeque and sat back with a few wines to enjoy dinner.

In the early hours of the morning it all changed. Suddenly we found ourselves in a forty-knot northerly gale. And as luck would have it the self-steering decided to give up the ghost at the same time. Then the engine overheated and stopped. Eventually we took shelter under Mallacoota on the Victorian coast, but not before I was knocked out by a flying breadboard in the galley while preparing a meal. The next morning a southerly came in and we managed to sail on to the busy fishing village of Eden where we decamped to the local hotel for showers and a much-needed drink. Honey left us here as she'd been dreadfully seasick on the way over and couldn't stomach the thought of soldiering on to Sydney.

'I know exactly how many damn flowers there are on those cushions,' she told me exhaustedly in the middle of Bass Strait, as I tried to coax her to eat something when she was lying prostrate in the cabin with a bowl beside her.

When we got to Eden she suddenly came to life. I've never seen anyone leap onto solid ground with such enthusiasm. She promised to meet us in Sydney where she assured us she'd cook a curry and have it waiting for us. Needless to say she wasn't there when we arrived (I suspect it was early on in the romance and Jim was waiting back in Hobart), but she never forgot. When Jim, as Premier, launched our Tasmanian photographic book *From the Sea* in 2002, Honey arrived with a packet of curry powder.

For the next three and a half weeks we sailed north, with Dan disembarking in Sydney where a couple of friends, Susie and Pete Knight from Canberra, joined us for the trip north to Coffs Harbour. But it was just Rob, Georgie, Simon and I who literally surfed over the treacherous bar at Southport on the Gold Coast (it was closed half an hour later due to the huge seas), before tying up at the Marina Mirage in an almighty electrical storm. Eugene and Charlotte were there to meet us as we were spending Christmas with Eugene and his family.

After a week or so, Simon flew back to Hobart and Eugene and Nicky, an exchange student staying with them from Austria, joined us on the trip north to Mooloolaba where we were leaving the boat for the next year.

'It's like riding in a rodeo,' Nicky exclaimed in delight, as we rode one monstrous wave after the next. Poor Eugene was turning a pale shade of green.

All in all it had been a challenging trip. In hindsight we should have gone at a different time of year when northerlies didn't predominately prevail, but this was the only time I could get off work and I was also keen to spend Christmas with Eugene. Yet I must admit there were times, when we were bashing into a head wind, with Rob in the engine room trying to coax the motor into life, that I'd wished I hadn't been quite so persuasive.

Reveille's temperamental engine was a constant battle the whole time we owned her. Rob spent many an hour fixing one problem after another, taking the shine off the trip for him somewhat. Even when it was purring along we always had to keep an ear out, listening for that bump that told us it was about to give up the ghost, particularly in tricky situations like going over the bar at Southport when Georgie was heard to pray, which wasn't one of her stronger points, 'Hail Mary full of grace…please…please keep the engine going. Just for another half hour.'

Chapter 34

From Humble Beginnings... Starting Peterswalds

When we were once again in Hobart we both went back to work, but I must admit, much as we tried, our hearts weren't really in it. Friends went up to Mooloolaba to stay on *Reveille*, using her as a base, and Georgie and Simon also had a holiday on board. So too Rob and I. Once when Rob went up to check all was okay he discovered the whole of the cabin floor crawling in cockroaches. We never really did get rid of them. They gave me the creeps, particularly when one crawled into my ear at night.

'The only way to get rid of 'em is to sink the bloody boat and haul it up again,' an old salt told us. 'That'll drown the buggers.'

We weren't game to prove his theory, although at times we were tempted.

After discovering a heavily wooded block of land on the bends at Mount Nelson, with wide views to the Derwent River and Eastern Shore, we decided to sell Albuera Street and build a pole house.

'They didn't buy a block of land,' Georgie told the newspaper reporter when they were doing an article on our new house. 'They bought a block of air.'

She wasn't far wrong, for the block fell away steeply down

the mountain at the front and the only house that could be built on it was a pole house. Firstly Rob took time off work and helped the builder erect the house. Then he painted it from top to bottom himself, no mean feat, as most of the time he was on a perilous ladder trying to reach almost unreachable parts. Built on three levels, Poppy had a separate flat underneath and the girls had two bedrooms and a small bathroom upstairs. Our bedroom, kitchen and living area were on the middle floor.

Once it was built and everyone was comfortably installed, I also decided to give up work so that we could take *Reveille* further north to the Whitsundays for a few months. Edwards Windsor had kindly said I could come back to work with them anytime I wanted. But in the end I felt it was time for a change and time for Rob and me to do something together. As Charlotte was still working at the Regent in Sydney, Georgie offered to look after Poppy; at the same time she was studying hard at her Economics Degree at the University of Tasmania situated at the bottom of the hill where she could walk.

So after a wonderful send-off for me, where Edwards Windsor hired the *Cartella*, an old steam ferry, to party on the Derwent with all the staff in fancy dress, I flew up to Sydney to visit Charlotte (where we were wined and dined at the famous Kables restaurant at the Regent, thanks to a prize Charlotte had won for excellent service), and then on to Mooloolaba where Rob was already installed on *Reveille*, preparing her for the trip north.

I was sad to leave Edwards Windsor and all the friends I'd made there, but was excited about the future. One of the things Rob Windsor gave me in my wonderful 'send-off gift basket' was a bottle of bright red hair dye.

'This,' he assured me with the huge grin he was renowned

for, 'is the only colour your hair hasn't been all the time you've been with us.'

He'd also compiled a tear-jerking photo album of my six years there, from the first and last auction I'd conducted, to our time at a seminar in Fiji – and the numerous office functions we'd had over the years. By the time the night was finished I hadn't a skerrick of mascara left on my eyelashes.

For three wonderful months, interspersed with the odd horrendous storm (during one we lost the dinghy), and engine breakdowns we sailed north and around the magical Whitsunday Islands with family and friends coming to stay on board. We adored ship life and despite at times fighting the elements (they never advertise the howling bullets in glossy brochures for the Whitsundays), we wondered why we hadn't done this before.

Yet we couldn't stay sailing forever. We had Poppy and Georgie to think of and bills to pay. One evening, sitting on the back deck of *Reveille* in Butterfly Bay, enjoying a late twilight, we decided to open our own real estate office in Hobart. We would call the firm 'Peterswalds'. We even more or less designed the logo, chose the colours of burgundy and gold (the Dunhill cigarette packet) and worked out a strategy. We would initially set up our office from home, downstairs in the spare bedroom and use our living room as a boardroom and reception area.

We left *Reveille* on a mooring at Airlie Beach, where a local yacht broker was to offer her for sale. It didn't take long until we found a buyer, exchanging her for part payment on a unit on Hastings Street in Noosa in Queensland. A good arrangement, as the unit was let out and we could certainly do with the rent coming in, rather than paying mooring fees at Airlie. Later we sold the unit for a reasonable profit. In hindsight we should have held on to it. At the time we needed the cash flow for the business. Of all the boats we've had, *Reveille* I mourned the least. Although she'd taken us on a long passage, there constantly seemed to be mechanical problems, and of course the cockroaches were still driving me balmy, no matter how much we sprayed and bombed.

Amazingly, I hadn't worked much on a computer before, apart from the basics. Georgie was a wonderful and patient coach. Before too long I was designing signboards, advertisements and promotional material on the large computer screen in the spare bedroom. At first I found working from home difficult to adjust to. I missed the interaction of other staff. The after-work drinks. The gossip. The fun we used to have going around as a group looking at new listings on what we called 'Groupie'. I also worried myself sick that we'd be a failure. What if no-one listed with us? Worse still, what if they listed with us and we couldn't sell their property? Would people laugh that we were trying to do it all from home? Was I being disloyal to Edwards Windsor? In fact with all the worrying I lost a stone in weight, which in itself wasn't a bad thing, although eventually even I realised I was getting a bit gaunt.

Rob was marvellous, full of confidence and loving being his own boss. It took a while to get going. It was a new concept in real estate to set up an office without being in a prominent position with a window display. This was well before the Internet revolutionised the real estate world. Also, most agents in Hobart belonged to a national group. Here we were setting up a totally independent family business from the spare bedroom in our pole house, much removed from the city.

Somehow it worked. Our signboards were distinctive; our advertisements different. I found customers I'd dealt with before at Edwards Windsor would seek me out and Rob did hours and hours of letter dropping around the suburbs of Mount Nelson and Sandy Bay. He enjoyed dealing with our clients and they, particularly the women, loved dealing with him. It wasn't long before we had more listings than we knew what to do with and sales contracts would spill out of the fax machine on a regular basis. As I was also the secretary, I would work long hours into the night typing letters and doing endless amounts of paper work. We sold four of the most expensive properties in Sandy Bay in one week, gaining much needed publicity through the *Mercury*.

To top it all off we were invited to join the Leading Agents of Australia, a tight group of top agents in every state of Australia. We attended our first conference at the Hyatt in Double Bay where I was photographed for the front page of the Business Section in the *Australian* newspaper, and the gregarious Max Christmas enthralled us for hours with stories of his somewhat chequered career.

With the Leading Agents' backing and a number of substantial sales now under our belt, I finally started to feel we were on our way.

Sadly, about six months into our new venture, my father became desperately ill in Ireland. Hurriedly I flew to be by his side, but unfortunately needed to return to Tasmania before he died.

When I took the phone call from Eugene to tell me my father had finally gone, I was beyond consolation. I couldn't believe that he wouldn't be at the end of the phone-line full of sound advice. Memories flooded my mind. How he carried me around in a bucket at Clonmoylan. Sitting with him as he dug the postholes at Reidsdale. Helping him on the milk run in Canberra. Collecting wood with him. Seeing him leaning over the gate of our Drominagh in Canberra with the girls laughing by his side. Walking stick in hand, tweed cap on his head, on the front steps of his own Drominagh and strolling through the fields by the lake to O'Kennedy's Castle. Helping us in the orchard at Windermere. His eightieth birthday party where he wrote a poetic speech, apologising for the angst he'd sometimes caused us, although he hadn't touched a drop of alcohol for the last thirty years of his life. I couldn't imagine a world without him. And I was devastated for my poor mother left behind at Cloneen without her soul mate to go walking up the river road with on long twilight evenings. How would she cope on her own?

Even now I think of him nearly every day. I was devastated not to be there for his funeral; however, finances and business was so that it was just impossible for me to do the long trip to Ireland once again. So sadly I wasn't there to say a final farewell with my mother and Viv as they buried him in the family plot at Terryglass on the shores of his beloved Lough Derg on the River Shannon, near Drominagh, where Esmondes have been laid to rest for many generations. Instead, I did what I knew he would have wanted me to do: knuckled down and got on with making our new business a success.

At the time not only were we listing houses in the centre of Hobart, suddenly we found ourselves out in the countryside too, selling farms and historic homes in places like the sleepy town of Kempton, an hour's drive north of Hobart or in the Huon or Derwent Valleys. So, as you can see, we were on the go often seven days a week.

Working together and living together had its moments, particularly as Poppy was there as well. In fact my office was right next door to his bedroom. With him so close we couldn't really have loud arguments, although there were times when we felt like killing each other, particularly when one of us had stuffed up on something important. However, on the whole we worked extremely well together and were a good team.

It wasn't long before we realised that we were growing out of our small office at home. Rob discovered some premises for sale at Magnet Court in Sandy Bay with a shop underneath. This we soon let out to a Dutchman, who started a successful patisserie, *The Golden Tulip,* the pastries adding inches to my waistline, I'm sure. Initially it was just Rob and me in these vast offices – a bit tricky when we had to go out on appointments. However, before what seemed like the blink of an eyelid, we were employing fifteen staff, including some of the best sales people in the business and were regarded by many as the top agent in Hobart, selling most of the prestigious properties. Charlotte and Georgie came back from teaching English in Japan to work with us and Simon and Rob became a successful commercial team.

Georgie did a sterling job with the accounts and property management, which Rob had handled until then and Charlotte went into sales, where she revamped our logo and advertisements with the help of Georgie, Rob and me. With much foresight she set up one of the first Internet Real Estate pages in Australia. After one presentation she'd given at a Leading Agents of Australia conference one of the prominent Sydney agents told her what a lot of people felt at the time: 'The Internet will never work for selling houses.'

How wrong he was.

For the next ten years Peterswalds continued to grow. So too did our competitors. Some followed our lead, setting up independent offices. It was a constant battle to stay at the top. But we had good staff and with Charlotte and Georgie there to keep an eye on things it allowed Rob and me to do some travelling. First of all we flew to England, starting off with a week in London, then another week exploring the English countryside and visiting the Imperial War Museum in Yeovil, where there was a detailed display commemorating my Uncle Eugene. Finally we ended up with Viv and Tim at Cilwych, who were enjoying a brief spell of warm weather. Being early summer, the daffodils were out in bloom and the countryside shone in the golden light. We strolled through the tall meadows covered in wild flowers, to where we had a picnic by the river and enjoyed warm late twilights on the front lawn. A few years ago Viv and Tim set up a huge marquee here for a reception, after the beautiful Dom's wedding to Alex Freeman at the stone church in the nearby estate of Glen Usk. Dom and Alex now have three boys, so once again Cilwych will ring with the mirth of children. Viv and I rode through the heavily wooded hills and I helped her with the stone cottages she had now successfully turned into a thriving tourist venture. And like me, Rob fell in love with this glorious corner of the world where Viv has made her life.

After Cilwych we drove to Scotland to stay at my mother's family home, Coul House, at Contin, just outside Inverness. It was now a private hotel, but alive with the history of the Mackenzie family, of which my mother was so much a part.

My mother's father, George Henry Louis, was the son of Sir Alexander Mackenzie, the 5th Baronet, to his second wife, Kathleen, daughter of Sir Henry Jardine. The title, bypassed the first part of the family, and it was my uncle, Sir Robert Evelyn Mackenzie, who inherited Coul House, where we were to stay.

Having heard so much about this wonderful piece of Scotland, we were looking forward to seeing it at long last. For two days we lived in splendour in the blue-stone mansion, relishing high tea and cucumber sandwiches on the lawns while watching a game of croquet, walking the extensive grounds and sitting in the wood-panelled library. At night we savoured delicious Scottish cuisine, including Haggis, served to us regally at a cedar table by the window overlooking the tranquil gardens, with a musician playing softly in the corner.

In a way I was pleased it was a hotel, for it had fallen into disrepair, just as so many English and Scottish mansions had done due to lack of funds. Now it was a grand and luxurious abode with many of the original features still in place.

From Scotland we flew to Ireland and my mother waiting at Cloneen. I hadn't seen her since my father's death a few years before, but she was faring much better than I'd expected. She was quite chirpy. Imelda was still there looking after her, as she'd faithfully done when my father was alive, coming from her house in the village each day to check she was okay and keeping the place in order.

After a few days at Cloneen we packed the car up and drove to Tipperary, staying at Gertalougha House next door to Drominagh. On my father's grave beside the stone church in Terryglass, I planted a fuscia, one of his favourite bushes, and hoped desperately that it would grow.

Having dropped my mother back to Cloneen, Rob and I then drove to Westport in the West of Ireland, where we rented a small white washed stone cottage on the shores of Clew Bay. Here Viv came to join us for a few days. Despite the howling winds we had picnics by the shore and later huddled around the peat fire in the kitchen, with Viv and I talking into the wee hours of the morning, well after Rob had retired to bed. On a freezing cold Sunday morning we drove to the isolated Achill Isles, where outcrops of grey speckled rocks sheltered scraggly sheep from the raging winds. Interspersed between bogs and wild heather, windswept cottages perched precariously on stony hills, as they've done for centuries gone by. Being the Sabbath, the locals were scurrying to Mass, snuggled into oversized anoraks and Aran pullovers with beanies pulled low over their eyes against the howling wind.

All too soon it was time to say goodbye to my mother at Cloneen. This was the first time I'd had to leave her on her own and come back to Australia. She looked so very small and sad standing there on the doorstep, waving us off with the trusty Imelda by her side. If I could have taken her with us I would have. But as she said: 'After a few days I'll get back to my own routine. And then I'll look forward to your next visit.'

Since then I've been back to Ireland over twenty times. And never once has it become any easier to leave her. I know it was my parents' choice to go back to Ireland; my mother's choice to stay on after my father died. Even so the guilt and heartbreak of leaving her there on her own is enormous. I am not alone in this. For all migrants, who've made Australia their home, there's always a relative separated from their loved ones. At least in this day and age, travel is so much quicker. In the time before my Uncle Eugene flew the first surcharged mail to Australia, the separation must have been horrendous.

As I've said before, a house with children and no dog is not the same, so too for Rob and I was a household without a boat. It wasn't long before the well-known Tasmanian yacht, *Tasman Isle*, built in 1952 of Huon Pine and celery top with a mahogany wheelhouse, became ours. Again she needed a great deal of work to bring her up to scratch, including a new deck; however, when the work was finished it was worth all the hours and money spent on her. Down below, the woodwork and brass lamps gleamed warmly in the cabin and on the topsides she sparkled and shone in the sun. For five years we relished owning her, keeping her at a secluded anchorage at the end of a dirt track in a small bay down the D'Entrecastreaux Channel. Most weekends, when work had finished, we'd grab some scallops or crays from the small shop in the seaside village of Snug and take them down to the boat and head out in the channel with schools of dolphins cavorting along beside us. Above the mast, flocks of shearwaters dotted the sky. Other times we'd head across to one of our favourite anchorages on Bruny Island, where I once went camel riding along the beach at Adventure Bay. Alexander's Bay was another of our favourite spots to anchor, where years later we'd party at Lennonville, an historic homestead with lawns rolling down to the shore (supposedly the oldest weatherboard house in the southern hemisphere),where our friend, Sally Cerny lived amidst a huge cherry farm she and her ex-partner had planted over much of the property.

Often we'd just sit on *Tasman Isle*, not even weighing anchor. It was bliss just to be away from the hurly burley of work. Other times it would be the glorious bay of Mickey's we'd sail into, where the same battered old seal would swim up to the stern and wait for us to feed him. Or a school of dolphins would play for hours, once jumping over Georgie and me huddled in the dinghy, terrified that one would land inside and sink the dinghy and us to the bottom of the ocean. Seeing those glorious creatures jumping and diving is one of the most spectacular sights I've ever seen. Another favourite spot was Woodbridge, where our friends Jill and Richard now had a wonderful vineyard overlooking the channel. Or it might have been Partridge Island, where years ago we'd gone with Sue and Don and the children on *Cascades* and tied up to the old jetty. In years gone by, we spent many days on the *Charlotte Rose* around the same haunts. And then we did it all again on *Oceania*, although this time we produced a photographic, coffee table book, *From the Sea*, to show the world how wonderful the sailing, seafood and wine is in Tasmania.

As time went on I was appointed to the Real Estate Agents Board of Tasmania and the Real Estate Institute Advertising Committee, at a time when a new paper, *The Southern Star*, was trying to break the monopoly of the Murdoch owned *Mercury Guide*. It was a traumatic time for all, as a battle raged between the two papers and agents were courted from both sides. Some agents moved to the new paper and some stuck with the old, causing huge friction within the industry. Eventually Murdoch won the battle.

For my 50th birthday we went to Bora Bora Island in Tahiti to escape a freezing cold Tasmanian winter. Much as I loved the white pearly beaches and coconut palms swaying in the warm breeze, I felt its natural beauty was no match to that of the Sepik, although we had a wonderful two weeks of swimming, snorkelling, walking and far too much food and wine.

Over the next three years we undertook two trips to Europe for Rob to research his historical novel on the Peterswald family, *The Castle at Peters Forrest*. After driving through Germany, Austria, and the Czech Republic, we discovered the Peterswald Castle in the small town of Piezyce in Poland, still standing despite being pillaged by years of war and communist rule. We even found the original Peterswald graves and crypts. Later, after a week in Prague, we discovered the magnificent Buchlovice Chateau built by the Roman Architect, Martinelli, for the Peterswalds at Buchlovice deep in the heartland of the Czech Republic, where a statue of Eleanora Peterswald stands proudly within the manicured acres of grounds, with peacocks roaming down to a rocky brook, which we picnicked by. This time Georgie and Simon joined us from Dublin where they were working for eighteen months. For hours we roamed the gardens, sat by the ornate fountains and perused the grandiose buildings with one of the best collections of art in eastern Europe.

When Georgie stood next to her Peterswald forebear up in the fourteenth century castle on the hill overlooking the chateau in Buchlovice there was a remarkable resemblance. Georgie's daughter, Eleanor, carries on the name, although sadly the buildings have long since gone out of the Peterswald family. We went back again this year with Charlotte when we were staying in Vienna, where amongst other things (opera and a Mozart concert) I went to the Spanish Horse Riding School and spent a couple of hours in horsey heaven. Although the chateau was closed we cherished a wonderful two hours ambling through the gardens, with the lawns a Monet painting of spring wildflowers. As there were no other tourists around, it almost felt as though we were the custodians of this magnificent piece of family history. Later, we headed up to the castle on the hill where a happy group of schoolchildren raced up the cobblestoned avenue, just like centuries ago, Rob's, Charlotte's and Georgie's ancestors had once ridden their battle-weary horses.

When we were in Piezyce in Poland, the local mayor was beside himself when he thought a Peterswald had returned to reclaim the castle and do it up, entertaining us in grand style in his mayoral offices in the centre of Piezyce. On discovering we were only doing research on the family history, his attitude changed in an instant and we were soon politely ushered out. But standing in the grounds of the castle that Otto Wilin von Peterswald, Heinrich von Peterswald, Arnold von Peterswald, (Governor of Richenbach), Heineman, Johan and many other Peterswalds had lived in and fought for many centuries before was an emotional time for both of us.

From a remote hillside in the Czech countryside I did an

interview by telephone for Telstra Business Woman of the Year. It seemed so strange to be sitting in this wayward spot discussing my business experiences back in Tasmania. After a few weeks in Ireland with my mother at Cloneen and Georgie and Simon in Dublin, we returned home to take up the reins of the business once again.

Chapter 35

The Next Generation and Oceania

Before Georgie and Simon went to live in Dublin they were married at Elizabeth Street Pier on the Hobart docks one balmy evening during the Tall Ships Regatta in 1998. We were delighted Simon was to become part of the family and that his parents, Geoff and Josie, who had become good friends of ours, were now to be our in-laws. Simon's sister, Sarah was Georgie's bridesmaid together with Charlotte, and his brother, Marcus, was Simon's best man. Rob gave a speech that brought a tear to everyone's eyes.

And he did it again when Charlotte married Stephen Auld, a dark-haired, dark eyed, good-looking fellow countryman of mine, a couple of months later. Stephen was brought up mostly in South Africa, arriving with his father to Tasmania when he was fourteen. He is a talented builder, having constructed a number of homes, showrooms and offices around Tasmania, plus doing his and Charlotte's own developments both in Australia and overseas. We are lucky, for like Simon, he is a great father to his gorgeous, but boisterous three sons. We held the marriage ceremony in our apartment in Brooke Street overlooking the docks where we'd moved the year before. Stephen's mother, Marion, came from South Africa and his father was his best man.

Within walking distance of thirty restaurants, and a short stroll from the fish punts, where we can buy local oysters, crayfish and scallops, the apartment is situated almost right on the finish line of the Sydney to Hobart yacht race, giving a bird's eye view of the yachts as they arrive into Constitution Dock. And below the deck is the busy working port of Hobart, where huge cruise and container ships from all around the world tie up to the wharf. To the right are the picturesque gardens in front of Parliament house and beyond that the thick row of plane trees and sandstone buildings of Salamanca Place. Each Saturday a colourful market bustles with locals and tourists, and the melodious sound of buskers wafts across the park.

Each week, when I'm in Hobart, I love to stroll to the market to wander amidst the stalls and buy fresh flowers, fruit and vegetables, crusty breads, herbs and spices. Most mornings I walk around the waterfront, stopping to admire whatever boats are in the docks or anchored in the river, sometimes meeting a friend for a coffee in one of the many restaurants and coffee lounges spilling onto the street.

At night we often dine out, as the restaurants in Hobart offer an amazing variety of cuisine. The seafood and other produce, particularly cheeses and berries in Tasmania, are world renowned, as are the wines grown and produced in many picturesque vineyards dotted around the island. Although Tasmania, particularly Hobart, has always been a popular spot for tourists from near and far, MONA, David Walsh's magnificent, if slightly controversial, Museum of Old and New Art, on the site of what was one of the first wineries in Tasmania (Moorilla, established by Claudio Alcorso in the 1950s), on the shores of the Derwent, has brought Tasmania a vast amount of fame and kudos. As have many other award-winning Tasmanian tourist ventures established by talented entrepreneurs.

Later in 1998 we were blessed with the arrival of our first

grandchild, Hubert, known as Hubie. Sadly, Poppy was no longer with us to meet him, for he had passed away at the age of ninety-three. We were all devastated that he was not with us anymore, for although when he first came to live with us I thought he'd be lucky to last more than ten years or so, he amazed us all and before we knew it nearly twenty years had passed. Most of the time we all got on famously; however, with three generations living together for such a long time there was understandably the odd occasion when we could all have happily killed each other. Poppy's brother, Keith, also came and spent the very last part of his life with us in Hobart. Unfortunately the brothers, just like at Windermere years before, didn't always see eye to eye, which was a bit tricky to say the least.

At the time of Hubie's birth, Charlotte was making an enormous success of the property management section, which she eventually bought and moved to new premises across the way in Magnet Court. For the first few months of his life Hubie lived in his bassinet, beside either Charlotte's or my desk at work, where the rest of the staff fell madly in love with his laughing brown eyes and wonderful sense of humour.

After over a decade of being together at Peterswalds, Rob decided he wanted to take time off to write, and possibly do more sailing. So in his absence I took three of the women working with us on as partners. Yet with Rob gone, much as I enjoyed working with the other partners, who were highly competent and good fun, it soon lost some of the shine for me. Although I was the Managing Director, I now had three other partners to consider (and quite often their partners as well), in any decision making. This was fair enough, but I missed having Rob as a sounding board.

So after eighteen months (and close to thirty years in the

Chapter 35 The Next Generation and Oceania

real estate business) I too decided to embark on a change of direction. Rob was biting the bit more than ever to go sailing and I was keen to join him. A couple of years before we had sold *Tasman Isle*, for we were finding we didn't have enough time in our busy work schedule to use her as often as we should have. Plus she was taking more and more money to keep up to scratch.

The saying goes: 'A boat is a hole in the ocean that you constantly pour money into.'

This was certainly the case with *Tasman Isle*, for although we'd totally refurbished her, including laying a new deck, she still required more and more work. Often this is the case with a wooden boat, shown only too clearly when we entered her in the Tasmanian Wooden Boat *Festival* and we could see all the other wooden boats needing work, despite others gleaming from bow to stern with years and years of tender loving care.

When we received a good offer to sell, we did.

Yet as soon as we sold we regretted dreadfully not having a boat. A year later, whilst on a Leading Agents of Australia conference in Brisbane, Rob and I took a side trip to Mooloolaba where we found *Oceania 11*, a William Gardner designed fifty-two foot ketch sitting at the yacht club marina. With her sleek lines and long bowsprit she was one of the prettiest boats we'd ever set eyes on. Later we learned that when she was at anchor in Sydney Harbour before we bought her, the super model Claudia Schiffer had supposedly demanded to be taken out on her. After one look inside we decided *Oceania* had to be ours. We soon made an offer to Mark and Rem Towers, who've since become wonderful friends, accompanying us on many sailing adventures.

So after selling Peterswalds to my partners we headed north to bring *Oceania* back to Hobart. Simon and Stephen sailed with us from Mooloolaba to Sydney, where we dropped anchor in front of our friends, Jill and Dave Henry's house in Birchgrove and next to their beautiful Buizzon yacht, *Sweet Chariot*, which they've since travelled across the world in and joined us at anchorages alongside *Sea Dreams* on the wonderful island of Elba in the Western Mediterranean and Split in Croatia. From Sydney Mark joined us on the trip to Hobart (I think he'd regretted selling *Oceania*), and Rob's brother, Dick, came on board in Ulladulla. After being holed up in Eden for over five days we eventually heard a good forecast and ventured out. Yet the forecast was way out, for around midnight the weather turned incredibly nasty and it was one of the roughest crossings we've encountered in Bass Strait. I remember huddling in the cockpit listening with terror to the roar of an angry sea and with monstrous waves crashing over the stern. Despite my safety harness, I was knocked to the cockpit floor where I banged my head hard against one of the lockers.

At times I've wondered if it's worse to be in a huge sea with waves crashing over the bow or the stern. That long night, with Rob and Mark taking it in turns to valiantly hold onto the wheel, I decided I'd prefer to be bashing into it, rather than waiting for a huge wall to come up behind. And then there was always the chance of a rogue wave that could make us disappear without as much as a whimper. There are a number of boats that have vanished without a trace in the middle of Bass Strait. Pam Corkhill, a partner at Peterswalds, lost her husband and father-in-law, who were on the yacht *The Charlston* travelling to Sydney for the start of the Sydney to Hobart yacht race, many years ago. The entire boat disappeared off the face of the earth with all on board presumed dead. Was it a whale that hit them? A lost container off a cargo ship? Or maybe it

Chapter 35   The Next Generation and Oceania

was a rogue wave. Who would ever know? For although there have been many enquiries and endless searches, not a thing has shown up that could give any clues as to their fate.

A few years ago on *Sea Dreams* we were sailing from Menorca to Sardinia when Rob pointed out a dark bulk ahead of us, moving slowly. As it was just on dusk it was difficult to see. At first we thought it was a huge log. On closer inspection it appeared to be a massive whale.

'Wow, look at that! I didn't know they had whales in the Med,' I exclaimed in amazement.

'Looks like they do,' Rob said, turning the wheel to avoid a collision.

We watched it pass our bow and then head along our starboard side almost close enough to pat. Soon another one came into sight and it too nosed closely to our hull and then continued on its way. As we had a long dark night ahead of us before reaching the coast of Sardinia I was a smidgen anxious. After all we weren't in *Oceania* now. She was twenty-four ton. *Sea Dreams* is just on twelve. Hitting a whale could do a lot of damage to the keel and the hull. Fortunately, when the sun rose the next morning and the towering sandstone cliffs of Sardinia came into view, we hadn't encountered another one. After referring to our sailing guide, we discovered that there are a number of Pilot whales in Mediterranean waters, though as yet we haven't seen any more.

At first I found I was missing real estate a great deal, particularly conducting the auctions and the interaction with clients and other staff. I still held my licence and remained on the Auctioneers Board, so was able to keep up to date with what was happening in the industry. As time went by I missed it less and less as I became more involved with writing and sailing. Rob pointed out to me one evening when I was procrastinating about whether to leave work or not, 'Do you still want to be selling real estate in ten years' time. Or would you like to have more adventures?'

Sitting here writing this on *Sea Dreams* in a stunning bay on the beautiful island of Poros in Greece, below the sun-washed ochre Villa Galini where Henry Miller wrote *The Colossus of Maroussi*, I'm more than glad I settled for the adventures.

Unfortunately, after a year or so, the three partners at Peterswalds disbanded. In the meantime Charlotte went from strength to strength, working under the banner *Charlotte Peterswald for Property* and I think it would be fair to say that her firm has become one of, if not the leading agent in Hobart and we are extremely proud of her achievements. And so for Rob and me, another part of our life began. For the next six years we sailed Tasmania and then the east coast of Australia on *Oceania*, producing two coffee-table books on sailing, seafood and wine, *From the Sea* and *Beyond the Shore*.

For the first time we discovered the magnificent waters of Port Davey in the South Coast Wilderness of Tasmania where we spent a month or so with Jill and Dave Henry as they undertook a maiden voyage on *Sweet Chariot*. It was a magical sail across the foot of Tasmania in the unpredictable Southern Ocean. Amazingly, we were able to hover off the notorious Maatsuyker Island in a calm blue sea chatting to Sue and Don on *Cascades* before continuing on to Port Davey; one of the most stunning and remote sailing wonders on this planet.

As Sue told me once: 'Port Davey is almost spiritual.'

And with its windswept waters abounding in abalone and crayfish, towering rugged mountains covered in native bushes, heather and wild flowers, horseshoe bays of sparkling white sand, secretive Aboriginal middens and mysterious coves of dark fathomless waters and hidden caves, I'd have to agree

Chapter 35 The Next Generation and Oceania

with her. In a way it reminds me of Connemara on the West Coast of Ireland or even the magical Kornati Islands in Croatia where we spent a month on *Sea Dreams*, yet in many ways it's far more dramatic and soul grabbing than either of those ethereal places.

After a couple of weeks of brilliant sunshine, just as Charlotte, Stephen and Hubie flew in to join us in Bathurst Harbour, the wind started to howl and the skies opened up, with rain pelting down for days on end. As the light plane was unable to weather the conditions to come back in to collect them, they had no option other than to sail back with us.

When we set off to round South West Cape the mist was so thick we could hardly see an inch in front of our bow and by the time we hit the Southern Ocean all hell let loose with an unforecasted forty-knot gale and huge seas breaking over the deck. At aged just two, Hubie sat up in the cockpit like a gallant little soldier for most of the whole fifteen hours as we continued to battle the howling gale on the nose, whilst Charlotte, now pregnant again, was violently ill down below. When Hubie wasn't sitting up in the cockpit he was holding a bucket for her to be sick into. I thought for a moment she would have the baby right there and then. Eventually we reached the fishing port of Dover where Georgie was there to join us for the run up to Hobart, allowing Charlotte and family to drive the rest of the way. I don't think I've seen anyone get off the boat with such relief, apart from Honey Bacon after our Bass Strait crossing ten years before.

Three months after this episode, Rufus, known as Ru, was born. A bundle of mischievousness since the day he arrived, he's kept us entertained and on our toes ever since. Then Georgie and Simon had the delightful Joseph, followed eighteen months later by the beautiful Eleanor Poppy, (so called after Poppy who Georgie had adored so much). Finally the larger-than-life Ferdi joined the Auld clan in 2006 and so far that is it.

When we came back from Port Davey, and after Jim Bacon, as Premier, had launched *From the Sea*, showcasing Tasmania's sailing waters, seafood, restaurants and wine, we headed north again across Bass Strait. For five days we were holed up at Flinders Island in almighty winds of over forty knots. Once again a few friendly Tassie fishermen (who were holed up as well) came to our rescue, arriving each day to *Oceania* with a couple of delectable crayfish or a huge fresh fish, which I'd cook down below. Normally we barbeque on deck, but the winds were such that it was difficult enough for us to put our noses out into the cockpit, let alone try to cook anything on the barbeque. However, on the fifth day when we were going a bit stir crazy with cabin fever, the winds abated and we headed across the strait in almost glass-like conditions. On board with Rob and me were Sue and Don and our friend from Canberra, Peter Knight. Sue and Don came with us most of the way to Cairns, although we would sometimes leave *Oceania* in a marina or on a mooring at various ports and come home for a few weeks here and there to catch up on things. Then Rob and I would go back to *Oceania* again and travel further north with other friends joining us, ending up at the spectacular Cape York on the tip of far north Queensland. I think it would be fair to say that *Beyond the Shore* showcases the ever-changing moods of Australia's spectacular east coast and the incredible array of restaurants, seafood, wine and amazing people as has never been seen in a book before or since. As with *From the Sea*, the restaurants were marvellous, inviting us into their kitchens to watch the preparation of meals and showering us with hospitality.

Chapter 35   The Next Generation and Oceania

When one of our tenants in Salamanca Square went bankrupt we had little option than to take over the business. And hence Maro Boutique was born. For the first year Rob and I ran it, together with a few staff, then Georgie joined us as Manager, allowing Rob and me to continue sailing. For seven years Georgie did the most wonderful job in managing, plus sourcing out new labels and handling publicity. Through her guidance Maro came to the forefront in Hobart fashion.

When we weren't on the water, I often joined her on buying trips around Australia. Sometimes Rob came too (once to New Zealand and Hong Kong and mainland China), or it could be just Rob and me. At times I knew Rob's mind was more on sailing than choosing the colour of an outfit, although I have to admit he had quite an eye for what would sell. One of the first brands we successfully won exclusively for Maro was Sass and Bide owned by Sarah Jane Clarke and Heidi Middleton, two highly motivated, talented and successful designers and business women, whom I'd had to woo at a meeting in Sydney when we were at anchor in Double Bay on *Oceania*. Without doubt it was our most successful brand for many years.

Eventually we opened another fashion boutique, Ruby Messiah, in one of the premises we owned further up in Salamanca Place. Georgie organised for the delightful Antonia Kidman to open it one freezing cold winter's night. However, it was a fairly remote position and although it worked quite well it wasn't nearly as successful as Maro. Eventually we joined Ruby to Maro back in Salamanca Square, where it remained until the girl to whom we sold it moved it into the centre of the city.

It was about this time that my mother moved from Cloneen to a nursing home at Arklow by the sea in County Wicklow. Sadly, when Gill went over to visit her from Australia one time, she discovered my mother wasn't coping. For years she'd had problems with her legs. Now they were getting worse. Viv had been at her for some time to look at various nursing homes, but my mother didn't have much enthusiasm. Now Gill travelled far and near until she found Asgard Lodge at Arklow.

Together with Viv, Gill helped her move to a sunny room overlooking the garden, taking her most precious pieces, including the treasured battered statue of the Virgin Mary we'd all knelt in front of for so many years both in Ireland and Australia.

To begin with my mother was miserable. 'It was worse than my first days at boarding school when I was four,' she lamented to me recently, looking back to those initial days at Asgard.

She grieved for her independence and felt confined within the small room. We were all desperately sad for her, but there was no option. She could no longer live at Cloneen on her own. Coming to Australia was not a possibility, as apart from not being able to get a visa, she was far too fragile to do the long trip. It was considered for a while that she may go over to Viv in Wales. In the end she decided to stay in Ireland close to my father in Tipperary, where she too wanted to be buried when her time came. So it was with a heavy heart that I went once again to Ireland to visit her and pack up Cloneen – thirty years, and many years before that, of wonderful memories. It was one of the hardest things I've had to do in life.

By the time I arrived, my mother had settled into Asgard somewhat. The nurses, under the guidance of the wonderful Una, Jimmy and Andrea Tyrill, are a true blessing, including my mother's favourites, Catherine, Ruth, Chris, Cecilia, and the pretty Sindu from India, who finally wheedled her way into my mother's heart, after having been told in no uncertain terms, 'You, my dear, are far too young to be a nurse.'

The problem with living to a great old age and having all

your faculties is that most nursing homes, Asgard included, are full of people with Alzheimer's. My mother is one of only two guests who are not affected.

On that first visit to Asgard I bought my mother a bird feeder, which Ruth and I set up outside her window. For hours she watched the birds feed and fly as she listened to their happy chirps. Before she got to the stage where she was unable to leave Asgard, we would take her out for lunch, drives in the country and down to the beach at Britis Bay, where an icy wind roars in from the Irish Sea, which she adored.

Despite my maudlin thoughts whilst packing up Cloneen, soon the job was done, with all the ancestors in their gilded frames placed carefully in cardboard boxes and the fine pieces of china that had been to Australia and back once more packed up. Viv came over to help me with the final clean-up, and later Tim arrived across on the ferry from Wales, towing the horse float to take the furniture and valuables that couldn't go to Asgard to Cilwych.

CHAPTER 36

A Setback with a Silver Lining

One of the things we missed about living in an apartment on the Hobart docks was a garden. On a perfect summer's day, when out driving with Charlotte and Stephen on the east coast, we came across a beach house for sale on Nine Mile Beach, north of the seaside town of Swansea. To say it needed work was an understatement, but it was in a brilliant position, up an avenue lined with agapanthus, right on the sand dunes, with the scent of eucalyptus and heather permeating the salty air.

With Stephen's help we totally redid the house, knocking out walls, adding others and re-wiring and re-plumbing the lot. For days on end Stephen and Rob, together with Paul, a wonderful man of all trades from Swansea who looked after the place in our absences, rendered the outside walls. Rob painted it from top to bottom and I painted the outbuildings and fences with Hubie's help. Rob also put in a small vineyard, as it was situated on an underground aquifer, providing us with enough water for both the garden and the vineyard. For a number of years we enjoyed family holidays, with the grandchildren playing and swimming on the beach, and long twilight evenings in the garden, or on the huge timber deck we'd added at the back.

It was whilst working in the vineyard that we noticed

Chapter 36 A Setback with a Silver Lining

Rob wasn't quite his usual self. He was getting tired and lethargic. Dizzy at times. He became even worse when we were renovating both the house and garden, mowing the lawns, planting a lavender hedge and a rose garden at Vernon, a wonderful historic old home on a huge block we bought in Battery Point. We discovered he was suffering from a heart condition known as Atrial Fibrillation, which was taking its toll. It also meant he had to be on blood thinners and have his blood monitored regularly in case he got a blood clot. As a result of this we were loath to venture back to sea again in *Oceania* – away from medical attention. What if he had a bad attack? If he did, we needed to be near a hospital, so his heart could be put back into kilter by electrical currents. Sadly, because of this, we had to sell *Oceania*, now at Hamilton Island in Queensland, from where we'd hoped to sail her abroad.

Eventually we decided to seek help for Rob's heart condition in Sydney, but without much success. Although there are excellent heart specialists in Hobart, including Rob's own talented Luke Galligan, the procedure Rob needed couldn't be carried out there. Our last hope was in Melbourne. Here the wonderfully named Dr Sparks, who literally did put the spark back in Rob's life, operated on him twice: once to fix the bothersome flutter; the next month for the fibrillation. To say Rob was like a new person was an understatement. Unfortunately Rob's brother, Dick, who suffers from a similar condition, is one of the cases that can't be operated on.

Yet, with Rob's success, there was a nagging thought in our minds. Had we sold *Oceania* prematurely? Possibly, for there was no doubt that we now wanted to go sailing again. As a compromise we decided to do a journey across the world on another sort of *Oceania*. This time on the cruise liner, *Nautica*, part of the Oceania fleet of small cruise ships.

After a buying trip to mainland China with Georgie for the dress shops, we set off from Hong Kong. Our route took us to Vietnam (where we traversed part of the Mekong Delta), Bangkok, Phuket, Singapore, India, Oman, Egypt (visiting the pyramids), Jordan (where we had a day in the wonderful ancient city of Petra and a romantic night under the stars in Wadi Rum desert where they made Lawrence of Arabia), and through the Suez Canal to Athens. From there we went to Croatia, Turkey and through the Greek Islands, finally ending up in Istanbul. It took us forty-five days and although we'd doubts about enjoying that amount of time on a cruise ship we loved every moment of it, meeting some wonderful people whom we later visited in America and who've since been to Tassie to stay. We ended up in the French Alps with Charlotte and Stephen, who had decided to move to France the year before. (Charlotte had left her real estate business in the more than capable hands of her fellow partners, who continue to make the business prosper in her absence.) Charlotte and Stephen and the boys were now living in the Haute Savoie in the small village of Lescheraine, not far from glorious Lake Annecy, an hour's drive across the French border from Geneva. Charlotte has always had a hankering to live in France. Most people only dream of such a thing; she and Stephen actually did it. I take my hat off to them, for none of the family spoke any French, apart from a smattering from a few French lessons in Hobart. Soon Hubie, at aged eight, and Ru, who was just five, were installed in a small school in the village of Le Chatelard, where they were the only English-speaking children. Now, of course, the whole family is fluent.

After six months in Lescheraine they bought the Hotel Chapet at Bout du Lac on the shores of Lake Annecy, near the delightful village of Doussard. Now they have totally refurbished and renovated the hotel and adjoining house, including the gardens running down to the lake in the front. To the side is a small canal where ducks and geese glide up and down and a naughty beaver lives, coming out in the cooler months to sabotage their garden. With stunning views of the tall mountains, often with the spectacular peaks covered in a thick coating of snow reflected in the lake as if in a gilded mirror, it's truly one of the most beautiful spots on this earth. They can swim, kayak, paraglide, and sail on the lake in summer and ski in the alps in the winter, when all the extended family have joined them for white Christmases, skiing nearby or at the popular resorts of Chamonix, Courcheval and La Cluza, only half an hour's drive away.

Rob and I don't ski so we usually have a few weeks there on the way to *Sea Dreams* for the summer and then on the way back to Australia. I adore dropping the boys off to school at Doussard (where I mingle with the mothers, but have no idea what they're saying) and then have a coffee at the small *boulangerie* on the corner of the main street where the locals gather for a gossip, before I walk home along the *pieste*, one of the most beautiful walks I've been on. With the sound of happy cyclists, walkers and roller skaters, and the towering alps in the distance I could walk, or ride the bike I recently bought, forever. I feel I can do this too when staying with Georgie at Trinity Beach in far north Queensland (where they moved with their property business, Merchants, which is now Australia wide, and turned a beach cottage into a work of art, encompassing a swimming pool with a bursting bougainvillea vine tumbling over the wall). There I get up early in the morning and power walk along the palm-fringed beach, as the sun appears across the ocean. Or it might be a gentle walk with Eleanor and Joseph at the end of the day, before we flop into the ocean to cool down and then have a picnic or barbeque under the palms with Simon's parents, Geoff and Josie, who live nearby.

CHAPTER 37

Sea Dreams in the Med

Back in Tasmania it wasn't long before the sailing bug got to us again. Rob was now healthy, and although I loved writing I was looking forward to another challenge, as was he.

With Charlotte living in France and Georgie and family ensconced at Trinity Beach, where Georgie finished her MBA and started work as a commercial valuer, Rob and I were left in Hobart on our own, for the first time in many years. So we too decided to head off.

One evening, when staying with Dave and Jill Henry in Sydney, we found our new boat on the Internet. She was lying in Gruissan between Montpelier and the coast of Spain in the south of France. A fifty-foot brand-new Beneteau Oceanis 50, she was still wrapped up in plastic. She seemed to have everything we aspired to on a boat, from in-mast furling, a bow thruster, to a healthy set of navigation equipment. What's more she had a blue hull, something I'd always coveted.

Soon she was ours. We called her *Sea Dreams* after a painting my mother bought in Dublin when she first married my father in Ireland in 1938. We've had that painting on every boat we've ever owned. Now that tousled-haired young boy, looking languidly out over the south coast of France, was to have his own boat called after him. Before we knew it we were fighting a huge Tramontane gale in Gruissan, waiting for her to be fitted out, where we rented an apartment from Linda Stoker, who told us ironically that her grandfather was Walter Thompson, Winston Churchill's bodyguard. In fact she had just collaborated with the BBC to produce a series, *Churchill's Bodyguard*. Over the next few weeks we spent fun times with her and her husband, even going down to see where they were doing up a two-hundred-year-old chalet situated on the banks of the Canal du Midi near the fortified city of Carcassonne.

After a month, where we filled in the time we weren't working on *Sea Dreams*, by driving around the wonderful Languedoc region and down to Spain, we hoisted the sails and set out with a friend from Mallorca for his island home. At the marina in Palma we had a generator and watermaker installed.

And so began, apart from the odd time when one of us could happily throw the other overboard, what Rob and I often describe as: 'The best time of our life.'

We are now in our eighth summer of sailing the Mediterranean, Adriatic and Aegean.

The first year we explored the beautiful waters and islands of Mallorca, Ibiza, Menorca and Sardinia, leaving *Sea Dreams* at Porto Rotondo on the Costa Smerelda under the watchful eye of Salvatorie, a delightful Sardinian, whose family has lived on the island for many generations.

The next year we sailed from Sardinia to Corsica, Elba, down the coast of Italy to Sicily and across to Croatia where we left *Sea Dreams* in Split for the winter. From France, Charlotte and her family joined us, renting a sixteenth century villa north of Dubrovnik where we anchored in the small bay out the front. The next year they found an ancient villa on the island of Brac, not far from Split, where Eugene and Jenny joined us, as well as Gill's Andrew, his wife, Jane (whose rendition of her own Welsh National Anthem had the whole anchorage on the island of Hvar spellbound), and their girls, Sian and Catrin. Georgie and family came to Sardinia and both families came to Greece and Turkey this year. We are also fortunate that many friends and other family members have joined us aboard for a few weeks here and there.

We take myriads of photos and are lucky enough to sample many fine local dishes and wines for our photographic sailing books: *Sea Dreams in the Western Mediterranean* and *Sea Dreams in the Adriatic*, mostly featuring Croatia, a country we both fell instantly in love with. Apart from the magical sailing waters of the Mediterranean, Adriatic and Aegean, it's the incredible history that this part of the world has to offer that keeps beckoning us back. To be able to drop anchor under a twelfth or thirteenth century fortress, as we often do, is not something to be taken lightly. Nor is the fact that one can anchor out front of a taverna or Konoba (as in Croatia) and hop into the dinghy to motor in for a very reasonably priced meal of local sea food overlooking our anchorage. Or it may be in the harbour of one of the 'old towns'. Or as in the case of the Gocek Peninsula in Turkey, wild boar from the hills behind where we anchored. Or just vegetables from *Mama's* garden accompanied by a wine of the region.

Or it could be, as we experienced on the Costa Smerelda in Sardinia (made famous in the 1960s by Prince Karim Aga Khan), the most expensive meal either of us has ever been served, organised by our gregarious friend, Lenny. Sadly, he is no longer with us after a twelve-year battle with cancer, during which time he and his wife Helen sailed with us on their own yacht, *Fourth Dimension*. So I don't regret it one bit. As I said to Helen recently: 'Who would have missed it for quids?' And I must admit it gave us great photos for our book, *Sea Dreams in the Western Mediterranean*.

Presently we are compiling another coffee table book depicting special havens throughout the Mediterranean, Adriatic and the Aegean.

I keep writing all of the time, for it is something I can never imagine not doing. To say we are blessed is an understatement; our only hiccup was that Rob was diagnosed with prostate cancer a few years ago. After Bracchy Therapy treatment in Brisbane by one of the best specialists in Australia (Hobart doesn't carry it out as yet, despite Rob's caring urologist, Michael Vaughan being at the forefront in his field), Rob's been given the all-clear and looks the picture of good health.

Good health is not something we take for granted anymore, so each day is lived to the full, keeping in mind one never knows what's around that corner – or in our case *over the horizon*. Sitting on the aft deck with a glass of local *vino* in our hands, watching the sun set over the olive groves and cypress-covered hills on the beautiful island of Corfu, I lifted my glass to Rob. Together we gazed across the bay to a rambling stone ruin on the shore that was bathed in the late golden glow of a warm twilight. 'Imagine we could have missed doing this.'

I've tried to work out which part of the Mediterranean, Adriatic or Aegean is my favourite. It's too difficult a choice for I've truly loved it all. From sitting on deck with my grandchildren, watching a blood-red sunset off the island of Formentera in Ibiza, to swimming at Isla Santa Maria off Sardinia, where the butterfly blue water laps gently onto snow-white beaches.

Then there was the rugged west coast of Corsica, with towering cliffs the colour of Ayres Rock, Napoleon's Elba, the romance of Amalfi and the tranquillity of the tiny unspoilt island of Procida in the Bay of Naples. Yet, when we sailed to Croatia, with her countless picturesque islands and sheltered anchorages with rustic *konobas* (traditional family restaurants) perching on the shore, and lemon and olive groves crawling up the rock covered hills, alive with lavender and wild herbs, I wasn't so sure that wasn't my favourite. For despite the memories of the dreadful war of the early nineties still etched into the landscape and carved deeply into some of the people's faces, it is truly one of the most beautiful spots in the world.

However, then there were the enchanting islands of Greece where white-washed villas danced in the sunlight and long twilights lit up the whole bay, donkeys brayed on the hillsides and goat bells resounded through the air. Or it might be the splendour of the fertile valleys and hulking mountains of the Peloponnese with its painted churches and rustic stone buildings amongst olive groves, vineyards and citrus groves, with tall cypresses dotted here and there, reminding us of the time we spent in Tuscany, but offering a much bigger, bolder canvas, on one of our rail trips from *Sea Dreams* to Annecy at the end of a sailing season.

For one of my birthdays we happened to be on the island of Skiathos, where part of the movie *Mama Mia* was made. The day before, I had even hiked up the hundreds of steps on the island of Skopelos, to where the wedding scene in the movie took place. All I can say is that Meryl Streep must have been a lot fitter than I am if she danced to the top as depicted in the movie. For by the time I reached the church on the summit I was somewhat out of breath.

When we sailed into Turkish waters with Georgie and her family on board I found that I fell in love all over again, both with the friendly and fun-loving people and the hidden bays and inlets where traders tied up to our boat to sell their wares. Later, we journeyed inland on local buses through the mountains and deep into the remote countryside where we stopped in small villages far away from tourists. In

Cappadoccia we went hot-air-ballooning above the vineyards set within a maze of historic rock caves where Cappadoccians once lived, and in some cases still do.

Rob and I look forward to many years of sailing on *Sea Dreams* with family and friends to wherever a warm breeze may take us. In between these adventures, we are so lucky to have Tasmania to come home to, where Dibs, Gill and Eugene visit us often, as do Charlotte, Georgie and their families and Rob's family too. We have now taken up bike riding and are once more enjoying exploring our state by land as well as by sea.

We are also enjoying discovering the Canberra district again where we spend part of the year, as Rob's sister Wendy enjoys Rob and their brother Dick being close by to the nursing home she is in. In Canberra it is fun catching up with many friends and their wives, who have also become dear friends, from Rob's time in the army dating back to 1962. Our apartment looks beyond verdant Glebe Park, now as I write in autumn, a spectacular sight of golden, rusts and oranges, to the Australian War Memorial. To our left are Ijong Street and the convent where I attended primary classes in Braddon. On our right is Duntroon where Rob was a cadet when Eugene first introduced him to me. We can even spy the spot where we shared our first kiss, not far from where I used to sit by the lake with Charlotte in her pram when Rob was in Vietnam. How the wheel of time turns!

This year we are planning to return by boat to Papua New Guinea for our 50th wedding anniversary with Eric and Eileen and Sue and Don, who also had their honeymoon in Tapini, like we did in 1966. In the meantime I will visit Eugene, both in Brisbane and on his new farm at Mapleton in the Noosa hinterland, Dibs at Glendalough Park in South Gippsland, Gill in Tamworth and Viv at Cilwych in Wales.

Last time I was in Ireland to visit my mother I purchased a packet of shamrock seed from the gift shop up a leafy laneway outside Avoca in County Wicklow. I sent it home to Georgie to see if it would grow in her lush tropical garden at Trinity Beach. For surely, if shamrocks can grow in the hot humid climate of far north Queensland, anything can happen, including peace and climatic stability throughout the world for my five precious grandchildren and all other children, no matter what race, colour or creed.

Epilogue

It was early on a warm summer's morning in Hobart when the phone rang. As soon as I heard Eugene's voice I knew what had happened. Viv had just rung him to say my dear mother had sadly passed away, two days after her ninety-eighth birthday. Even though I knew she couldn't go on much longer, it was still a dreadful shock to realise she had left us and gone to join my father in another world. I couldn't believe that she would no longer be there to talk to each week; to visit and laugh with; to read my books to, and then seek her advice; to answer my questions about her life.

After I used to write up what she had told me I would read it back to her and hear her say: 'No…no, darling. You got that bit wrong. This is how it happened.'

Her advice had been invaluable to me throughout the writing of this book, so specifically about our family. Her memories were of utmost importance to me. And now that she has gone, how I wish I had asked her more. Listened more.

I miss her being there, giving us her strong opinion, sometimes too sharp for comfort, particularly regarding how we presented ourselves.

'Oh, but I so much preferred your hair the other way.'

Yet she left us peacefully. Only four hours before she died she'd been talking to Georgie on the phone from Queensland about the Irish elections. Two days before that, Viv had helped her celebrate her birthday with a glass of champagne. We had all rung her for her birthday and thought she sounded tired, but happy. She remembered each and every one of her grandchildren, and great-grandchildren, enquiring after them all.

Within thirty-six hours I was once again at Dublin Airport awaiting Eugene, who'd flown in to Ireland the day before. Together we drove down to Cloneen at Glendalough to reminisce and take a photo of each other by the Glendasin River. We tried not to be sad, remembering the happy times. After that we drove through Laragh and Rathdrum to the Woodenbridge Hotel where Viv was also staying.

It was the first time the three of us had been together for close to fifty years, although I'd seen Eugene just the week before in Hobart and Viv last year. After a quick lunch, Eugene and I went over to Asgard, where all the staff were devastated. And once again I sat with my mother. Although now I sat beside an open coffin talking to someone who could no long answer me back. She looked so peaceful, dressed in creams and blues and with her rosary beads intertwined between her delicate fingers next to her gold wedding ring, which to my knowledge she'd never taken off her finger since 1938. The small Vegemite koala I'd given my father when he was dying was tucked up beside her.

'When I leave this world I want Vegemite Ted to come with me,' she told me last time I was with her. 'Your father left him behind. And I'd like that photo of your father amidst the flowerbeds at Ijong Street. It's such a lovely photo of him.'

So my father, digging amongst the petunias, hollyhocks and rose bushes, was with her too, as she lay there with fleeting rays of autumn sunshine lighting up the room and providing a comforting warmth. Her unlined creamy skin was now so cold it gave me a dreadful shock when I touched it. In Ireland it seems the custom to have the deceased lie in state so those who wish may pay their last respects. In some ways I wanted to remember my mother as she had been. In other ways it was a poignant, if heartbreaking, way for me to say a final goodbye to her, as Eugene sat beside me, holding my hand.

After a moving service at Asgard, where I was flanked by the tearful Lila and Imelda, who had looked after my parents for so long at Cloneen, we took her back to Terryglass in Tipperary to be with my father by the shores of Lough Derg close to their beloved Drominagh, where I was born. It was a long drive up the busy M50 and then down the N9; through the rolling fields of Kildare, where racehorses grazed contentedly behind white post and rail fences; and down to the green fields of Tipperary, with Ned, the undertaker from Arklow, driving the glistening black hearse, his stiff bowler hat perched high on his head. Behind the hearse, Viv, Eugene and I sadly followed. It was close to four hours later when we drove through Terryglass, where the local folk stopped by the side of the road and dipped their hats in her honour. At the same time the church bells resounded through the village. This was my undoing.

When we pulled up at the front of the stone church we were greeted by my cousins, Alice and Anthony, his family and the wonderful sound of Helen Fox, the caretaker at Drominagh, singing *Amazing Grace* over the outside loudspeakers. It was one of the most beautiful and moving renditions I have ever heard.

Ned, bowler hat still proudly in place, together with his dapper offsider, carried my mother's coffin inside the church and sat it before the altar. We then had a short service conducted by the parish priest, Father Michael. I was loathe to go, leaving my mother there alone, her coffin covered in white lilies, candles burning in tall candelabras; however, Viv had organised for us all to stay at Lisheen Castle in Thurles, also in Tipperary, about an hour's drive away. As it was now getting late, very dark, and bitterly cold, I patted the coffin goodbye and headed to Viv's car to drive with her and Eugene through the dark country roads and byways to this magnificent turreted castle where Charlotte was waiting for us with a roaring fire throwing out a welcoming warmth. Later my nephew Andrew and his family from Wales and Viv's two daughters Laragh and Dominee arrived.

We were lucky to have the run of this fully restored 18th century bastion, set in acres of thick woods and green fields, to ourselves. I know my mother would have been so happy to see us all gathered there together. We set up the huge oak table in the massive room off the kitchen and sat around it until the early hours of the morning, reminiscing about a wonderful woman who had touched our lives in so many different ways, even taking it in turns to sip from a bottle of her favourite Schooner Medium Dry Sherry, which we'd saved from her room at Asgard.

The next day we drove back to Terryglass for her funeral. It was so bitterly cold I literally had two sets of clothes on, as did Eugene, who was also sporting one of the black ties Ned's beautiful daughter Finola had provided for the mourning party. Rugged up as we were it was obvious we were not as hardy as the relations living in the northern hemisphere. Although the Mass was immensely sad, it was also a beautiful memory, when young and elderly relations, friends, village folk, and a few men who'd once worked on Drominagh and Clonmoylan came to pay their respects. One of the mourners was Young Danny's son from the lodge at Drominagh.

'I remember when I was only about eight years old I had to put on a white shirt and tie one evening and go and help serve cocktails on the lawn of the big house,' he told Eugene and me with a huge grin. 'Your parents were indeed gentle folks and my father had a grand time working for them.'

Eugene gave a truly moving eulogy, which had everyone remembering a wonderful, if sometimes stubborn, lady. And Dibs and Gill, who couldn't make the long journey from Australia, wrote of amusing memories, which Andrew read out. After the service Eugene and my cousins carried her coffin and laid her to rest next to my father overlooking Lough Derg. The wonderful Una, Jimmy, Andrea, Cecilia and Catherine from Asgard made the long trip down from Arklow for the funeral and then came for a true Irish wake at Drominagh, which Viv had organised. As I walked into Drominagh's front hall, with a huge log fire burning brightly in the stone hearth in the corner, I could just imagine my mother and father all those years ago, standing there ready to head out for a hunt meet or dressed in their finery, welcoming guests into this dearly loved house. Just as Eugene, Viv and I were doing now.

For the first time I met a few of my cousins who'd travelled up from Cork and down from Dublin and Belfast. And I met again two of my parents' greatest friends, including my godfather, Rickard Deasy's beautiful widow, Sheila. I also talked to the truly elegant Pauline Hickey of Slevyre, whose father had admonished my grandmother so sternly for hiding the shooting guns at Drominagh during the 1920s' Civil War, telling her in no uncertain terms. 'You could all have been shot to smithereens.'

The following morning, with slightly throbbing heads, Eugene, Charlotte and I visited Eugene and Jenny's friend, Garech, at his magnificent family estate, Luggala, built in 1787 in the Wicklow Hills, which has been in the Guinness family since 1937 when Ernest Guinness bought it for his daughter, Oonagh. Thereafter it became the home of literati, painters, actors, scholars, hangers-on, toffs, painters and poets. In recent years it has been used as a location for the movies

Zardoz, *Braveheart* and *Excalibur*, and even more recently, it was the setting for the historical TV drama series, *The Vikings*. As we drove up the wonderful tree-lined avenue, past running brooks and the glorious lake set against a backdrop of soaring mountains, even our pulsating heads couldn't dim our impressions of this incredible 'Gothic' home in one of the most stunning settings I've ever seen. After a delicious lunch with Garech, served around the ancient dining room table with all of the best silver, we continued on to the Woodenbridge Hotel, where the genial proprietor, Billy, who'd sent a beautiful bunch of flowers for the funeral, had a roaring fire and a glass of Guinness waiting to welcome us back.

The day after, I boarded the ferry from Roslare to Wales with Viv, whilst Eugene returned to Australia. Viv and Tim had now moved into the main centuries-old farmhouse at Cilwych, where Tim had spent his youth. The restoration Viv and Tim carried out had been a huge job; however, they have created a superb home for all the family to enjoy. A week later, I bade farewell to Viv at Cilwych and drove up through the almost mystical mountains of Snowdonia to my nephew Andrew and his family in north Wales before catching the ferry at Hollyhead to traverse the Irish Sea once more. For just on a week I stayed in Tipperary where I tended my parents' graves and sat with them for a time. I also took the opportunity to visit old childhood haunts, including Clonmoylan, where I was welcomed with open arms and later led into the kitchen (heated by the same Aga stove, which I had warmed my bottom on in the 1950s), for a steaming cup of tea and a piece of cake. Afterwards, I strolled down to the lake and gazed across to Friar's Island where years ago the herd of wild goats lived. Although it was freezing cold, I dipped my toes in the lake and remembered how my father used to push me around in the 'bog cart' with the older ones screaming in delight. It was all I could do to drag myself away and drive back down the tree-lined avenue and on to the road to Powers Cross where Viv used to ride her bicycle along to the shop at aged five. She wouldn't do that now, as it's a bustling road leading down to the picnic grounds and holiday cottages by the lake.

From Tipperary I wound my way through the countryside to Kilcullen near the Curragh and savoured the familiar smell of horses filling the air. Here I visited an old friend of Dibs from her Mount Anville school days in Dublin. She and her family have a thriving horse stud next door to the Aga Khan's sprawling estate, (reminding me of my mother's outings with his eminent father at the Savoy in the 1930s). Then I treated myself to a stay at the famous K Club at Kildare, where I walked with my memories for hours around the golf course, sat by the tranquil ponds covered in water lilies and watched the fish jumping in the river.

The next day, as I flew out of Dublin and over the green and gold patchwork fields, I made myself a firm promise: I would return to the land of my birth whenever possible, even though I no longer have the tug of my dear mother's heart strings pulling me to her side.

However, Ireland will always be there. Waiting. Calling me back.

Besides, graves need visitors and tending – and memories must be refreshed.

And Then There Was…

As the plane dipped low over the emerald patchwork fields towards Dublin Airport that feeling of exhilaration at returning to the land of my birth filled me with joy. Although I had been back many, many times since leaving in 1954, this particular time was extra special. In February 2023 I was diagnosed with ovarian cancer and one of my wishes was to return to Ireland before it was too late. It was now the Irish summer of 2024 and I found it almost impossible to believe I was here with Rob for a four week stay in my beloved Tipperary and a week or so in Wicklow where my parents spent their last years. But more of that later.

A great deal has happened since the first edition of this book was published. And one of the questions I am often asked is when are you going to write the rest of the story? So here it is.

After a memorable trip by ship back to Papua New Guinea with a group of friends, organised by Eric and Eileen Tang who we first met in Wewak back in 1972, we decided to sell *Sea Dreams* where we had left her in Greece and buy a boat on which we could explore the Dutch, Belgium and French waterways. Sadly, *Sea Dreams* was not the sort of vessel to navigate the narrow canals. There was no way that her mast would fit under many of the bridges and although we could have lowered the mast flat onto the deck, we decided we needed a sturdier hull for the many locks we would encounter. It wasn't long before we found a New Zealand couple to love her as much as we did and after a season in the Mediterranean, they sailed her home to Auckland. While in New Zealand at a Duntroon reunion for Rob, Eugene, and their fellow classmates we visited her on a freezing cold day nestled in a berth at Westhaven Marina where we enjoyed a delicious afternoon tea with her new owners below decks in her familiar cozy saloon. We then spent Christmas with the family in Bali, staying in a rambling Balinese-style villa nestled within a lush tropical garden lined with swaying palms and frangipani trees and adjoining rice paddies.

In 2017 *Linna* came into our lives. We found her in a rather fancy undercover sales marina in the picturesque canal town of Sneek in the Friesland area of Holland and fell in love right away. She was just what we were looking for. Built of steel, as many Dutch cruisers are, she had a beautiful interior of wood and leather, a bright and sunny saloon, cosy dining area off the galley, two spacious cabins and two bathrooms. Ideal for Rob and me, but also great for our friends and family, many of whom joined us for a leg or two. We spent three very happy summers meandering along glorious canals and lakes traversing the length and breadth of the Netherlands, into Belgium and on to France, mesmerised by the stunning countryside we passed.

At nearly every village we passed in the Netherlands there was a canal-side restaurant to dine at, busy markets to stock up the galley and friendly fellow sailors to pass the time with. We spent a lot of time sailing with an Irish couple, John and Win from Cork, who had a magnificent traditional flat-bottomed shoal-draught barge, *Avesol*, built in 1909 and originally used to carry cargo in the shallow Zuiderzee and the waterways of Holland. In those bygone days such barges were pulled by horses or unlucky men or women, children even.

Hubie joined us twice and my brother Eugene and his wife

Jenny were on board a couple of times. Friends came and went, including Don and Sue from Koonya and I must admit I missed our guests dreadfully after they left, for apart from their terrific company it was great to have the extra hands to help navigate the locks and bridges. Some days we would pass through 15 locks a day which made us realise that we were not as young as we used to be. Many of the smaller bridges were manned by cheery folk who hopped on their bicycles and rushed from one bridge to the next, where they would manually open the bridge, often using long poles to push one side of the bridge to the other in order to let us through. At times, particularly up north on the Winschoterdiep Kanal, there was barely an inch to spare as we squeezed through the narrow openings.

The Dutch countryside was an endless landscape of verdant flat land dotted with windmills and fields of wildflowers, or farms with horses and cows grazing contentedly. Sometimes there was a field of late tulips and often the canal with fishermen on each side wound through wooded forests. Around each bend was another surprise. It might be a castle or a village with plenty of places to tie up to the shore or it could be a large town, where we would pull in to a marina. Often, we could almost reach out and touch the people sitting sipping a coffee or cool drink on the verandah of their canal-side homes. Nearly every garden we passed had an array of whimsical ornaments placed in manicured gardens rolling down to the water. Many of the homes were built in the traditional Dutch barn style and had jetties out front or boat sheds for the boats to escape the harsh winters. The Dutch dress their windows for the outside world to enjoy, so there was always something to grab our attention. Every now and then there was a small rivulet leading to a hidden pond and beside many locks cheery patrons sat in bars or restaurants to wave to the passing parade, gleeful when a boatie stuffed up – as we occasionally did!

During this time, Rob and I kept writing and in 2018 I was excited to discover a novel I had been working on for many years, *The Homestead on the River*, was sold by my agent, Selwa Anthony to the world-wide publishers, *Harper Collins*. I had set the novel in County Kerry in Ireland as well as in the northern rivers area of New South Wales. To do the final edit required by the publishers Rob and I decided to take a cottage in County Kerry for a few weeks, so we left *Linna* in a tiny marina near the beautiful town of Utrecht and flew to Shannon Airport. Firstly, we spent a few days in a quaint lakeside hotel in Tipperary where once again Helen showed us over Drominagh, and we went out to Clonmoylan. We then drove across Ireland to the little stone cottage we had booked overlooking vast acres of green rolling fields separated by stone walls rolling down to the Kenmare River in County Kerry where I spent hours editing my novel. But it wasn't all work, for we loved exploring the countryside, and visiting the nearby towns, villages and driving the Ring of Kerry. Our favourite haunt was the Parknasilla Hotel, where Rob, Georgie and I had taken my mother many years before and where she had spent school holidays back in the 1920's. Viv came over from Wales and we spent a week in a converted stone coach house just outside Gorey in Wexford, close to Ballynastragh.

Back in Australia, after we had left *Linna* in the picturesque city of Maastricht for the European winter, my novel was published nationwide and there were many book signings and public speaking events around Australia, including numerous bookshops in Sydney, Tamworth, Hobart, Canberra and small country towns, plus a large luncheon gathering at the historic Parliament House in Sydney where I was the guest speaker.

When we returned to *Linna* for our third summer we found her just as we had left her at the expansive marina in Maastricht nestled below the rambling castle where the famous Dutch violinist and entertainer, André Rieu, lives. After stocking up with supplies we navigated our way through the canals of Belgium and down to France, where our friends, Carmel and Phill, who we first met at Koonya in 1980, joined us at Givet. It was great to have them on board as apart from enjoying their company, there were many long, narrow tunnels to squeeze our way through and with all three of us holding lanterns it made it that much easier for the captain to avoid hitting the dark, steep sides. Mind you, the odd scream and shout was also needed, together with a stiff drink when we were finally through and tied up to a grassy bank for the night. Some of the tunnels were up to five kilometres long with not a skerrick of light, apart from our lanterns, so you can understand why a drink was necessary. We did have a flashlight on the front of the boat, but for some reason it lit up the roof of the tunnel, not the sharp, dark, unwelcoming sides waiting to gouge large holes in *Linna's* sides, should Rob go off course by an inch.

Despite the beauty of the surrounding countryside, we preferred the Dutch canals to those of Belgium and northern France as the Dutch seem to be more organised and friendly towards boaties. In northern France a church steeple heralded an approaching village but often those villages were almost deserted and the boulangeries and restaurants were mostly closed, and many shops boarded up. Like in the rest of the world the young had left to chase the bright lights of Paris or other large cities, leaving the villages to the elderly. Tourism hadn't found this part of France. Or if it had arrived it had left before we got there. Sadly, a pizza or kabab shop was more likely to be found than an enticing canal-side restaurant or a boulangerie. But the countryside was stunning and often there was a sheltered bike or walking track winding between the plane trees alongside the canal and golden fields and mountains surrounded us on both sides. And there was nothing quite like a French market with endless stalls of fresh vegetables, fruits, cheeses, wines, breads, pastries and condiments to linger over for hours on end. Often, we would return to *Linna* with overflowing baskets of goodies and have a feast sitting on the back deck. As we ventured further south we stopped off at larger towns and cities, Charleville-Mézières, Verdun and Nancy being our favourites.

In a tiny hidden away anchorage off a tree-lined canal, we met a lovely Australian couple, John and Jill, who accompanied us to our destination in the stunning canal city of Strasbourg where restaurants, boulangeries, fancy shops, cathedrals, ancient buildings, and glorious window boxes of colourful flowers greeted us warmly. After exploring Strasbourg and surrounding villages we took the train to Paris to renew Rob's passport (which had been water damaged) and then flew to Wales to have a week with Viv and family. On our return we decided to leave *Linna* in Strasbourg and fly to Frankfurt to board a small commercial cruiser to navigate the Rhine and Mozelle as we had decided to produce another coffee table book on the canals of Europe.

When we returned to *Linna* in Strasbourg and bedded her down for the winter ahead we had no idea that we would never see her again. For in 2019 the deadly Covid virus arrived with a vengeance, and the world came to a standstill. Lockdowns occurred in almost every country, many died, and the world as we knew it was changed forever. Offices, shops and restaurants closed down, people worked from home and in many cases were never to return to the office. With borders closed worldwide we were unable to travel back to Strasbourg. At the time it seemed that the virus and travel restrictions were here to stay indefinitely so we made a sad decision to sell *Linna* to a Swiss couple, who (with borders now open again) continue to sail her along the European canals.

When the Australian borders eventually opened for a short while we decided to escape the huge bushfires engulfing Canberra and investigate moving further north, where we could keep a boat close to us. We settled on a lovely apartment at Bayview Harbour in Runaway Bay in Queensland overlooking the vast expanse of the Broadwater across to Stradbroke Island in the north, and south to the Gold Coast. Our new yacht, *Water Music*, sits happily in a berth below our verandah where vibrant pots of pink and red geraniums remind me of our time sailing in the Med. We love to hop on board *Water Music* and explore the waterways of the Broadwater, Moreton Bay and further afield, or otherwise just sit on her deck enjoying the expansive view across to Stradbroke Island. Rob uses her for an office and loves nothing more than to pack up his computer and spend the morning writing in her sunny saloon. She is a 44ft Catalina Morgan built in California, which we found during the pandemic and we fell in love with her instantly. She has two large cabins, a raised saloon, spacious galley just below the expansive cockpit and two spacious bathrooms. Throughout, gleaming woodwork gives a warm welcoming glow.

Rob and I have now produced three more coffee table books which are distributed around Australia and overseas: A new version of *Beyond the Shore*, called *Coasting, A Sailing and Dining Odyssey Along Australian Shores*, *101 Greek Islands, A Sailing and Dining Odyssey* and *Beautiful Waterways, Slow Boating Through the Netherlands*. Rob has also published two terrific books: *History of the World from the Back of a Boat, Volumes 1 and 2*. And much to the delight of the family he has also produced a book about his time in the army in Papua New Guinea in the 1960's and early 70's and detailing the many patrols he carried out with his soldiers into the rugged interior. He has also produced a book for the family on all the ports we have visited over our extensive sailing life together.

Sadly, in 2022 my eldest sister Dibs and her husband Kevin left us. Firstly, Kevin with a massive heart attack and then Dibs of a broken heart. Gill, her daughter Mia and husband Doug, Eugene, Jenny, Rob and I went down to tuck her in beside Kevin at the cemetery at Inverloch, where we had buried Kevin a few months before, not far from their beloved property, *Glendalough Park*, where they had lived for so many of their happy years together.

It is now the year 2025 and I am eternally grateful to still be alive. For, as I have mentioned, in February 2023 I was diagnosed with ovarian cancer, and I must admit I thought that was it. Sadly, ovarian cancer is known as the silent killer, mainly as it is almost impossible to diagnose. When it was discovered I had succumbed to the 'big C' it was advanced. But miraculously after ten weeks of intensive chemotherapy, a huge operation and another ten weeks of chemo I was declared to be in remission. Now it is a matter of living each day as it comes, multiple tests and scans a year and crossing my fingers the tightest they have ever been crossed in my life. When diagnosed I made up my mind to be positive and keep busy. So, I published another novel, *Love in a Far Place* and started a radio show at 4rph Reading Radio in Brisbane, called *Lots to Chat About*, where I chat to incredible Australians. For the past 20 years I have volunteered with radio stations for the vision impaired in Hobart, Canberra and Brisbane, reading newspapers on air. But with my cancer diagnosis the early mornings commuting by train to Brisbane to read the newspapers proved difficult, so 4rph came up with the idea of my chat show, which I can record later in the day. My first guest was General Sir Peter Cosgrove, past Governor General of Australia, and my great friend and Brisbane's first and only female Lord Mayor, and still a dynamic force throughout Australia, Sallyanne Atkinson, has been a guest. Other guests have included a young woman who smashed world records by kayaking solo around Australia, national and international authors, sports personalities, professors of medicine, TV stars, as well as many incredible ordinary Australians with amazing stories to tell. I enjoy travelling up each Wednesday by train to the radio station in central Brisbane and often catch up with Eugene afterwards for a coffee and a quick sandwich. Never having conducted an interview show before, I am amazed at how much I love it and how well it has been received.

When first diagnosed with ovarian cancer the one thing I wanted to do was to return to Ireland to visit Drominagh, Clonmoylan and my parents' grave in Terryglass in Tipperary and to see Viv again. Luckily, I was able to do this. As I had suffered complications during my chemo treatment by way of blood clots and other nasties (including a stroke), my doctors advised it was best to avoid long flights if possible. So, Rob and I decided to travel most of the way by ship. From Brisbane we flew to Osaka and boarded a small cruise ship, which took us up the coast of Japan, across to the amazing snow-covered alps, forests, and barren landscapes of Alaska and down to Vancouver, traversing the magnificent Inside Passage and Glacier Bay. From there we flew to Los Angeles and boarded another ship for a sail along the coast of Mexico, Guatemala, Costa Rica, through the incredible Panama Canal, Columbia, the Caribbean, Morocco, Canary Islands, Miami and across to Spain, enjoying the unique culture, colours, and traditions of each place we visited. From Barcelona we flew to Dublin. For four marvellous, if slightly wet, weeks we enjoyed the land of my birth. The highlight was our stay in the walled garden cottage on the splendid estate of Gurthalougha, next door to Drominagh on the shores of Lough Derg and once owned by the famous American Getty family. Before that, Gurthalougha House, where we were invited by the present owners for cocktails, was a hotel. Rob and I took my mother to stay there not long after my father died back in the early 1990's. The cottage, (our home for three weeks this time) and surrounding gardens are stunningly beautiful and with Drominagh a short walk through the woods next door I was in heaven. Eugene and Jenny came with us, and Viv and her husband Tim arrived from Wales and stayed at Drominagh, (still owned by the same family the Esmondes sold it to back in 1948) where we were able to spend many happy hours living as in the 'old days'. We also visited Clonmoylan and then drove across to Glendalough in County Wicklow where my parents had spent the last years of their lives.

I continue to be cancer-free, although the cancer suppressant tablets I take do knock me around somewhat, but it is a small price to pay in order to continue my 'blessed' life, which is made all the more 'blessed' by Rob and my cherished family and friends, old and new, who have been so supportive of me during my illness. We go back to Tasmania at least once a year to visit friends, including Sue and Don at their property, *Cascades*, still that piece of paradise nestled by Norfolk Bay at Koonya just down the road from *Windermere* where we had our apple orchard back in the early 1980's. Only this year we drove from Bayview Harbour here in Queensland to as far south as one can drive in Tasmania, catching up with old friends and visiting old haunts, plus some new ones. Tasmania was as green as I have ever seen it after much rain. In fact, the whole of the east coast of Australia was unusually lush for mid- summer. As we drove around Tasmania, I saw so many signs for *Peterswalds*, which is still one of the most prominent property companies in Hobart. I smiled to myself as I thought of the very first property I sold for *Henry Jones* as a newcomer to the Tasman Peninsula in 1981and how Rob and I started *Peterswalds* in our spare bedroom at Mount Nelson in 1991. And how our name has become so well-known in Tasmania, not just for property but also our books.

Charlotte, Stephen, and her family now live in a waterside property in Vaucluse in Sydney and Georgie, Simon, and their family live in a home beside a canal five minutes away from where we live at Bayview Harbour. Charlotte continues successfully with her own property firm, *Charlotte Peterswald, Sydney*, and Georgie is still an accomplished property valuer, now on the Gold Coast. Hubie has qualified as a Certified Building and Construction Manager and continues to work in the building industry, Ru has graduated from university as a Bachelor of Engineering and also works in construction, Joseph has completed his military training at both the Australian Defence Force Academy and Duntroon Military College (like his grandfather and Eugene) and will complete an Engineering Degree this year, Eleanor is in her fourth year of a Business Law Degree and Ferdi is in his second year of a Mechatronics Engineering Degree. Rob and I are extremely proud of our beautiful daughters and their families. As often as we can, we get together to celebrate Christmas, birthdays and other family occasions.

My sister, Gill and her husband, Colin have moved to

Kiama in NSW to be close to their daughter, Mia and family and we caught up with them, and their son, Andrew and wife, Jane who were over from Wales, on our trip south. Allison lives north of Sydney where she keeps her much-loved horses. Eugene and his wife Jenny are still in Brisbane commuting to their lovely farm near Mapleton in the Noosa hinterland most weekends where we visit often. Godfrey is close by with his family, Eugene and family are in Canada and Grania and family in London. Viv and Tim continue to live on their wonderful farm, *Cilwych*, by the River Usk in South Wales with their daughter Laragh where Dominie and family live close by. Rob's brother, Richard and his wife, Franny and family live on a property with their daughter, Joanna and family outside Murrumbateman in NSW close to Canberra, where their son James and his family live. Rob and Richard's sister, Wendy is still in a nursing home in Canberra, and both brothers read to her by phone each day. Sadly, a number of Rob and Eugene's Duntroon class of 1965 have passed away, however we catch up regularly with those who are still with us, together with their wives.

As I sit at my computer researching the internet for my future guests appearing on *Lots to Chat About* and working on a new novel, before meeting my good friend, Helene, for a coffee at the small café across the road, I worry that it is a difficult world we live in right now. I fear for the future of our young ones, for there seems to be many changes to life as we once knew it and copious bloody wars are raging right across the globe.

However, as Rob and I celebrate 60 years together, I'm sure there have been many like us who have thought just the same through the centuries, including our ancestors. For now, I look back on a wonderful life and hope for more to come.

All the family in Bali for Christmas 2018.

At the cottage we rented in County Kerry overlooking the Kenmare river for me to edit my novel, the Homestead on the River, *partly set in Kerry*

First novel a big leap from real estate ads

JESSICA HOWARD

HER name is synonymous with real estate in Tasmania and now Rosemary Peterswald is taking the literary world by storm.

Mrs Peterswald recently secured a book deal with the publisher HarperCollins/Mira for her first novel, which she has written under the nom de plume Rosie Mackenzie to honour her late mother.

Somewhat drawing on her own background of growing up in Ireland, The Homestead on The River is about an Irish family who moves to Australia for a fresh start.

"This is a story I've always wanted to write so it's been a work in progress for many years," Mrs Peterswald said.

"I had a lot of rejections before HarperCollins accepted it.

"It's quite a bit different to writing real estate ads for the paper."

Mrs Peterswald came to Australia with her family from Ireland in the 1950s.

She moved to Tasmania with her husband Rob in 1981 and the couple started their own real estate agency, Peterswalds, in 1992 as one of the few boutique firms in Hobart at the time.

Retired from the real estate game, the couple now split their time between Tasmania, Canberra and spending five months of the year on their yacht overseas.

The Homestead on The River will be launched at Fullers Bookshop tomorrow at 5.30pm.

MOVING: Author Rosemary Peterswald. Picture: CHRIS KIDD

Article in the Mercury for the launch of my novel,
The Homestead on the River.

Navigating the beautiful Vecht River in Holland

Rob with Linna in Verdun, France.
We spent three years sailing the Dutch and French waterways

Rob negotiating one of many large locks in France

With Eugene while traversing the Dutch canals on Linna

In the Canary Islands on way back to Ireland. My hair growing back after chemo

Drominagh in 2024. I was keen to return to where I was born after my cancer diagnoses.

With Dibs and Gill in 2019

With Viv and Eugene, in front of Clonmoylan by Lough Derg 2024

Interviewing General Sir Peter Cosgrove, past Governor General of Australia on my radio show, Lots To Chat About on 4RPH Brisbane, Reading Radio.

Our latest yacht, Water Music at anchor off Stradbroke Island

The view from our apartment at Bayview Harbour north of the Gold Coast with Water Music in her berth in 2024

Hubie, Ru, Joseph, Eleanor and Ferdi – forging their own lives and careers.

Charlotte and Georgie, who have brought such joy to Rob and I and given us five beautiful grandchildren.

Acknowledgements

First of all I would like to thank my siblings, Deborah Scott (Dibs), Gillian Rosewarne (Gill), Eugene Esmonde (Eug) and Vivienne Cresswell (Viv). For without them this story would not be.

To Rob, and our beautiful daughters, Charlotte (who came up with the wonderful name for my book) and Georgie for their love and support. This story is also theirs.

To Hubie, Ru, Joseph, Eleanor, and Ferdi for giving me more pleasure as a grandmother than I could ever have imagined.

A special thanks to Rosie Dub for her initial input when I first thought of writing this book. To Ormé Harris for her expertise and patience with helping me get this manuscript up to scratch, whilst I was on our yacht in Greece and she in Victoria. To Luke Harris for making this book look as good as it does. To Selwa Anthony, my wonderful literary agent and Annie Seaton, award-winning author who has helped both Rob and I with edits on a number of our other books.

To our many friends who have added so much to my life.

And finally, to my parents, Owen James and Eira Margaret Antonia (Toni) Esmonde for their memories and for making me who I am today.

References

Eugene Esmonde, VC, DSO by Chaz Bowyer Channel Dash by Terrence Robertson

The Way Things Happened by Owen Esmonde

Discussions with my mother: Eira Margaret Antonia Esmonde and my siblings, Dibs, Gill, Eugene and Viv.

My own memories, although others may sometimes remember events slightly differently.

And, of course, Charlotte, Georgie and especially Rob, whose patience with my constant questioning about our life has been almost endless.

ALSO BY THE AUTHOR

Rosemary's other books are: *From the Sea, Beyond the Shore, Sea Dreams in the Western Mediterranean, Sea Dreams in the Adriatic, 50 Romantic Havens, Coasting, 101 Greek Islands* and *Beautiful Waterways,* all of which she wrote and photographed with her husband, Rob Peterswald. Rosemary has also published a novel, *Bird of Paradise* set in 1960s Papua New Guinea. Harper Collins (Mira)published her novel, *The Homestead on the River* under her pen name Rosie Mackenzie, a name she also used for her most recent novel, *Love in a Far Place.* She is presently working on another novel and conducts a radio show on 4rph, Reading Radio in Brisbane called *Lots to Chat About.* She has a Youtube channel called: *Lots to Chat About* with Rosemary Peterswald.

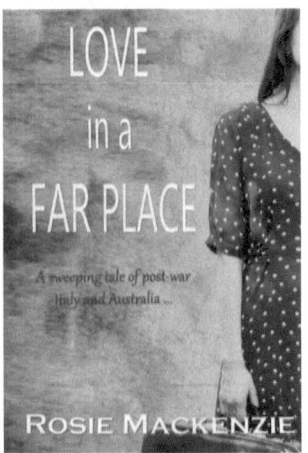

This book and the ones above are available in selected bookstores or www.ballynastraghbooks.com.au

www.ingramcontent.com/pod-product-compliance
Lightning Source LLC
Chambersburg PA
CBHW020635300426
44112CB00007B/118